As If Learning Mattered

Reforming Higher Education

As If Learning Mattered

Richard E. Miller

Cornell University Press   Ithaca & London

First published 1998 by Cornell University Press.

Printed in the United States of America

Library of Congress Cataloging-in-Publication Data

Miller, Richard E. (Richard Earl), 1961–
    As if learning mattered : reforming higher education / Richard E. Miller.
        p.   cm.
    Includes bibliographical references (p.) and index.
    ISBN 0-8014-3483-1 (cloth : alk. paper).
    —ISBN 0-8014-8528-2 (pbk.: alk. paper)
    1. Education, Higher—United States.
2. Educational change—United States.
3. Universities and colleges—United States—Sociological aspects.   I. Title.
LA227.4.M555   1998
378.73—dc21   97-39221

Cornell University Press strives to utilize environmentally responsible suppliers and materials to the fullest extent possible in the publishing of its books. Such materials include vegetable-based, low-VOC inks and acid-free papers that are also either recycled, totally chlorine-free, or partly composed of nonwood fibers.

Cloth printing   10 9 8 7 6 5 4 3 2 1
Paperback printing   10 9 8 7 6 5 4 3 2 1

For my first teachers,

Warren C. and Elinor S. Miller

Contents

Acknowledgments

This book could not have been started without the early support and guidance of my teachers, Ann E. Berthoff, Louise Z. Smith, David Bartholomae, Joseph Harris, and Mariolina Salvatori, who introduced me to composition studies and taught me how to use writing to advance my own thinking. I owe a special debt of gratitude to them and to Neil Bruss, Robert Crossley, Monica McAlpine, Jean Ferguson Carr, and the members of the Committee for the Evaluation and Advancement of Teaching: together they created learning environments at the University of Massachusetts–Boston and the University of Pittsburgh that productively blurred the institutional distinctions between teaching, scholarship, and service. In retrospect, it is clear to me that part of my interest in the hybrid persona of the intellectual-bureaucrat evolved out of my experiences watching these teachers at work in their classrooms and in their offices humanely administering the business of undergraduate and graduate education.

I could not have completed this book without the assistance of my colleagues in the English department of Rutgers University. Kurt Spellmeyer has been tireless as a friend and mentor, generous with his time, his insights, and his inimitable wit. Dean Richard Foley and Barry Qualls provided me with a crucial research leave; Marcia Ian helped me find a publisher. They and others have offered encouragement and challenged my thinking by reading drafts, treating me to lunch, introducing me to the university's internal logics, and just keeping the conversation going: I thank Emily Bartels, Wesley Brown, Ann Coiro, Susan Crane, Harriet Davidson, Marianne Dekoven, Elin Diamond, Don Gibson, Marty Glisserman, Marjorie Howes, George Levine, John McClure, Michael McKeon, Marc Manganaro, Bruce Robbins, Larry Scanlon, Cheryl Wall, and Carolyn Williams. James Livingston read the manuscript in full and taught me the importance of using history not only to learn *about* one's sources, but to learn *from* them. Marc and Elise Manganaro welcomed me and my family into their lives. They have watched over this project from its inception and have provided me with a thorough and rigorous critique of the fifth chapter. I am lucky, indeed, to have such administrators, colleagues, and friends just down the hall.

My involvement with the Conference on College Composition and Communication has sustained my interest in this project over the years. This annual gathering of writing teachers has made it possible for me to continue meeting with and learning from my dear friends Donna Dunbar-

Odom, Barbara McCarthy, Tom Laughlin, and Howard Tinberg, who have helped me to see how deeply the past shapes present thoughts and actions. Their unfailing honesty, skepticism, and support defines, for me, the essence of intellectual integrity.

I presented drafts of Chapter 3 at Penn State–Erie and Michigan Technological University and of Chapter 6 at the University of Washington. The book as a whole has benefited from this early exposure. My thanks to Kirk Branch and Wendy Swyt at the University of Washington and to the remarkable community at Michigan Tech, particularly Diana George, Stephen Jukuri, Dennis Lynch, Cindy Selfe, and Tim Fontaine, who suggested that I name my approach "deliberative." John Champagne, as always, offered support, gave me a hearing, and helped me find an audience.

My thanks to Leslie Morris of Harvard's Houghton Library and R. J. Rockefeller of the Maryland State Archives for permission to quote from their collections. An earlier version of Chapter 4 was published by *Cultural Studies*: I thank the journal for allowing me to draw on that article here. Don Whitehead of the Open University sent me a wealth of material concerning student responses to U203 that, in turn, led to my reconceiving my project. I am grateful to him and Stephen Sherwood for allowing me to quote from these materials. The discussion of the monitorial method in Chapter 1 appeared in an abbreviated form in *JAC* 16 (1996): 41–60; I thank the editors for granting me permission to reprint that discussion here.

Over the past three years, the directors of the Writing Program at Rutgers and the members of the Composition Discussion Group have been ideal partners for exploring the complexities of overseeing the solicitation and assessment of so much student writing. Anthony Lioi and Julian Koslow have always been willing to read another draft, to offer suggestions and warnings. Patrick Kavanagh has been a first-rate research assistant: without his help in the final stages, this book would have been populated with an array of citational red herrings. Elinor Miller and John Keith provided vital feedback in the final stages and Mark Estes provided life support throughout. Special thanks, finally, to Bernhard Kendler for believing in this project.

I have learned the most about history, both personal and institutional, from my partner and most valued interlocutor, Barbara Cooper. By teaching me how to listen to others, Barbara, Cara, and Rachel showed me how to finish this project. Now, finally, we can talk about something else!

R. E. M.

As If Learning Mattered

Introduction

Orr was crazy and could be grounded. All he had to do was ask;
and as soon as he did, he would no longer be crazy and would have
to fly more missions.

(HELLER 46)

Perhaps no novel has better captured the absurdities of life in a highly bureaucratized society than Joseph Heller's *Catch-22*. Indeed, though the novel is primarily concerned with exposing the incompatible logics that structure military experience, the phrase "Catch-22" has since become shorthand for *any* bureaucratic situation that places one at the mercy of intertwined but mutually exclusive lines of reasoning. As the common currency of this term suggests, "the catch" names an essential characteristic of modern life, as everyone is shown, at one time or another, to be vulnerable to the whims of a baroque and wholly incoherent power structure. There is no escape; there is always, as Heller insists throughout his novel, a catch.

Shortly after I graduated from college, I became entangled in one such "catch," when a major research university, which had just rejected me both from its doctoral program in English and its master's program in creative writing, turned around and hired me to teach in its college for remedial students. One moment the university was telling me, "You aren't qualified to study here," and the next it was saying, "But we're glad to have you teach here." My inability to make sense of the university's actions was compounded by my belief that my credentials made it clear that I was well prepared to go on being a student and quite ill prepared to commence being a teacher. Indeed, that I was even considered for the position of learning skills specialist seemed nonsensical, since I didn't meet any of the "minimum re-

1

quirements" listed in the university's job announcement. Rather than the three years of teaching experience called for, I had none. Rather than the requested master's degree in science, I had a B.A. in the liberal arts. And, perhaps most important, not only was I unqualified to run the study skills workshops that were to be the centerpiece of the job, I was actually wholly ignorant of the fact that there were *strategies* for taking tests, for reading textbooks, for organizing lecture notes. Like most people, I thought everyone went about this work in pretty much the same way and that some people were just better at it than others. It never occurred to me that study skills could or should be taught.

Thus, while the position of learning skills specialist in math and science required the ability to assist remedial students in mastering the study skills central to success at a large university, I had no firsthand experience with the skills my students needed to master or of the educational system they had to navigate. Instead, my undergraduate experience had come at a small liberal arts college where the classes were run exclusively as tutorials, where the shared objective was understood to be ongoing engagement in the discussion of the Great Books, and where the business of assigning grades was treated as a peripheral matter, a mere formality. While my shortcomings in these areas seemed to me sufficient cause for disqualifying me from further consideration, for my future employer, suddenly understaffed late in the summer, the obvious weaknesses in my application were insignificant instances of "content deficit," which could be corrected with a little reading. And so, when my boss concluded the interview by handing me the job, I gave myself over to the rich contradictions that institutional life so dependably provides.

At one point in *Catch-22*, Yossarian, the novel's protagonist, reacts to the contradictory demands that have been placed on him by removing his clothes and taking to the trees. Yossarian's symbolic return to a "natural state" prior to the creation of human society is short-lived, of course, but it is indicative of Yossarian's overwhelming desire to place himself on the farthest fringes of the military establishment. Indeed, Yossarian's enduring appeal surely resides in his limitless talent for devising ways to reduce his own active involvement in the war effort to an absolute minimum. One could even argue that Yossarian transcends the absurdities that surround him and salvages his own integrity by steadfastly maintaining a state of ironic detachment. At the same time, though, one could argue just as convincingly that the novel amply, if inadvertently, documents the ultimate futility of Yossarian's favored mode of resistance. After all, while Yossarian does manage to keep his superiors guessing by shuttling back and forth between critical resignation and social withdrawal, he never succeeds in escaping or altering his conditions of constraint.

Within the world of Heller's novel, we clearly are meant to believe that given the power Yossarian's superiors had over his life, there was little else he could do. And, by extension, it is certainly tempting to read Yossarian's plight as an expression of the more general modern condition: like Yossarian, we are helpless and vulnerable; like Yossarian, we have only our humor and our wry observations to distinguish us from those wholly at the mercy of the systems of oppression that dominate our lives. The problem with seeing Yossarian as Everyman, though, is that Yossarian resides in a total institution, where the hierarchical relations among members are rigorously policed and each member's actions are subject to continuous and potentially endless review. For those who aren't in the military or in prison, there are other, more productive ways of responding to the constraining conditions of life in a bureaucracy than sinking into ironic detachment. Most of us have other options available to us, and my specific concern in the chapters that follow is to show what some of these options have been for those dissatisfied with that other major bureaucratic institution of social control—the academy.

There are, of course, very sound reasons for seeing the world of higher education as a jumble of meaningless contradictions that can never be changed or understood. One need only point to the long and venerable tradition of declaring one educational crisis after another to see that willed ignorance about the bureaucratic intricacies of life in the academy is often understood to be both a virtue and a sign of elevated intelligence. But, to stand apart from the academy like Yossarian in the trees in order to express shock and outrage at its manifest absurdities and injustices does little or nothing to change the day-to-day workings of this bureaucratic machine. An alternative approach, which I rely on throughout this book, is to seek out the logics that lie at the heart of local incarnations of the educational enterprise. Thus, to return for a moment to my opening example, the apparent contradiction in the university's decision to employ me as a teacher rather than admit me as a student can be disentangled by recognizing that universities have one set of standards for those it deems possible members of the future professoriate and another set for those it aims to hire to work with students on the lowest rungs of the academy. The apparent disjunction between this particular university's admissions process and its hiring practice is actually a straightforward reflection of the division of labor in the academy more generally, where marginal students get help from "marginal" academics and graduate students are permitted access to "the best" the university has to offer. In this case, then, disentangling the university's contradictory actions serves to expose the strictly coherent organizational logic governing the university's use of human resources. Like to like.

While I hope to show in the pages that follow how efforts to reform educational practice have been shaped and distorted by the widespread belief in the academy's ability to reliably sort people into the "right" categories, I don't mean to suggest by this that maintaining such a belief is an easy task. To the contrary, those who accept the idea that "the best" teachers are to be found at "the best" schools working with "the best" students are inevitably driven to endow the academy and its bureaucratic instruments with almost magical powers of prescience — powers that enable administrators and teachers to know who belongs where and which disciplinary sectors need to be policed more rigorously than others at any given time. In practice, though, what finally matters most is not that this system for sorting the nation's undifferentiated masses into a hierarchy of credentialed citizens operate fairly, but only that it generate hierarchical relations and the logics that support them, including a belief in the possibility of accurate placement. Of course, with so many students and so little time, the academy cannot, in fact, "know" much at all about any of the individuals it has placed here or there, up or down, in or out, beyond what can be learned from test scores, transcripts, a personal statement, a writing sample, a few letters of recommendation.

In the three years I served as a learning skills specialist in math and science in the university's remedial two-year college, I came to see just how little one can learn from such data. Although the students I worked with had been sorted to the bottom of the university, they bore little resemblance to the ill-prepared, unruly, and underprivileged kids one might have been led to expect would be found residing in this holding tank for the American Dream. Indeed, while my own sense of entitlement had led me, somewhat foolishly, to expect a smoother ride to advanced study, the students I tutored felt equally entitled (equally foolishly, I would say) to expect academic success simply because they had paid for it. They were not, in short, the kind of students who automatically evoked a sympathetic response. Instead, more often than not, they were highly privileged underachievers, most of whom didn't excel in school because success in this realm simply didn't matter to them. But though they often came to the university either uninterested in or alienated by the educational process, they learned soon enough that they should be ashamed of the fact that they had been placed in what other students referred to as "The Coulda Been Something School," "The Coloring Book School," and "The Charlie Brown School." Once exposed to these taunts, the students quickly came to feel that what mattered most was getting out of this remedial eddy and back into the mainstream where all the other, "normal" students were to be found.

It was not, on its face, an ideal teaching situation. But, as I will argue in the following chapters, there are *no* ideal teaching situations, because all institutionalized learning occurs under conditions shaped by contingencies beyond the control of any of the individual actors. This fact is the source of nearly all the frustrations that teachers voice about life in the classroom: "If only I had better students, fewer administrative demands, smaller classes, fewer preparations, more time for my own research, a higher salary, then I could do my job," teachers say. Indeed, one of the abiding paradoxes of the teaching profession is that those who work under conditions that are anything but free endlessly sing the praises of education's emancipatory powers. Thus teachers, dreaming that life must be better somewhere else, teach their students to dream this same dream. In my case, this paradox was sharpened all the more by the fact that I was proffering "the emancipatory possibilities of critical thinking" to students who could, and did, escape the demands of studying by spending a long weekend in Cancun or Aruba, winter break in the Swiss Alps, summers sunning on islands in the Aegean.

And yet, however much I might have been repelled by the lives of privilege that many of these students led, it was also quite clear to me that few of them were being well served by the education they were receiving at my college. To begin with, the students were primarily taught by a transient, visibly disenchanted junior faculty who were always actively and openly seeking employment elsewhere; the students were presented with a common curriculum that each teacher was required to follow; the instruction they received was almost exclusively in the lecture format, frequently when they were massed together in groups of four hundred; and finally, nearly all of the students' learning was assessed through multiple-choice exams. The most obvious problem with this approach is its striking resemblance to the pedagogical practice that the students had encountered — and failed to learn under — in high school. For those students who sought the assistance of the learning skills staff, there was an additional problem: everything they heard in their classes seemed to emphasize the idea that the right answer was the most important part of learning, but once they entered the Learning Skills Center, they found tutors less interested in the right answer than in the process of coming to know. This battle between method and content, deep understanding and surface learning, is a commonplace of academic life, of course. And, in this case, the students and the support staff found themselves pitted against one another, with each side feeling the other couldn't see what being successful in the academy required. It was also a battle that both students and the learning skills specialists were certain the teachers would win, since the teachers wielded the grades and thus were understood to control access to the "real" university just beyond the walls of our remedial college.

Although we all succumbed, from time to time, to the temptation to cast "the teachers" as the real enemies of education, we knew that, in this instance, the teachers actually exercised very little control over the content of the courses they taught or the grades their students received. In the science course with which I was involved, for example, the final grade given to a particular student in the course was not a reflection of any single teacher's decisions; rather the final grade reflected that student's averaged results on a multiple-choice midterm and final exam collaboratively produced by all the science faculty. Once these exams were electronically scanned and the scores collated, the averages for each class were placed on a graph so that the performance of the different instructors could be readily compared. These averages were, in turn, interpreted as evidence showing which teachers had veered from or failed to cover the prescribed curriculum and which ones had stuck to schedule: high scores equaled good teaching, low scores equaled bad teaching. Like to like. In this system, for a teacher to teach away from the prescribed curriculum was a kind of folly that had unambiguous material consequences: such actions produced documented evidence of "poor" teaching; complaints from students and parents about inferior instruction would follow; a meeting with the department chair and the dean would occur; a decision not to renew the contract of the teacher in question would be reached. This drama regularly played itself out during my time at the college; one new faculty member after another, disillusioned by the disparity between the life the academy had seemed to promise and one it actually provided, would respond by setting out to teach whatever it was he or she wanted in whatever way seemed appropriate. The results were invariable.

When I finally understood how the administration and the curriculum worked in tandem to constrict the faculty's actions in these ways, I realized how oddly fortunate I was to be tinkering along the margins of the academy in an institutional space that almost no one of importance took an interest in. Although my own encounters with the students were certainly constrained, as I've already suggested, I did have a measure of freedom unavailable to those faculty members in the higher-paying, more visible positions. While they had to plod along in the traces of the assigned curriculum, I could structure my courses around the needs of whoever happened to attend my classes; I could focus on fundamental concepts that the lecture series had long ago left behind; I could spend an entire period on one word problem; I could help the students generate questions about a field of study that, from their vantage point, seemed concerned only with answers. Furthermore, since my classes were all voluntary, I had to deal only with students who wanted to work with me—students who were motivated to succeed but who, for one reason or another, couldn't translate this desire into something their teachers could see or understand. And what I learned from these students was that they were all deeply ashamed of their need for help and that many of them felt "the system" had it in for them. They knew their failure was inevitable: it was only a matter of time. If only, they would tell me, they had had a different teacher, a different assignment, a different family. If only they had gone to a better school, had tried harder, had taken the test on a different day. If only things were not the way they were, then they would be different.

In this environment, each and every one of us—the teachers, the support staff, and the students—felt misplaced and trapped by a set of institutional circumstances that we could only dream of escaping. And, as I have since made my way through graduate school and on into the profession as a faculty member, I have found that students are not alone in being trapped by the fanciful notion that learning occurs only under conditions of absolute freedom: that assumption often renders us, their teachers, unprepared to respond to the array of material, cultural, and institutional constraints that both define and confine all learning situations. In other words, for every student who says, "I could have written a really excellent paper if my teacher had let me choose my own topic," there's an educator ready to proclaim at a faculty meeting, "It's an outrage that this administration is treating education as if it were a business," and someone else in support services complaining, "All the faculty cares about is product, not process." In each arena, the parties imagine an alternative, free space where a different kind of learning and teaching might go on; and in more cases than not, this utopian space is deployed to justify the speaker's own nonperformance or political ineffectiveness in the fallen world of the academy.

In an intellectual environment populated by such utopian visions, it is clear enough that the administrator's pragmatic decisions can only appear as a form of deviance—as the way of those who have fallen out of favor with sweet Reason. Or to put it another way, because the academy's central concern is with the production of critique, everyone in the system can be counted on to detail why whatever can be done is not, in fact, what should or must be done. Heller's send-up of the military works within this tradition, exhausting itself in the work of repeatedly exposing the absurdities and the horrors one must simultaneously acknowledge and disavow to participate in organized society. But however successful Heller may be at making the contradictions of bureaucratic life available to be read, the novel itself never offers a sense of how one might or should act in light of its critique; beyond resigning oneself to the impossibility of meaningful change, it is unclear what one is being invited to do.

Though despair of this kind can be quite reassuring to those who have decided to retire from the world of social action, in the chapters that follow I will be concerned to focus on a very different line of response to the discontinuities, disappointments, and disturbances that define life in the academy. Concentrating on the question of what changes are possible or desirable for those employed in the academy, I look in detail at past efforts to reform educational practice. And, perhaps because I am keenly aware of the ways in which my own circuitous route through the academy has brought me to this project, I have made every effort in what follows to stress how profoundly local educational practices and possibilities are shaped by local constraints. For this reason, I have not set out to reveal some master pattern in the deep structure of the past that inexorably expresses itself across time in movements to reform the academy; nor have I argued for a national revision of standards, modes of assessment, or plans for teacher training that can and should be applied here as well as there; nor finally have I suggested some ludic approach that will allow us all, à la Dr. Strangelove, to stop worrying and start loving the contradictions afforded by bureaucratic life. Critical research on education and calls for educational reform tend to sound the battle cry in these ways, but as the history of educational reform amply illustrates, a mountain of similarly hortatory educational tracts have left no real traces in the world beyond the paper on which they were written.

With this fact firmly in mind, I have insisted on seeing every educational program as being the product of a series of complex, contradictory, compromised, and contingent solutions whose permanence is never assured. And, as the following analyses of particular programs show, this approach reveals that any bureaucratic decision about who should receive an education, in what form, at what cost, and to what end is susceptible, over time, to considerable — if slow-moving — revision. Indeed, by attending to the play between the policy statements and the enacted pedagogical practices of the administrators, curricular planners, teachers, and students, one finds a place where individuals acting alone and collectively have an opportunity to express their agency, albeit in the highly restricted realm of relative freedom. In other words, while the critique of educational practice sets out to highlight the limits of any given bureaucratic arrangement, the historical approach I employ here begins with the assumption that such bureaucratic limits are ultimately inescapable and moves on to a consideration of what has been thought possible under the less-than-ideal conditions educators have inevitably faced, where there has been and always will be a slippage between the worlds that can be created in words and the worlds lived in by real people.

In my case, the slippage between the world suggested by the want ad I responded to more than a decade ago—a world of credentials, experience, expertise—and the pressing reality of my employer's need for someone to staff a suddenly vacated position was fortunate: it permitted me to join in a discussion and a kind of labor from which, at another time, I might have been excluded or from which I might have excluded myself. The results certainly could have been otherwise. Indeed, as we will see in the chapters that follow, the very impossibility of either planning for or protecting against such contingencies is *the* defining condition of work in the academy. While this fact is often presented as the occasion for despair, I will argue that meaningful intervention in the business of higher education becomes possible only after the constraining forces that shape local labor practices are acknowledged. That is, it's easy enough to put together a reform proposal, but actually seeing any of the proposed changes through requires anticipating and responding to, among other things, the reigning discourses of fiscal crisis, the expressed needs and abilities of resident student and faculty populations, mandated controls over class size and course load, and the physical plant's available facilities. Of course, to relocate the discussion of education's "emancipatory powers" on such seemingly mundane grounds is to suggest that teaching is not and never has been an activity free of material constraint. It is also to recognize that denying, bemoaning, or critiquing this state of affairs does little to affect prevailing working conditions or to improve the delivery of a meaningful educational experience for undergraduates. But as we will see, there are many ways to work within extant constraints to modify both the form and content of higher education. Indeed, if the history of educational reform may be made to teach us a lesson, it is this—that sustainable educational ventures have always worked *within* local, material constraints and that, more often than not, they have papered over their involvement in such bureaucratic matters with rhetorics that declare education's emancipatory powers. To pursue educational reform is thus to work in an impure space, where intractable material conditions always threaten to expose rhetorics of change as delusional or deliberately deceptive; it is also to insist that bureaucracies don't simply impede change: they are the social instruments that make change possible.

1 Thinking with Students

Deliberations on the History of Educational Reform

> *When we look at the 1870s, it is the tension between our opinions and theirs, our ideologies and theirs, that matters most, that enables us to be aware of some of our blindness and its causes. If emancipation can come from a study of the history of opinion, it is not from disembodied intellectual history, not from a mindless record of social events, but from...the history of ideas as they are hammered out and encountered in action.*
>
> (SILVER 96)

In *Education as History*, Harold Silver argues that efforts to historicize educational practice have favored the "easier route of describing the structure of educational systems, the motives of providers, [and] the intricacies of policies" rather than face "questions relating to educational realities, to the impact of education, to its role in cultural and social processes" (21). One way to illustrate the problem with this "easier" historical approach is to turn to the work of the three figures who have dominated discussions of educational reform over the past decade—Allan Bloom, E. D. Hirsch, and William Bennett. There can be no question that these men and their ideas have garnered a great deal of attention in the media and in the academy. Indeed, it is easy enough to believe that these reformers embody the zeitgeist of the Reagan-Bush era, for it was during this time that Bloom and Hirsch both produced best-selling books about the crisis in the academy's values and that Bennett came to power as Reagan's polemical secretary of education. And to this day the work of these three men continues to symbolize the conservative threat (or promise) to put an end to academic freedom, affirmative action, critical education.

But what do we actually know about the material consequences of what these educators have said or of how their words have been used? We know that each has sold a lot of books. And we also know that Hirsch and Bennett have, separately, established their own publishing ventures, spinning off an array of anthologies and textbooks to help nervous parents provide their children with the cultural information and moral guidance that the schools now apparently refuse to disseminate. Finally, we know that critics of this conservative movement have not come up with any comparably marketable alternative.[1] As suggestive as the popularity of these conservative tracts on educational reform may be, though, the truth is we don't know, in anything approaching concrete detail, how Bloom's *Closing of the American Mind*, Hirsch's *Cultural Literacy*, and Bennett's *Book of Virtues* have been put to use once they've been acquired. Nor do we know whether these authors or their arguments have played a significant role in altering the structure of the educational system or the content of the students' educational experiences. As of this writing, all we do know is that Bloom called for a return to the Great Books, Hirsch for the abolition of cafeteria-style curricula, and Bennett, most famously, for the elimination of the Department of Education he once headed — and that, so far, not one of these reforms has come to pass.

This is not to say that we know they have had *no* effect on the educational system in the United States. Nor is it meant to imply that we can never know whether they have made any difference or not. Clearly, these three educators have all had an effect at the level of national debate by serving, if nothing else, as reliable straw figures to be repeatedly dismembered at academic conferences from coast to coast. But here, too, we don't know whether the fusillade of countercritiques, rebuttals, and denunciations has had any material impact on shape of educational policy or on the experience of students currently in the educational system. Around the country the coffee tables of intellectuals now display Gerald Graff's *Beyond the Culture Wars*, Henry Louis Gates's *Loose Canons*, bell hooks's *Teaching to Transgress*, and Michael Bérubé and Cary Nelson's *Higher Education under Fire*, but have these books succeeded in answering the "conservative backlash"? That is, have they successfully supplied those committed to multiculturalism with a strategic arsenal for making the academy more responsive to the needs of students outside the mainstream? Has all the criticism heaped on Bloom, Hirsch, and Bennett led to a detectable change in the material practices that structure the academy? in the systems for evaluating student work? in the mechanisms for policing and maintaining current hierarchies of distinction at work sites across the university? The critiques and the metacritiques proliferate but, we must ask, to what measurable or discernible consequence?

It is easy enough to overestimate the importance of such critical work. As Ian Hunter points out in *Rethinking the School*, the enduring interest that historians have in the educational theories of Wilhelm von Humboldt and John Stuart Mill persists despite the fact that, as Hunter bluntly puts it, "the line of critique that flowed through Humboldt and Mill has had no discernible impact on the development, organization or reform of the modern school system" (140). From Hunter's vantage point, it would be much more fruitful if educational historians attended to school designers and teacher-trainers like Samuel Wilderspin and David Stowe, who, though obscure now, played a pivotal role both in organizing the physical space in which students learned and in developing the hybrid pedagogical practice for promoting self-formation and citizen formation that teachers rely on to this day. This ongoing interest in the ideas of Humboldt and Mill, despite their irrelevance to the history of actual institutional practices, is reinforced by histories that give ideas center stage and a surrounding academic culture that traffics in the production and dissemination of ideas. We see and value what we are trained to see and value. And, within the academic environment, this means we attend to critiques, interpretations, methodological elaborations — to the development and testing of, as Hunter puts it, "principled positions"; we are much less likely to consider whether or not such intellectual work has material effects in the world at large or in the local sphere of academic practice. We know, of course, that texts act in quite unprincipled ways when they fall into the hands of actual readers. (If this weren't the case, what need would there be for such extended training in learning how to read according to academic standards?) And we know as well that texts, by themselves, don't and can't make anything happen: texts require readers. Thus, for a critique of education to have a material effect on the structure of the school system or on the students' experience of that system, that critique would have to be taken up and put into practice by someone — or, better yet, a group of someones. And for this to happen, the reader of Humboldt or Mill, Stowe or Wilderspin, Bloom or Graff would have to put the book down and take some kind of action that would go beyond critique, such as altering classroom practice, training teachers, redesigning the curriculum, assuming an administrative position. Ideally, there would be time prior to such action for deliberating over how best to proceed. But to remain trapped in this deliberative space, critiquing the critiques and pursuing all imaginable alternatives, is to restrict oneself, a priori, to acting in the ideational rather than the social world.

For those securely employed in the academy, being trapped in the realm of ideas has its material rewards, as the central figures in the culture wars are well aware, since this ongoing struggle has provided the academy's headliners with countless opportunities to speak at conferences, to engage in public debates, to appear in special issues of academic journals, and to generate more text, more books, and bigger, fatter c.v.'s.[2] In other words, trafficking in ideas *does* have material consequences for academics and others involved in the business of higher education, by making an even deeper rut in the most well-worn of pathways for the circulation of cultural capital. But, again, to know that careers are made through visible participation in central academic debates does not mean that we know what effect this critical activity has had or might have on those other residents of the academic scene—the students. To date, most accounts of educational reform have factored students out of the equation, perhaps on the assumption that students always do as they're told. Because working under this assumption significantly reduces the challenges involved in historicizing educational practice, factoring students back into the history of educational reform is bound to be perceived as unnecessary and as counterproductive by those who think that the students' experience of education can be deduced from mission statements and policy papers. Nevertheless, placing the student at the center of discussions of educational reform can serve to reinvigorate interest in versions of those neglected questions that Silver was cited posing at the opening of this section: What forces shape the students' experience of educational reality? How does one measure or determine the impact of educational reform on students? What role does the education of students play in relation to other cultural and social processes?

A brief example will illustrate how productively disruptive it can be to attend to the construction of "the student" in rhetorics of reform. Gerald Graff, an institutional historian and educational reformer, has received a good deal of attention for pointing out that while spirited disagreement defines the core of academic life, the undergraduate curriculum seems designed to conceal these disagreements from the students. Graff's awareness of this problem grew out of his groundbreaking work on the institutional history of English Studies, *Professing Literature*, where he argues that a "university is a curious accretion of historical conflicts that it has systematically forgotten" (257). Having tracked the rise and fall of the ideological battles for the soul of English Studies between philologists and generalists, scholars and critics, and theorists against themselves and all comers, Graff concludes that revitalizing education in the United States would require reforming the curriculum so that it would begin to focus on these forgotten and submerged conflicts.[3] If this reform proposal is followed, Graff suggests, the gap between students and their professors may be narrowed, and students may learn that knowledge itself has "a history that they might have a personal and critical stake in" (258).

While Graff's commitment to historicizing academic debates has led him to outline a laudable project of curricular reform, that same historiographic approach has, unfortunately, allowed him to rely on the most readily familiar representation of "the student" to justify his program for teaching the conflicts. Thus, the problem, as Graff defines it, is that students currently "are exposed to the *results* of their professors' conflicts but not to the process of discussion and debate they need to see in order to become something more than passive spectators to their education" (*Beyond the Culture Wars* 12, original emphasis). Elsewhere he depicts students as "nervously stammer[ing] questions" before their professors, as made "confused or indifferent" by the chaos of the curriculum, as the ones "most vulnerable to ideological coercion," and as currently "bullied by their teachers' political views" (82, 107, 146, 169). Students are, in short, the victims of an educational system that successfully transforms potential agents for change into "cynical relativists who care less about convictions than about grades and careers" (106). The power of this commonplace to organize our perceptions may be felt in its utter obviousness: no one — and particularly no teacher — has trouble calling to mind relevant experiences to support this vision of the student as alternately victim and villain.

There's a rhetorical necessity, though, behind the seemingly effortless conjuring of this commonplace, for the representation of the student as victim/villain covers the proposed reforms with moral dignity. And with this version of the student secured, it is but a small step, whatever the reform proposal, to listing the opposing attributes one is striving for: a student who is an active learner rather than a passive memorizer, eloquent rather than stammering, confident and committed rather than bored and indifferent, devoted to learning for its own sake rather than to grades and increased earning potential. Thus, with regard to Graff's approach, we learn that his program of reform aims "to make entrenched positions open to question, to destabilize established views, and to tap a greater part of the enormous potential of our educational diversity"; that it has helped to get students "to appreciate central disagreements and to be more critical of prevailing categories"; and that teachers have reported its ability to encourage more students to "become independent, self-motivated, and willing to try out intellectual styles" (172–82).

As laudable as these goals are, it is worth noting that on either side of the reform process "the student" tends to remain an absolutely anonymous, deracinated, ahistorical, malleable, infinitely penetrable being, as quick to embrace cynical relativism as critical, self-reflexive thinking; conservativism as conscientization; a pedagogy of despair as one of possibility. In other words, deploying the commonplace representation of the student as a victim on the verge of becoming a villain tends to foreclose further consideration of what students actually do in school, making a fool of anyone who would ask how we know students experience school in the ways described.[4] To put it yet another way, invoking the ever-pliable student helps cover over the embarrassing fact that we know almost nothing about how students experience the culture of schooling or why some students fail and others succeed. And, as we will see, this use of the student also helps conceal the bureaucratic role that teachers and reformers play in giving order to the heterogenous student population. We tell ourselves we are doing it for their own good.

An Unwelcome Discovery and Its Uses: Intellectuals as Bureaucrats

Silver has his own example of how historical research into actual sites of educational practice can serve to unsettle common assumptions about the ease and the benefits of pursuing educational reform. He describes a research project he and Pamela Silver set out to do involving a church school that relied on the monitorial method for educating the poor in Kennington, South London, during the nineteenth century. Silver explains that he and his coauthor brought to their study the expectation that they would find all the known horrors of the monitorial system confirmed: there would be evidence that students were ruthlessly disciplined, that education consisted of nothing more than rote instruction carried out by a series of barely literate functionaries, that anything would be an improvement over this exercise in instruction by the clock. And yet, once the Silvers delved into the school records, they had to concede that their evidence told quite a different story about the practice of the monitorial method at this particular school. As Silver describes it, "The school sources revealed a more imaginative and humane approach to children and to school affairs, and stronger school-community links than we had expected, or could explain" (18). Although the Silvers could have remedied this problem easily enough by declaring the Kennington school "atypical," doing so would have required accepting the "typical" account of the monitorial system, something that they felt they simply could not do, for their own investigation had uncovered the fact that "historians had surprisingly done no research on the monitorial system as it was operated in practice" (19).

Silver sees two causes for this gap between how much we know about principles of educational management and how little we know about what happened at the local level once those principles were implemented. First, he asserts that educational historians have accepted "crude models of social structure and social change," producing state-centered accounts of educational practice that are then used to provide retroactive explanations: in Britain, these explanations are used to account for the development of the twentieth-century welfare state; in the United States, they are used to explain the development of industrial democracy (24). Compounding the faults of this methodological approach, by which only those events in the past that confirm one's view of the present are perceived as warranting attention, research on educational history has been further constrained by a profound sense of "embarrassment" about how little is actually known about the implementation of educational principles, about diversity among schools ascribing to the same principles, and about what was taught and what was learned (26–27). To probe beyond the central, most visible documents of debate, legislation, and public policy only further exacerbates this sense of embarrassment, since probing of this kind inevitably reveals that there is no necessary or direct correlation between what gets said about education and what actually happens in the schools.[5]

To embark on such localized research into institutional practices is also to trade the perspective of the broad overview for an unmistakably narrowed focus on individual cases, an exchange that comes at considerable cost since a "case" only becomes meaningful by being situated within some larger argument—say, the dramatization of an alternative historiographic approach, or the revelation of findings that confirm, deny, challenge, or complicate common conceptions of intellectual practice. In other words, the "turn to cases" must be followed by a *return* to generalities, hypotheses, overarching observations, and speculations if this methodological interest in the local is to have any chance of escaping the charge of mere parochialism. In the case studies that follow, I have elected to focus on institutionalized instances of some of the more frequent referents in the ongoing debate over multiculturalism and the role of education in contemporary society: Matthew Arnold and "the best that has been said and thought in our time," the Great Books approach, British cultural studies and the interest in popular culture, and the introduction of ethnographic methods to the class-room. By historicizing these separate attempts to reform educational practice, my admittedly narrow preoccupation with concrete efforts to establish specific reforms at specific institutions during specific times opens out to the most important educational questions of our time: What responsibility does the academy have to its students and to society more generally? Is it the academy's job to prepare students for future employment? to raise consciousness? to expose students to academic codes and conventions?

As it turns out, the initiatives discussed here do establish that educators in Britain and in the United States have struggled with these issues for well over a century. But, to my mind, this inadvertent discovery is much less important than what the case studies reveal about how the various answers given to these questions have been transformed into institutional practices that define the work of students and teachers. Specifically, they show how the horizon of possible educational reform has been defined by prevailing figurations of "the student" and the general assumption that intellectuals and bureaucrats stand in opposition to one another. My method throughout has been to read the absent figure of the student back into the institutional history of English Studies. In this instance, thinking with students—that is, using "students" as a concept with which to think anew that institutional history—has had the paradoxical effect of problematizing the reform ideal dear to the hearts of those of us who dream of making the classroom function as a more humane, democratic space. In such a democratic classroom, which one finds celebrated most notably in those two classics of educational reform, Peter Elbow's *Writing without Teachers* and Paulo Freire's *Pedagogy of the Oppressed*, the hierarchical relationship between teacher and student is replaced by a learning community in which collaboration reigns supreme and teachers think along with, rather than over or against, their students. It is an attractive vision—one that powerfully shaped my own early interests in becoming a teacher—but it is a vision that does not, and I now think cannot, engage with the bureaucratic realities of teaching in an institutional context.

This was not a welcome discovery. Indeed, this book began as an effort to marshal evidence to support a position I held long before the "research" ever began: that under the right conditions, the classroom could operate as a free space for learning, where passive students would be jolted to life and the groundwork for radical social change would be laid. However, because my interest in "the student" recentered my attention on conjunctions and disjunctions between educational theory and educational practice, my own work in the archives compelled me to concede what *everyone* working in the academy already knows at some level—namely, that all teaching occurs within the context of a deeply entrenched bureaucratic system that exercises any number of material constraints on what must take place in the classroom, on who and what may be allowed in that space, and on how those entities and materials may interact. What made this discovery particularly unwanted was that it seemed to eliminate the possibility of substantial structural change. One might hope to tinker with, say, extant mechanisms and methods for soliciting, assessing, and responding to student work, or with schemes for attracting a more diverse student population, but the historical inertia of the institution and its practices will ensure that even these modest changes will encounter a general, if low-level, resistance. In this way, my interest in the student inadvertently led me to view higher education's bureaucratic apparatus as inescapable at both the macro and the micro levels: that is, where teachers see a liberatory practice and rising opportunities, most students see a set of requirements, an arbitrary system of assessment, an impediment to advancement—a bureaucracy, in short. Thus, looking at education from the student's point of view compelled me to see what I, as a teacher, preferred not to see.

However unpleasant this was, I knew my disappointment at discovering the inescapable presence of bureaucratic mechanisms in the academic sphere was not, in fact, "mine" alone. Few teachers have warmed to my suggestion that we are all, essentially, bureaucrats toiling away in bureaucracy's embrace. Once I understood the significance of this shared revulsion, I realized that my affective and intellectual responses to my own research could be used to situate me as an historical subject. To give a brief example: when this research began, I had meant for Matthew Arnold to figure, as he does throughout much of the academy, as the whipping boy whose whipping would inaugurate my own "oppositional" project. I would identify him as a bookish elitist, out of touch with the world, blind to the needs of real students. All that remained for me to do was connect the dots and move on to the next exercise in critical historiography. And, as it happened, I discovered that there was no shortage of evidence to support such a project: opening *Culture and Anarchy* to almost any page effortlessly provided me with all the damning quotes I would ever need; contemporary work that decried Arnold's influence, such as Chris Baldick's *The Social Mission of English Criticism* and Edward Said's *The World, the Text, and the Critic,* was everywhere ready to hand. Everything was going quite smoothly until I stumbled on a footnote that brought my developing argument crashing to the ground.

As it turns out, Arnold was not the wealthy aristocrat I assumed him to be. Rather, he had spent his life as one of Her Majesty's inspectors of schools, traveling the country to visit the nation's poorest schools and to inspect the often gruesomely disappointing results. This unwanted discovery led me to read in parts of the Arnoldian corpus that originally had held no interest for me—Arnold's book-length reports on foreign education, his annual inspection reports on British schools, his anonymous tracts concerning the Revised Code. In order to understand these works, I had to move to other parts of the archive altogether: parliamentary papers, histories of popular education, pamphlets for the design and implementation of the monitorial method of instruction, handbooks describing the duties of school inspectors. In place of Arnold the literary and social critic, there slowly began to emerge a complex field of bureaucratic relations in which Arnold and his writings often seemed wholly inconsequential. And this field, shaped by competing political interests and the available technologies for producing and transmitting knowledge, proved to be populated by a cast of charismatic figures and lowly functionaries who, working in and out of concert, invented the duties of government as they went along, endlessly establishing, following, and flaunting procedural regimes concocted on the fly.

To be confronted with how little I knew about the history and the mechanisms for disseminating mass education *was* embarrassing, and my failure even to consider these matters important to my study was a further sign of the "conceptual crudity," as Silver would put it (26), of my original approach to these materials. My plan, after all, had been simply to critique Arnold's ideological position and assume both that his position had shaped future practice in significant ways and that it had also reflected the sentiments of fellow travelers in his own time. But this tidy and manageable research project stayed tidy and manageable only so long as I steered clear of such thorny and ultimately inaccessible matters as the nature and constitution of the "student experience" in history. The unwelcome news about the material conditions of Arnold's life as a school inspector, however, propelled me into the murkier, messier regions beyond the well-charted waters of ideological critique. And, in turn, the sense of surprise and restriction that I felt in embarking on this new project became the means by which I was able to begin to historicize my own relationship to the material I was studying; it gave me a way, as Silver would put it, to think about my "blindness and its causes."

Thus, to know that Matthew Arnold was a poet, essayist, and social critic committed to promoting "the best that has been thought and said" and to know that he is now referred to regularly in discussions of canon reform is to be "culturally literate" about Arnold at this time. And, perhaps paradoxically, to know almost nothing about the advent of popular education in either Britain or the United States during the nineteenth century is also a sign of one's cultural literacy, for at the present time the educational theories of Louis Althusser and Antonio Gramsci are more likely to appear on graduate syllabi than are historical accounts of the bureaucratic maneuvers, legislative decisions, and individual initiatives that gave rise to the university. So what I knew and didn't know about Arnold reflected my own educational history, as did my expectations about what I thought the material I uncovered would reveal. Or, to put it another way, since my educational history is the result of my personal circulation to and engagement with a number of distinct and necessarily impersonal institutional locations, "my own" educational history is only partly mine.

With this insight in mind, I realized that I could use my own ignorance and expectations as signs of a state I shared with many others. This, in turn, enabled me to historicize the connections between what I knew and didn't know and the areas of thought I had and hadn't been introduced to in school, as well as the teachers, writers, and ideas that I had and hadn't been given access to throughout the educational system; the autodidactic pursuits that that system had and hadn't given rise to; and, most important, the ways I had and hadn't been taught to define, think about, and respond to ignorance. Once these connections had been elucidated, it became clear to me that my "surprised," "personal" reactions to the material were, in fact, trace elements of an historically produced, schooled response to the business of knowledge construction.[6]

Before I fill out this notion of "the schooled response," though, it may be best first to summarize my methodology. In seeking to offer an alternative approach for defining and studying what work it is that schools do and how that work might be reformed, I have chosen to focus on how the student has been figured both rhetorically and pedagogically by specific institutional practices within specific educational systems. In order to find evidence of the actual reading and writing students have been required to do within a given educational system, I turn to a set of archival materials less likely to be consulted in more traditional intellectual histories of the institution— textbooks and book collections produced by educators alongside their reforms, personal accounts of the educators' teaching practices, moments when educators quote students in their texts, and, in one case, course evaluations. By juxtaposing plans for reform with evidence of what a given reform looked like when implemented, my aim is to throw into high relief the dynamic interplay that exists between intellectual desires and bureaucratic realities, as all utopian aspirations encounter inescapable, historically produced material constraints.

What Can't Be Changed:
The Grammar and the Game of Educational Reform

Some will surely balk at my unqualified invocation of "bureaucratic re-alities" on the grounds that my approach transforms an accident of history into a transhistoric inevitability. And others may further adduce an essentially "conservative" bent to this enterprise, since I discount the possibility of fomenting a radical revision of the structure of the academy as we know it. I can only respond that my concern in what follows is not with assessing versions of what the academy *might* be if freed from its fetters to business, bureaucracy, a skeptical public, a declining tax base, an ambivalent student population. Though trafficking in such utopian visions is a time-honored academic pastime (one that, as we will see, serves the important institutional function of manifesting and securing the academic's mark of distinction as a moral figure), my interest here is with the academy as it is and has, in fact, been for some time—that is, as a bureaucratic institution for sifting, sorting, and credentialing the otherwise undifferentiated masses. Reseeing the educational enterprise through this lens makes it clear that any serious effort to reform the academy *must* work within the bureaucratic constraints that reign at the local and national levels. This argument may appear obvious enough—indeed, from a certain earthbound vantage point, it *is* obvious—but conceding the reality of academic working conditions is not so easy as it might at first seem, since it entails recognizing how much the purportedly opposed figures of "the intellectual" and "the bureaucrat" actually have in common. It also requires the admission that institutions of higher education are susceptible, at best, to modest rather than radical change and, furthermore, that when such change occurs, it will be slow, uneven, and with unpredictable consequences. Conceding the essentially bureaucratic nature of academic work demands, in other words, an acknowledgment that making hortatory declarations about what must be done and extended critiques of what has been done is not, by any stretch of the imagination, the same thing as engaging in the entirely unglamorous, often utterly anonymous work of figuring out what *can* be done within a given institutional context, where one is certain to run up against extant, competing, undoubtedly unreasonable, and unquestionably unfair constraints.

In their award-winning book *Tinkering toward Utopia: A Century of Public School Reform*, David Tyack and Larry Cuban use the phrase "the basic grammar of schooling" to describe the remarkable stability of educational institutions. As they define it, this grammar consists of "the ways that schools divide time and space, classify students and allocate them to classrooms, splinter knowledge into 'subjects,' and award grades and 'credits' as evidence of learning" (85). Tyack and Cuban recount numerous efforts to transform this basic instructional design; they chronicle, as well, the eventual failure of all attempts that sought to fundamentally alter either the organization of the schools or the delivery of education. Defining successful projects as those that lasted long enough "to register as institutional trends," Tyack and Cuban extracted the following attributes of sustainable reform efforts: the reforms could be added on to the existing structure without interfering with standard operating procedures; they were, as a rule, perceived to be noncontroversial by the public and by the larger governing bodies; they produced influential constituencies committed to their perpetuation (such as drivers' education in the high schools, which gained the support of insurance companies and car dealers); they were required by law and easily monitored; and, finally, they were implemented by school administrators and teachers rather than by outsiders (57–58). For those interested in radically reshaping educational practice in order to address the gross inequities in the extant system, these findings are bound to be disappointing, since they confirm the notion that the institution is fundamentally conservative and suggest the impossibility of "meaningful" change, however that might be construed.

Of course, educational systems do not actually have a "fundamental nature." Rather, they have assumed a historically produced character that manifests itself in our time as an immensely complex bureaucracy with an inherent resistance to structural change. The fact that there is no logical necessity to the system's procedures frequently becomes the occasion for educational reformers to argue that schools might, in fact, function quite differently—that schools could, for instance, be more collaborative, liberating, inclusive, efficient, and fair. To head down this road, however, is to mistake the relative arbitrariness of the form that the school currently has assumed as proof that any imaginable alternative form could be adopted at this historical moment. It is also to believe that the histories of all the students, employees, and administrators who have circulated through the current educational system are an insignificant detail—a minor impediment—standing in the way of radical change. But as Tyack and Cuban sagely observe, "rarely have start-from-scratch reformers with their prefabricated innovations really understood the tenacity of the grammar of schooling or the need to adapt change to local knowledge and needs" (132). The people outside the system trying to get in, the people already in the system, and the system itself, already so deeply ingrained in both groups: all of these "problems" inevitably make themselves known once a reform proposal is introduced and they all work, in various ways, to ensure that managed change is never so rapid as it was planned to be, never so radical as it promised to be, and never so fully successful as on paper it seemed it would be. Thus, to produce plans for changing the schools that wish away these historically produced material constraints—including economic necessity, resident human capital, and extant institutional structures—is to reject from the outset learning how to speak using "the basic grammar of schooling" and to consign oneself to the Platonic exercise of building an ideal system in words.

In observing that such utopian exercises are regularly rehearsed without consequence, I do not mean to suggest that all one need do to bring one's plans for reforming the educational system to fruition is to become fluent in the "grammar of schooling." This is a seductive notion, one that is particularly appealing to those who think that all the world's a language and we but speakers who need only open our mouths and speak the truth to alter the workings of that world. Indeed, to think that learning the grammar of a culture alone makes change possible is to fall into the deepest and most capacious trap awaiting those who venture onto the field of pedagogical relations. That is, in imagining that under ideal circumstances, all one has to do is teach a given content in a certain way for "learning" to occur, one constructs "the student" once again as infinitely malleable, ready and able to take on a new grammar, a new way of thinking, a new consciousness if only the right information is made available in the right way. I term this error in thinking about the lived realities of the social sphere the *teacher's fallacy* because it imbues teachers with an almost magical power that, under the right conditions, can be unleashed to transform the objects of instruction into whatever the teacher pleases.

I discuss the tremendous and ultimately inescapable allure this particular fallacy has for teachers and cultural critics alike in Chapter 6; but for the moment, it is worth noting that Tyack and Cuban do not include as part of the grammar of schooling this captivating image of the teacher as an autonomous subject, uninterested in material rewards, selflessly committed to the spread of knowledge, fluent in the languages and mental procedures that set the mind free. I think this omission is unfortunate, for just as schools structure time and space in such uniform, predictable ways as to warrant being compared to a grammar, there can be no question that schools also attract followers to the profession through an equally uniform and predictable mechanism for allocating rewards and dividing the labor force. That is, the grammar of schooling must also include as one of its attributes a labor force drawn to a profession that promises to maintain a sharp distinction between intellectual and bureaucratic work, teaching and management, freedom and servility. The "mind-set" of this labor force is no more amenable to radical reform than is the division of the school day or the awarding of grades as evidence of learning. To put it another way, any reform project that sets out to radically reorient the teachers' mind-set is bound to fail.

No one has done more to advance the understanding of how schools create and reward this intellectual revulsion for bureaucratic work than the sociologist Pierre Bourdieu. Indeed, *Distinction: A Social Critique of the Judgement of Taste* is best read as Bourdieu's effort to expose the social mechanisms that infuse a taste for "legitimate culture" with value, thereby distinguishing it from tastes for other kinds of work and other kinds of cultural artifacts. Bourdieu is quick to declare his preliminary findings to be "self-evident," since most people, without doing any research at all, would say that the two most important factors influencing the level of taste an individual acquires are class of origin and level of education (99). Bourdieu's project, however, is to systematize the processes by which taste is either inherited from one's forebears or acquired through education. This, in turn, will allow him to track the "series of different *effects*" that acquiring an academic's tastes will have in the lived experience of individuals (22, original emphasis). Establishing an analogy between the market in taste and the economic market, Bourdieu argues that taste itself indicates the amount of "cultural capital" an individual has accrued: the more cultural capital an individual accumulates, the more likely that individual is to manifest a disdain for economic capital and for the concerns of the material world. Within such a cultural market, the surest way to make it known that one has attained the highest level of taste and, therefore, that one is an order of being quite distinct from those who possess greater economic wealth, political power, and social mobility is to openly declare and to ceaselessly manifest one's preference for the idols of culture — great literature, high art, avant-garde theater, antiques, the life of the mind, a freedom from constraint.

Because cultural capital circulates in this way, "it brings to those who have legitimate culture as a second nature [that is, those who have a 'natural' appreciation for 'the best that has been thought and said'] the supplementary profit of being seen (and seeing themselves) as perfectly disinterested, unblemished by any cynical or mercenary use of culture" (86). With respect to the highly educated, this means that they come to see themselves as being beyond the reach of politics and the bureaucratic world. For this reason, "culture" itself becomes, in Bourdieu's famous formulation, "the site, par excellence, of misrecognition," where the highly educated individual's appreciation for "higher things," which actually results from a complex collusion of economic, historic, and social forces, is "misrecognized" as a sign of the individual's natural superiority over others.[7] Bourdieu goes on to elaborate:

> This means that the term "investment," for example, must be understood in the dual sense of economic investment—which it objectively always is, though misrecognized—and the sense of affective investment which it has in psychoanalysis, or, more exactly, in the sense of *illusio*, belief, an involvement in the game which produces the game. The art-lover knows no other guide than his love of art, and when he moves, as if by instinct, toward what is, at each moment, the thing to be loved, like some businessmen who make money even when they are not trying to, he is not pursuing a cynical calculation, but his own pleasure, the sincere enthusiasm which, in such matters, is one of the preconditions of successful investment. (86)

With this in mind, we can say that Bourdieu's analysis points to the impossibility of radically reforming any highly developed educational system, since that system will, of necessity, be predominantly inhabited by individuals who have profited from that system, who are invested in that system, and whose felt sense of distinction has been established and certified by that system. Furthermore, to follow out this train of thought, it would appear that no academic can escape the allure of this game, not even those overtly interested in fully democratizing current educational practice, since such activists implicitly believe that education is the preeminent site for organizing relationships between individuals. One could even argue that those driven to reform the academy are the ones most fully involved in "the game which produces the game," since such individuals aim to establish their own distinction from others by assuming the position of the oppositional critic and by teaching others to see what is often all too appropriately described as the reformer's "vision."

Given Bourdieu's insistence that the game of culture rests on a persistent act of misrecognition whereby culturally produced differences are felt internally as naturally realized matters of taste, it is not surprising that he is routinely labeled a fatalist.[8] Indeed, with respect to academic culture, his analysis would appear to suggest that intellectuals are not qualified to oversee academic reform, since they themselves are blind to their own conditions of possibility. For whether schooling is conceived of as constrained either by a grammar or by the rules of a game, the only option available to the participants, given these analogies, is conforming to expectations. In this maddening way, Bourdieu's work not only elucidates the structural tensions within educational institutions between knowledge producers and knowledge managers, but it also anticipates how intellectuals, regardless of their political or disciplinary commitments, will respond to such an account of the game of culture. That is, Bourdieu knows only too well that one way we intellectuals manifest and misrecognize our economic and affective investment in our own cultural superiority is through ritualized public performances of our revulsion at the suggestion that our hard-earned insights into the ways of the world may not be our own at all.

Utopian Delusions and Bureaucratic Realities: Bourdieu, Guillory, and the Sphere of Intellectual Autonomy

In an effort to counter the charge that his analysis leaves no room for meaningful intervention, Bourdieu has since set out his guidelines for reforming the academy. Specifically, in "The Corporatism of the Universal: The Role of Intellectuals in the Modern World," Bourdieu urges intellectuals "to work collectively towards the defense of their own interests and towards the means necessary for the protection of their autonomy" (103). For too long, Bourdieu asserts, intellectuals have been paralyzed by a "guilt complex" about the underprivileged, which has led them to forget "that the defense of the universal [the downtrodden] presupposes the defense of the defenders of the universal" (103). The intellectual's desire to participate in rational dialogue with other intellectuals has been further restricted by "the fact that the most autonomous practitioners are endlessly exposed to the disloyal competition of the most heteronomous [practitioners], who always manage to find a way to compensate for their weaknesses by appealing to outside powers" (104). To counter these forces, Bourdieu believes that intellectuals must unite to protect the autonomy of "the most autonomous" from further incursions by the state, from the arbitrary decisions of funding agencies, from "second-rate intellectuals," and from outside evaluation in general. The creation of an organization that has these objectives is desirable for two reasons. First, in this newly autonomous sphere of intellectual engagement, "competition...is [to be] organized in such a manner that no one can succeed over anyone else, except by means of better *arguments*, *reasonings*, and *demonstrations*, thereby advancing reason and truth" (104, original emphasis). Second, because such an organization would recognize that protecting the autonomy of intellectuals is a political cause of paramount importance, it would provide the necessary infrastructure to ensure that intellectuals from around the globe could be "mobilized against all attacks on the autonomy of the intellectual world, and especially against all forms of *cultural imperialism*" (108–9, original emphasis). Thus, as Bourdieu would have it, it is in the self-interest of intellectuals to act collectively, not only to preserve their sphere of relative autonomy but also to create an even purer environment for the circulation of cultural capital.

In the new environment Bourdieu envisions, working conditions for intellectuals would be even more distinct from those under which others labor. This is a desirable outcome in itself, Bourdieu believes, because these secure working conditions would increase the intellectuals' "inclination to *assert* this independence by criticizing the powers that be ... [and the] *symbolic effectiveness* of whatever political positions [the intellectuals] might take" (100, original emphasis). Ultimately, then, Bourdieu's plan for future action takes his findings about the social laws governing the construction of taste and the establishment of hierarchies within intellectual communities to their logical end point: to survive in these increasingly threatening times, intellectuals must work together to protect the sense of privilege that they have come to feel is rightfully and naturally theirs. Regardless of whether or not one finds this project to be distasteful, Bourdieu's own analysis of intellectual culture makes it clear that such collective action among intellectuals is unlikely, since establishing an organization for preserving and protecting this common interest in remaining disinterested requires "neutraliz[ing] the tendency inscribed in the very logic of the intellectual field toward division and particularism," a tendency that makes intellectuals "surely among the least adept when it comes to discovering common interests uniting them" (109). If the goal of establishing a space where intellectual work would be uncontaminated by bureaucratic realities, cultural constraints, and "second-rate" minds seems uninviting, perhaps even revolting, this may be because the articulation of such a goal foregrounds the self-interest of a cultural class whose prestige and position is founded on the very assumption of its own disinterestedness.

The shared distaste that intellectuals have for organizational work does not mean, of course, that it would be impossible for them to unite to protect their own interests. Rather, it means that for collective action to occur, intellectuals must become "disenchanted" with the alluring image of themselves as free-thinking individuals whose mental work escapes the logic of the marketplace. As the following passage attests, Bourdieu believes his "reflexive sociology" can be instrumental in relieving intellectuals of their self-deluding fantasies:

I believe that sociology does exert a disenchanting effect, but this, in my eyes, marks a progress toward a form of scientific and political realism that is the absolute antithesis of naive utopianism. Scientific knowledge allows us to locate real points of application for responsible action; it enables us to avoid struggling where there is no freedom—which is often an alibi of bad faith—in such a manner as to dodge sites of genuine responsibility.... The political task of social science is to stand up both against irresponsible voluntarism and fatalistic scientism, to help define a rational utopianism by using the knowledge of the probable to make the possible come true. (Bourdieu and Wacquant 196–97)

As Bourdieu knows, few intellectuals are likely to embrace the "rational utopianism" he proffers, partly because his project "does not look radical enough" for their tastes and partly because it lacks the aesthetic component so central to intellectual work (197). One could even say that Bourdieu has made a serious rhetorical miscalculation, since his decision to adopt the persona of the disenchanter transforms his highly educated audience into "the enchanted," few of whom are likely to be pleased at being so designated. For, as we can see, Bourdieu labels those who disagree with the fruits of his analysis as dupes of "naive utopianism," "irresponsible voluntarism," and "fatalistic scientism." In contrast, he characterizes his own unqualified belief in a "scientific knowledge" of the laws governing social action as paving the way to a "rational utopianism."

In sum, Bourdieu makes no rhetorical concessions to those who might be skeptical of his argument. Rather, buying into the *illusio* of the teacher's fallacy, he imagines all those who accept his position to have exercised their Reason and all those who reject his argument to be fools of the system—the truly "dominated dominators," those blind to the fact that "being in possession of one of the major means of domination, cultural capital, they partake of the dominant order" ("Corporatism" 109). And because he accepts the results of his research as revealing a set of historical—and therefore fundamental—truths about the organization of contemporary society, Bourdieu can't help but see his own responsibility to lie with disseminating these scientific results throughout the academic community, where, under ideal conditions, they would be dispassionately digested and evaluated. Thus, even though his own research suggests that it would be highly unlikely for his proposal to receive such a hearing, given intellectuals' profound investment in the game that both depicts them as and rewards them for appearing disinterested, Bourdieu himself must play by the rules of this game. Indeed, it would appear that he has no other option but to believe in the game's *illusio* and to be its puppet like everyone else. Consequently, he must eschew the arts of persuasion and all other discursive traits that might reveal a weakness for anything other than Reason: he must "speak the truth," whatever the material consequences (which, of course, in his case are few); he must be an intellectual and not a bureaucrat; he must embrace the ideals of the former and flee everything the latter represents, including, paradoxically, the anonymity that comes from working in a larger collectivity.

Although he is indebted to Bourdieu's approach, John Guillory has developed an alternative reform proposal that is both more conservative and more rhetorically savvy than Bourdieu's. Guillory's specific concern in *Cultural Capital* is to address the failure of liberals to generate "an effective response to the conservative backlash" created by debates about multiculturalism and the teaching of noncanonical literature (4). Insisting that the revisionists have been fighting a losing battle, Guillory argues for the necessity of shifting attention away from the curriculum and onto "the school itself, which regulates access to literary production by regulating access to literacy, to the practices of reading and writing" (ix). It thus becomes possible "to repudiate the practice of fetishizing the curriculum, of locating the politics of pedagogy in the anxious drawing up of a list of representative names" (51). This, in turn, enables a "strategic" reformulation of the canon debate, as one abandons the argument that it is necessary to teach "noncanonical" works in order to represent social minorities, insisting instead "that the school has the social obligation of providing access to these works, *because they are important and significant cultural works*" (52, original emphasis). In this way, Guillory's awareness of how the canon debates have contributed to the erosion of academics' ability to appear as impartial arbiters of cultural disputes leads him to devise a rhetorical strategy for restoring academics to their former positions of power: first, declare everything that appears on the syllabus a valuable cultural commodity *in itself* and then, to fend off charges of elitism, declare a commitment to giving everyone access to these cultural treasures.

As we will see, there is a striking compatibility between Guillory's hypothesis "that a total democratization of access to cultural products would disarticulate the formation of cultural capital from the class structure and from the markets" (337) and the arguments made by those who formulated the Great Books movement beginning in the 1920s. But whatever rhetorical force may be gained by labeling one's own reforms "democratizing," it should be clear that for Guillory, as for Bourdieu, the ultimate goal is to establish an autonomous intellectual sphere exclusively under the control of disinterested cultural critics. Thus, universalizing access to cultural goods would, in Guillory's terms, enable "a vast enlargement of the field of aesthetic judgment," since the value of any cultural good would be assessed not on the basis of its inaccessibility but on "aesthetic grounds" (339). This "democratizing" gesture would wrench control of the universities from the hands of those "technobureaucrats" who have found an institutional home in expanding composition programs where—however unlikely his claims may seem to those familiar with the field—Guillory informs us, students are taught "the speech of the professional-managerial classes, the administrators, and bureaucrats" (79).[9] By beating back these forces, Guillory believes it will also be possible to strike at the heart of the internal restrictions that constrain instructional freedom: such work is necessary, he insists, because "in the situation of the bureaucratized educational institution, pedagogic autonomy must defend itself against the heteronomous pressure of the *educational institution itself,* insofar as it bureaucratically administers pedagogy, and not only against the pressures that seek to constrain or determine pedagogy from outside the school" (252–53, original emphasis).

Ian Hunter describes rhetorical moves of this kind, where a purely educational space outside the reach of governmentality is understood to be the educator's ultimate desideratum, as the "practice of exemplary withdrawal or 'world flight' " (29). When intellectuals resort in argument to this gesture they are manifesting what Hunter elsewhere calls their "secular holiness" (167). We can see the traces of Guillory's "exemplary withdrawal" from the world of material concerns in his assertion that the academy controls access to "the means of literary production." If one deems the assigned texts in a literature course to be the academy's "cultural goods" and then thinks about the work that students are habitually asked to do with those goods, it seems an extraordinary stretch of the imagination to say that this process regulates access to "the means of literary production." Such an assertion presumes that access to literary production is granted only to those who have been taught to generate exegetical or critical essays on literary or critical texts. In any event, there is little historical evidence to suggest that English Studies has understood its mission to be preparing students to produce literature: to the contrary, a survey of course requirements for English majors around the country would show that the bulk of the undergraduate's writing experience is taken up with multiple-choice exams and the composition of short essays and longer research papers.

In short, Guillory has got it wrong. Because schools regulate the circulation of students and the credentialing process, what they actually control is access to the means of *critical* production. Guillory, for his part, would certainly acknowledge that this is what schools currently do. Indeed, he sees the increased emphasis on theoretical texts in the literary curriculum as the technobureaucrats' other line of attack. Guillory even goes so far as to claim that the rise of theory must be seen as "a historically specific routinization effect," whereby a formulaic mode of reading—most notably de Manian deconstruction—is transmitted to graduate students, who, in turn, apply it throughout the literary curriculum (259). And what deconstruction has provided, particularly through Paul de Man's project of rhetorical reading, is "the means of transforming the method of reading into a rigorously iterable *technical* procedure" that, Guillory asserts, "directly incorporated into the protocols of rhetorical reading a mimesis of the technobureaucratic itself" (262, original emphasis).

For evidence of theory's dominion over the literary syllabus, Guillory need look no further than the final preserve of academic autonomy—the graduate seminar:

> We can emphasize, to begin with, that it is only in the graduate seminar that theory can emerge as such, as a distinctive "canon" of writers and texts. The institutional conditions for the emergence of literary theory are therefore related to the institutional distinction between the graduate and undergraduate levels of the educational system. The signal feature of that distinction will already have been apparent: the relatively greater autonomy of the graduate teacher, which is in turn the condition for the transferential cathexes necessary for the propagation of theory. The relative nondetermination of the graduate syllabus by any higher administrative power is the sine qua non of theory, and for that reason theory itself is the vehicle of a claim to autonomy; it is the discursive field in which that autonomy can be negotiated, even when it is negotiated ideologically, as the perennial theoretical problem of the relation between language and the agency of the subject. The development of theory was always premised on the inviolability of the graduate seminar, the site of an autonomy not possible at the undergraduate level, where the syllabus of literature was subject to much greater oversight. (261)

While Guillory himself is obviously indebted to theory for "refunctioning" the work of those at the highest levels of literary study, he nevertheless sees this transformation of the content of graduate education and the marginalization of the literary curriculum as evidence that the university is being molded "into the institution designed to produce a new class of technical/managerial specialists possessed of purely technical/managerial knowledge" (261). With the literary curriculum being attacked from below by composition and from above by theory, he concludes that the only safe haven for the literary is the graduate seminar itself. For here the small class size, the intimate surroundings, and the self-selecting student body provide the harried graduate professor with some relief from the intrusions of "higher administrative powers" and the disciplinarily enforced constraints of teaching on the undergraduate level.

Of course, the relatively autonomous working conditions afforded by the graduate seminar are to be found only at the upper echelons of the academy: they certainly are nowhere in evidence in the pedagogical configurations more regularly produced by our systems of mass education, particularly in the "technobureaucratic" enclave of composition. In these places, the feelings students have for their teachers or for the assigned materials are quite unlike those at play in the dynamic that most interests Guillory, where there is a "love for what the master teaches, his 'teaching,' and beyond that…a love for the very texts the master loves" (182). And, as we will see in the concluding chapter, the pedagogical relationship Guillory deems necessary for "the propagation of theory" is even less likely to appear at the graduate level if one happens to be teaching a *required* course in composition studies. Yet however remote may be the world of pedagogical relations Guillory imagines, he persists in the hope that the rarefied conditions of educational exchange in the graduate seminar might be made to give way, as we've seen, to a system that allows for "a total democratization of access to cultural products" (337). In this utopian world, cultural capital would not disappear—a disastrous result that would rob intellectuals of their hard-earned prestige. Rather, at some future moment, everyone will be able to get in on the game, thereby producing "a vast enlargement of the field of aesthetic judgment" (339) and, one must assume, a new domain for first-rate intellectuals to exercise their influence.

The Twilight of Professional Purity: The Intellectual, the Bureaucrat, and the Undergraduate Curriculum

As Bourdieu and Guillory build their alternative worlds in words, there can be little question that both educators are reacting to the fact that we are now working in the twilight of the academic profession.[10] And it should be clear as well that both Bourdieu and Guillory advocate plans that are essentially thinly veiled reaction formations designed to protect and preserve the "relatively autonomous" intellectual sphere. Though they cover their acts of "world flight" with arguments about a deeper engagement in the political sphere (Guillory even says, at one point, that his approach to the canon debates may help "to bring the imaginary itself under more strategic political control" [37]), they can't escape the debilitating plight of being trapped in a prestige-based economy, where one's failure to effect change can be misrecognized as the successful adoption of a principled position. As the following chapters will show in some detail, however, there is a way out of this self-induced powerlessness. Specifically, the historicizing of actual educational practices provides ample evidence that sustainable reform occurs when educators move toward rather than flee from the world of bureaucratic demands that structure academic life. As we will see, no one involved in the reform efforts discussed here completely escaped the gravitational pull of what Hunter terms "intellectual fanaticism" (133) — that way of thinking that captures all of us who work in the academy, tempting us to believe that the material world can be changed through rational argument alone, drawing us deeper into the teacher's fallacy. Nor, for that matter, did any of these reformers manage to engage with the extant mechanisms for delivering education *without* compromising their original goals. It is for precisely this reason that each of these reform efforts warrants our attention, for taken together they allow us to see how any plan meant to have a direct and measurable effect on the institutional practices that govern what constitutes "higher" education and who will be given access to that education is inevitably altered during the implementation phase. Thus, unlike the utopian visions of educational reform alluded to above, the reform efforts I discuss had no alternative but to engage in what I have come to call "a politics of impurity."[11]

Lest embracing a politics of impurity sound grander and more heroic than it, in fact, is, we might usefully recall Evan Watkins's argument in *Work Time: English Departments and the Circulation of Cultural Value*, where Watkins offers irrefutable evidence that academics are necessarily deeply mired in and complicit with the massive bureaucratic machinery of higher education. As he puts it, "nobody becomes an English professor in order to grade papers, write committee meeting minutes and letters of recommendation, or argue with the dean about the need for a Xerox machine in the departmental office," but the the vast majority of one's "work time" in the academy is taken up with these very activities, rather than in "documenting the frontier myths informing *The Great Gatsby*" or some other such project that one was ostensibly trained to pursue (1). To illustrate this point, Watkins describes completing a form surveying how faculty spent their time during the previous quarter, a task he discovered he could perform "with depressing ease":

> I taught two undergraduate classes, requiring then two sets of decisions about what texts to order, what to read, what written work to assign. I read 211 student papers from those classes, assigning a grade to each one and a final grade to each of the total of 64 students who finished the

quarter. I directed 2 graduate students in independent reading courses, helped write and evaluate 9 Ph.D. examinations, and directed 1 M.A. thesis. I wrote 18 letters of recommendation for students, to various ends, and 2 letters of recommendation for faculty. I read and wrote evaluations of 2 essays submitted to journals for publication. (81)

Watkins's list continues, but this much of it is sufficient to illustrate his point that the profession looks different depending on whether one focuses on the content of graduate education or the content of its members' work time. This does not prove — nor does Watkins intend to imply — that the intensive training graduate students receive in preparation for a kind of intellectual labor that will never occupy a central place in their actual "work time" is utterly without meaning. To the contrary, he insists, such training in literary criticism and critical theory is preeminently important precisely because "theory recruits a labor force into English" (8).

Building on the notion that theory's job is to attract future laborers to the profession, Watkins explains this mismatch between the intellectual and bureaucratic demands placed on those who work in the academy: "English as a university discipline always foregrounds theory in one way or another, under whatever name, because it is always in the business of recruiting. As a discipline, however, it recruits a labor force for English *departments*, whose social functions and educational importance were not determined on the basis of recruiting promises. Nor can they be changed simply by rethinking the discipline" (9, original emphasis). Or, to put this somewhat differently, it is no accident that those recruited to study at the highest levels of the academy are regularly trained to do a kind of intellectual work that will consume little of their time in their future places of employment — if, that is, they are lucky enough to land a job. The suppression of this disjunction between the intellectual promise and the bureaucratic realities of work in higher education is simply a marketing strategy. Clearly, those attracted by this ploy are more likely than not to share the intellectual's visceral distaste for life in a bureaucracy and to see an academic career as providing the promise of at least momentary freedom from the constraints of the material world. Indeed, announcing one's utter disregard for what the job market portends and refusing to confront the consequences of going into considerable debt to finance one's education are only the most obvious ways to demonstrate that one is an ideal recruit, too given to the pleasures of the mind to care what deprivations might await the body. By the time these initiates are ready to enter the job market and find themselves competing for jobs that regularly require teaching composition and entry-level survey courses, the problem is out of everyone's hands: the recruit is usually too deep in the system to tunnel out; the sympathetic recruiters who helped train the graduate student regret that they have no control over the market; and the new employers explain that the content of the teaching load at their institutions is based not on the training the recruit received elsewhere, but on the needs of the resident student population.

If it is fair to say that English Studies attracts people to the profession by suppressing its own conditions of possibility, it does so for the very good reason that teaching undergraduates, working in composition, and being a bureaucratic functionary have all come to circulate as synonyms for disreputable work. All of these activities pose a threat to the notion that employment at the highest levels of the academy leads to a life of relative autonomy. In fact, the common assumption is that such work is "better suited" to teaching assistants, part-time lecturers, and second-rate minds—the bottom feeders in the intellectual food chain. By speaking this open secret aloud, Watkins's intent is not to heighten the resident antagonisms that exist between "teachers" and "scholars," "bureaucrats" and "deep thinkers." To the contrary, his argument robs the accusation that one is a bureaucrat of its power. Watkins illustrates this point by drawing a distinction between the concrete labor that students perform in a specific course and the "abstract labor" that circulates from that course once the work has been completed. As he put it, when teaching a course,

> You don't report to the registrar that *Paradise Lost* is a revolutionary fusion of contradictory ethical claims, or even that John has a remarkable grasp of English history for a sophomore. You report that 60239 got a 3.8 in Engl 322, which in turn, in a couple of years, is then circulated to the personnel office at Boeing as 60239's prospective employer. There's a chance the workers in the personnel office at Boeing will hear something from 60239 about the fusion of ethical claims in *Paradise Lost*, but not a very good one. (18)

Given the shared bureaucratic and administrative structure of nearly every educational organization in this country, this is what all teachers do, regardless of discipline or position in the academic hierarchy: they produce and put into circulation evaluations; they solicit, assess, and respond to student work; they perform the bureaucratic function of sifting and sorting individuals.

Obviously, there are ways to reduce being directly implicated in this bureaucratic process whereby the unique character of any specific classroom practice is erased and transformed into a homogenous experience equivalent to any other course in any discipline with any instructor. One can seek out lighter teaching loads with smaller classes; with the acquisition of seniority, one can further insist on teaching only electives at the upper levels. Under "ideal" circumstances, one can make oneself available only to graduate students. Certainly, those "fortunate" enough to attain this level of distinction experience a greater sense of relative autonomy than those placed elsewhere in the system; indeed, as Guillory's discussion of the erotics of de Man's seminar suggests, it may even be the case that those who work under such conditions enjoy a learning environment where casting the teacher as a "master" and analyzing the pedagogical relations in terms of "love" might be of some use analytically. Whatever opportunities seminars of this kind may provide, though, the availability of such working conditions is steadily declining and the gap between the unfettered life of the intellectual and the beleaguered life of the bureaucrat is shrinking to the point that, as we have seen above, even the best and the brightest in the profession have begun to sense that the academy is changing. Of course, for those in the academy who have never enjoyed the now-disappearing privileges and for those who never fully bought into the logic of the game of the academy's monopoly of the circulation of cultural capital, the call from on high to band together to defend the institution against the "sudden" encroachment of arbitrary methods for managing human capital is bound to produce a range of conflicting responses. Socrates may have been willing to drink the hemlock, but nearly everyone who has followed after him has opted to comply with the broad demands of systems of domination.

In *Rethinking the School*, Ian Hunter provides the historical background and the theoretical framework necessary for making sense of our view of the academic and the bureaucratic spheres as both fully enmeshed and fully incommensurate. Hunter turns to the historical record to make the argument — shocking in this context — that the bureaucratized educational system embodies "one of the central ethical and political achievements of the administrative state" (xxii). This is so, he maintains, because the educational system is an unprincipled, hybridized institution that has succeeded in separating the state's business of training citizens from the religious interest in managing the development of an individual's inner life and conscience. By way of explaining this almost unthinkable notion that a school system administered by unprincipled bureaucrats is superior to one under the control of highly principled intellectuals, Hunter insists that

> The ethical attributes of the good bureaucrat — strict adherence to procedure, acceptance of sub- and super-ordination, esprit de corps, abne-

gation of personal moral enthusiasms, commitment to the purposes of the office—are not an incompetent substraction from a "complete" (self-concerned and self-realizing) comportment of the person. On the contrary, they are a positive moral achievement requiring the mastery of a difficult ethical milieu and practice. They are the product of definite ethical techniques and routines—"declaring" one's personal interest, developing professional relations with one's colleagues, subordinating one's ego to procedural decision-making—through which individuals develop the disposition and ability to conduct themselves according to the ethos of bureaucratic office. (156–57)

And what "good bureaucrats" have done historically, according to Hunter, is to assist in the creation of a similarly hybridized school system, one that uses a pastoral model of pedagogical practice, defanged of its religious fervor, to meet the government's need for an educated citizenry. Thus, in place of an idealized instructional scene, where the teacher is the shepherd tending with loving care to the flock, Hunter bids us to see the material advantages of placing the bureaucrat between the figure of the teacher, as self-reflective moral subject, and the students, as citizens-in-the-making. With the classroom roles redefined in this way, the teacher's genealogical relationship to the pastor is found to reveal itself in an overriding inclination toward "intellectual fundamentalism," which insists on seeing schools "as the expression of a coherent set of ethical or political principles." This fanaticism does not pose the threat that it has in religious institutions, however, partly because the historic achievement of the bureaucratic system of education is its "unprincipled coherence," which allows it to resist dogmatic idealisms in favor of creating "a new horizon for political action and reflection: the optimal management of mundane social and economic life" (89–91).

Hunter's celebration of an administered state is bound to appear woefully out of step at a historical moment ruled by the Foucauldian critique of disciplinarity. Hunter is not, however, ignorant of Michel Foucault's observations. Rather he would have us see that

It was the administrative state that created a non-violent, tolerant, and pragmatic sphere of political deliberation, by forcefully separating the public comportment of the citizen from the private persona of the man of conscience, and by subordinating spiritual absolutes to governmental objectives. Perhaps the foremost instrument and effect of this historic development was the education "bureau," through which states conceptualized and organized that massive and ongoing program of pacification, discipline, and training responsible for the political and social capacities of the modern citizen. (60)

One way that the administered state established this "pragmatic sphere of political deliberation" was by developing "new political and intellectual technologies of government... [that] allowed the life and labor of national populations to be known in a form that opened them to political calculation and administrative intervention" (47). And what this involved, specifically, was the creation of mechanisms for collecting and assessing statistical data on the population, exposing problems that were then understood to be susceptible to governmental management. As evidence of the beneficial side of the government's intrusion into the private lives of its citizens, Hunter turns to what can only seem, at first glance, to be the most ludicrous of examples — the creation and implementation of "intelligence testing." These tests, he insists, "played a key role in changing ability from something that government should recognize and reward into something that it could form and distribute, for its own ends" (121). That is, over against the designs of those who would restrict access to the intellectual sphere to those exhibiting, say, an ineffable "quality of mind," the government's reconfiguration of "ability," "intelligence," or "smarts" as a statistically measurable attribute needs to be seen as a significant advance precisely because the data produced by this reconfiguration has subsequently provided the material for de-naturalizing academic success. With such statistics, it becomes possible, for instance, to correlate test scores with race, class, and gender and to use such information to build a case for the necessity of legislative intervention to ensure that equal educational opportunities are made available to all citizens. The statistical assessments, in other words, *can* be used to give body to abstractions about restricted access to cultural capital, thereby making visible the need to address the system's manifest injustices with specific structural adjustments — such as increased spending, additional support services, curricular reforms to improve performance.[12]

Obviously, such statistical information can also be used in the service of promoting even greater social injustice. Indeed, the discussion of Matthew Arnold's tenure as an inspector of schools in the next chapter shows how the government's overarching interest in measurable results can shape in ways that are far from ideal the work students must do. Granting the point that statistical evidence can be used for good or ill, Hunter points out that critical intellectuals have been too quick to judge empirical evidence of the system's failure to deliver the same educational product to all as yet one more sign of the moral and ethical weakness of the bureaucrats who have rigged the system to preserve their own privilege. He insists that the statistics drawn from "intelligence testing" must be read differently:

> Critique distinguishes itself, and its exponents, only through the hypermoral reinterpretation of the figures as measures of the gap between class difference and moral equality. In thus presuming to judge the ethics of social governance by the standards of personal conscience, this gesture runs the risk of intellectual fanaticism. For what the figures in fact measure is the gap between class differences and an optimal social training and utilization of the population, the "talent reserve." It was this gap—opened by government itself as the means of problematizing the divided school system—that first made educational equality into a governmental objective and that fuelled the drive for comprehensive schooling. (133)

It is easy enough to imagine this claim being greeted with a cascade of catcalls, followed by the usual litany of accusations that accompany the articulation of such an impure position: without even reading *Rethinking the School*—and indeed, if Hunter is right, some intellectuals would refuse to read his book on principle—there will be those who, on the basis of my summary alone, will find cause to dismiss Hunter as a dupe of the ideological state apparatus, someone willfully blind to the role education has played in promoting social injustice.

While this line of response is predictable, it is also unwarranted, for Hunter presents his argument in hopes of providing intellectuals with a more useful way to think about how school reform might be tailored to combat social injustice. His goal is to develop a more successful set of strategies for approaching the ever-receding objective of educational equality. Thus, by arguing that the critical intellectual and all others who see themselves as self-realizing individuals can "claim no absolute ethical privilege" over any other entity produced by the administrative state—"the statesman, the bureaucrat, the jurist, the citizen"—Hunter's aim is not to justify the status quo but rather to lay the groundwork necessary for retheorizing what work it is that schools do and what work they can be made to do, given reigning social, political, historical, and economic constraints (36). In order to advance this project, Hunter argues,

> [Intellectuals] must give up "principled" critique and develop a far more pluralistic and supple bearing toward the ethical and organizational reality of the school system. Instead of holding it accountable to a single

ideal of the person we must learn to respect the restraints imposed on our intellectual conduct and, more importantly, on our conduct as intellectuals, by the plural assemblage of persons, disciplines, conducts and objectives that comprises the school system. (164–65)

It is in this spirit that the following analyses of particular reform efforts have been written. And, because they are the result of the deliberative approach I have outlined here, these case studies in the history of educational reform confirm Hunter's sense that there's little reason to believe individual institutions act like reasoned individuals or that such institutions respond to critiques made by those whose work they oversee and authorize.

Agents of Change:
Improvising the Hybrid Persona of the Intellectual-Bureaucrat

Like Hunter, I too hope that reflecting on the largely ineffectual role intellectuals have played in the history of educational reform will help us "to improvise a more sober and supple intellectual persona" than those seen to be available to us now (176), but I'm much less sanguine than he about the likelihood that "in obedience to its own governmental ethic, the school system would eventually itself give rise to a form of equality" (103). Bureaucracies are certainly good at generating data, producing information about the social world on a scale that no individual or team of individuals could ever approach. Even so, there is little evidence to support the idea that bureaucracies are driven by some internal compulsion to interpret the collected data in ways that *effectively* result in a more egalitarian distribution of educational and employment possibilities. Furthermore, when Hunter asserts that the bureaucrat and the critical intellectual "represent different stations in ethical life" and therefore "give rise to comportments of the person that are non-transferable," he leaves the impression that there is little the intellectual can do to assist the bureaucratic system in moving toward "a form of equality" (164). As the following cases make clear, there is, in fact, a good deal that can and has been done to improvise a "more sober and supple intellectual persona." To varying degrees, the reformers discussed here succeeded in fabricating the persona of that hybrid figure— the intellectual-bureaucrat—that Hunter only briefly entertains as an available option. For despite their different ways and different motivations, each of these reformers sought to harness the energy of the critical impulse to engage effectively with the bureaucratic realities that govern what can occur in the classroom.

Having invoked the intellectual-bureaucrat, I must underscore that the work lying ahead for those committed to educational reform will require *improvising* this persona under conditions of considerable constraint. For evidence of these constraints, we need look no further than the numerous ways in which my own argument has ensnared me in the very activities I have been at such pains to critique. Indeed, the very fact that I have engaged at such length in *critiquing* the critique of educational practice squarely places me in the ranks of those same self-reflexive theoreticians whose work I have criticized for endlessly deferring constructive action. One of the constraining conditions of academic life, though, is that in order to be heard, one must first establish a familiarity with, if not a mastery of, the institution's authenticating practices. This particular conflict between the form and the content of my argument may be explained away as an institutional inevitability; but the other contradictions that have made themselves felt over the course of my exposition may seem less the necessary responses to extant constraints than the traces of a second-rate mind betraying its limitations. Thus, if I may be said to have improvised a persona in all this, to some it may seem that I have produced little more than a series of dissonances: the critic of critique, the intellectual writing in defense of the bureaucrat (or perhaps the bureaucrat who dreams of being an intellectual), the teacher using the student to show how other teachers have used the student, the pure practitioner of a politics of impurity.

I do not seek to evade such charges; indeed, my being caught up in these contradictions points very clearly to what it means to say that we always are working within constraints. Though the ivory tower is an omnipresent image of academic freedom, among other things, those involved in the business of education are well aware that all academic work actually occurs under conditions that circumscribe what statements may be made as well as how and where those statements may be made. The processes of peer review, tenure, and promotion are only the most overt examples of the operative mechanisms of constraint in this sphere; recalling Bourdieu's work, we note that these constraints are also internalized and experienced as freely elected choices by the highly educated. In addition to these evaluative mechanisms, which exercise an array of material, conceptual, and experiential constraints on all members of the academic community, the form and content of discussions about educational reform are also regulated. These specific discursive constraints include dominant representations of teachers and students, the scene of instruction, and the educational process itself, as well as the shared assumption that the educational enterprise stands in opposition to business concerns and bureaucratic organization.

There is no escaping this array of constraints, no argument that will allow one to elude their grasp, no way of speaking or writing that can fully succeed at suppressing their contradictory force or their contaminating presence. If the by now tiresome exercise of pure deconstruction has taught us anything, it should be this. But to acknowledge that one's words and actions are constrained need not be a prelude, as it so often is, to yet another utopian vision where no such constraints operate and the free market for the circulation of cultural capital reigns supreme. Rather, recognizing the inescapability of these constraining conditions at this historical moment may well be the necessary first step toward a fuller engagement with the extant social sphere. For the figures who populate the pages that follow, this engagement has taken the form of improvising educational possibilities out of the restricted materials available, plunging into the impure business of building a functioning alternative to current educational practice, and working with and against the waves of internal and external resistance to change. In other words, these figures have done what Bourdieu has taught us intellectuals can see only as the "dirty" work of education—work that academics in particular have been happy enough, more often than not, to leave to a different order of being.

Ironically, perhaps, I was initially brought to pursue this study by my own dissatisfaction with the general current of the academic debate about multiculturalism, because the debate never seemed to get around to addressing the consequences of past and current academic practices that established and then hierarchized categorical and essential differences between peoples—to examining the academic assessment practices that marked certain peoples and certain acts of literary production as "dirty." Thus, in setting out to explore previous efforts to reform the academy, I wanted to gain a better understanding of how actual changes in the material practices of the educational system were realized; I wanted, in effect, some guidelines for how to move our discussions about difference forward so that they would provide pedagogical approaches and institutional environments that might be more responsive to the diverse histories our students bring with them into the classroom. For these reasons, I selected touchstones in the debate about multiculturalism, hoping to historicize the institutional practices that have served to naturalize cultural differences. But I also wanted to study those institutional practices that have attempted to recognize and accommodate differential ways of knowing by problematizing transhistorical differences—those approaches grounded in noncanonical cultural artifacts and practices as well as those that draw on ways of using language that stand outside the mainstream. Thus, one way to understand this book's organizational principle is to see it as exploring two "elitist" points of reference in the debate about multiculturalism—Matthew Arnold and the Great Books approach—and two "progressive" points of reference—British cultural studies and the introduction of ethnographic approaches into the curriculum.

As the individual analyses unfold, however, it will become clear that those preliminary labels, which accurately depict current understandings of the implicit political agendas of these projects, are of little descriptive or analytical value when applied to moments of actual educational practice. Indeed, the deliberative approach employed throughout the chapters that follow works to detail as fully as possible what Hunter calls "the plural assemblage of persons, disciplines, conducts and objectives that comprises the school system" (165). For this reason, I focus less on the fugitive ideological interests roiling beneath the educational rhetoric of the reformers than on the material practices and consequences that have followed, often quite unexpectedly, from particular efforts to institutionalize reform. In this way, the process of educational reform is cast as ever an uncertain project, one that involves anticipating the constraining forces that constantly threaten the possibilities of educational innovation and responding to the inevitably unforeseen contingencies, resistances, and outright ruptures that follow a plan once it is put into practice.

What I hope to show as being true of the process of educational reform is also true of the process of studying the process of educational reform, since my selection of cases occurred within a similarly constrained field of choice. That is, to do historical research on educational practice, one must rely on what the archive has preserved, and this reliance itself is quite constraining—particularly if one's interest lies with student work, which the academy endlessly produces and endlessly discards. The cases I examine here "paid off" as research sites because the archive could be made to release considerable amounts of previously untapped information about these curricular innovations: parliamentary records contain reams of testimony concerning the British government's reluctant venture into popular education; much of the discussion about the issues pertaining to the creation of the Great Books curriculum preceded the spread of the telephone and so is preserved in detailed correspondence among the founders; the initial effort to bring cultural studies to the masses circulated through the Open University's distance learning apparatus, which left behind mass-produced pedagogical materials and, by chance, a record of how students evaluated the work; and, finally, the sole extended ethnographic study that seeks to capture the whole of undergraduate life, Michael Moffat's *Coming of Age in*

New Jersey, concerns students from my own university. One always studies what one can, shaping a project in response to what can be found, what can be reasonably argued, and what can be accomplished in the allotted time, then covering one's tracks to make the absences, gaps, and shortcomings either disappear or seem a matter of principle.

In this instance, the absences, gaps, and shortcomings in our knowledge about how the student has figured in and been figured by educational reform is intimately related to institutional decisions about what educational materials warrant preservation. One virtue of pursuing research on the history of educational reform, though, is that whatever the library has on the subject is almost certain to be on the shelf—the availability of the desired reference matter being a concrete manifestation of what isn't now circulating as cultural capital. Even so, ready access to the small body of relevant materials doesn't make up for the absence of representative bodies of student work completed within any of the educational systems I study here. One may well ask, Why on earth should that material have been preserved? It is a reasonable question. But the apparent absurdity of proposing that student work be preserved may be another trace of the belief that "the student" functions as a transhistorical subject whose work remains everywhere and in every way the same. That is, such a question may just be another way of saying that student work warrants as little attention as one can get away giving it.

That my study has been cobbled together from within this field of material constraint, where I have resorted to any number of strategies for reading along the margins of official documents, textbooks, and teacher accounts to tease out the historical fragments of the figure of the student, doesn't explain my failure to consider those two movements that have clearly had the most to do with placing the debate about multiculturalism in the national spotlight: women's studies and African American studies. It would be a mistake to read their absence from my book as indicating my lack of interest in these areas or in the curricular and pedagogical initiatives they have given rise to, just as it would be an error to construe the presence of any of the areas covered in the chapters that follow as indicating my implicit commitments. To the contrary, efforts to make academic practice more responsive to the needs, concerns, and achievements of women, African Americans, other racial and ethnic minorities, and other marginalized groups are never far from my analysis of the reform approaches discussed here.

My commitment to improving both access to and the content of higher education does not manifest itself, however, in the form of an ongoing assessment of each program in terms of the degree to which women or other marginalized groups are represented on that program's curriculum. Rather, my concern with making the academy a more hospitable environment for all those disenfranchised by the current system for disseminating cultural capital is expressed in my attention to the profound material consequences that regularly result from constructing reform movements on the back of an idealized student who, more often than not, is understood to be entirely free of cultural commitments, fully deracinated, infinitely malleable, and absolutely receptive to any and all reform objectives. By "thinking with students," I draw attention to the ways that specific assumptions about race, class, and gender construct specific learning subjects. Woven into the very fabric of my methodology, then, is an array of questions that serve to reveal how "the student" has been gendered female within the institutional space of the academy; one consequence of this gendering has been the designation of resistance to pedagogical practice as evidence of the student's unreason, while compliance is understood to reveal fertile possibilities for the social reproduction of the institution.

This approach also makes it clear that those truly committed to increasing access to all the academy has to offer must assume a more central role in the bureaucratic management of the academy. For, as I argue in my final chapter, it is at the microbureaucratic level of local praxis that one can begin to exercise a material influence not only on how students are represented or on which books will be a part of the required reading lists but also, and much more important, on which individuals are given a chance to become students and on whether the academy can be made to function as a responsive, hospitable environment for all who work within its confines. This is a modest enough goal, but it is firmly grounded in the belief that what we do as teachers and intellectuals does matter and that this work matters most immediately and significantly within our local institutional contexts. In other words, it is just the kind of goal that Tyack and Cuban might approvingly characterize as tinkering toward utopia: it concedes the existence of a grammar of schooling and bids those of us who know the most about the daily practice of education to speak using this grammar, to recognize the weight of historical constraint, and to engage with the bureaucratic systems that makes academic work possible. By pursuing this goal, we may find it possible to begin to change what it means to "succeed" in the academy and to provide greater access to such success. It may also allow those of us who are in the business of education to begin to exercise some small measure of control over the circumstances, conditions, and content of our employment. And this, in itself, as the following chapters illustrate in quite different ways, can be the first step toward actually experiencing and thereby preserving the "relative autonomy" that academic work can, indeed, be made to provide.

2 Ministering to a Mind Diseased

Matthew Arnold, Her Majesty's Inspector

In 1875 Matthew Arnold was invited to make a public toast at an anniversary banquet for the Royal Academy, a space created in 1768 by George III for the exhibition of contemporary art. Arnold, who by this point in his life had served as an inspector of schools for nearly a quarter of a century, found himself in rich company: there "were two English 'royal highnesses' present, as well as several from the Continent" (qtd. in Super 478). According to a reporter for the London *Times*, following "the toasts to the Queen, the Royal family, the Army and the Navy, the President of the Academy proposed 'Prosperity to the Interests of Science and Literature,' " Sir John Lubbock provided the toast for science, and then Arnold, as requested, spoke on behalf of literature (373). With the stage thus set, Arnold turned to those present—the royalty, the aristocrats, the president of the Academy, a group of his superiors from the Education Department—and made this remarkable statement:

> Literature, no doubt, is a great and splendid art, allied to that great and splendid art of which we see around us the handiwork. But, Sir, you do me an undeserved honor when, as President of the Royal Academy, you desire me to speak in the name of Literature. Whatever I may have once wished or intended, my life is not that of a man of letters, but of an Inspector of Schools (a laugh), and it is with embarrassment that I now stand up in the dreaded presence of my own official chiefs (a laugh), who have lately been turning upon their Inspectors an eye of some suspicion. (A laugh). ("Three Public Speeches" 373–74)

That Arnold was disappointed not to have been able to lead the life of a "man of letters" is clear enough: his professorship at Oxford had ended eight years before this speech and he had never been able to support his family solely through his writing or his lecturing. In fact, Arnold had been driven into public service twenty-four years earlier because the life of a man of letters did not permit him the means to start and support a family.

There is also ample evidence that Arnold was not particularly taken with the bureaucratic work of school inspection. Although Arnold wrote his wife after receiving the appointment, "I think I shall get interested in the schools after a little time," within two months he had a clearer sense of how demanding his job was to be: "I have had a hard day. Thirty pupil teachers to examine in an inconvenient room and nothing to eat except a biscuit, which a charitable lady gave me" (*Letters, 1848–1888* 20–21). And a little more than a year later, in early 1853, he was dreaming of a different life altogether: "I don't know why, but I certainly find inspecting peculiarly oppressive just now; but I must tackle to, as it would not do to let this feeling get too strong. All this afternoon I have been haunted by a vision of living with you at Berne, on a diplomatic appointment, and how different that would be from this incessant grind in schools" (30–31). Around this time, as well, Arnold observed with resignation, in a letter to his friend Arthur Clough, that "a great career is hardly possible any longer.... I am more and more convinced that the world tends to become more comfortable for the mass, and more uncomfortable for those of any natural gift or distinction — and it is as well perhaps that it should be so" (*Letters to Clough* 122).

And so, although Arnold neither "wished" nor "intended" it, he spent his working hours living the life of an inspector of schools, under conditions of economic necessity few of his listeners in the Academy that evening were likely to have ever experienced. When we keep this in mind, the audacity of Arnold's toast becomes apparent, for he used this public occasion to criticize those in power — both his immediate superiors and the aristocracy in general — for their support of a political system whereby it was impossible for a man (and Arnold most certainly would have meant "a man") to make a living by writing poetry and criticism. What Arnold wanted his auditors to understand, apparently, was that while they stood surrounded by works of art, he lived in a world in which teaching others about sweetness and light, Hellenism and Hebraism, culture and anarchy did not put food on the table. And yet, if Arnold really was expressing his bitterness about what he perceived as the injustice of the system of social relations that dominated his life, how are we to make sense of the reporter's parenthetical observations that each moment in this opening salvo was met by laughter? Who is laughing? And why?

Perhaps those present thought Arnold was being ironic. After all, given the amount of work he had published by 1875, his claim might well have seemed a comic gesture of self-deprecation. Arnold, not a man of letters? Imagine! While it is certainly possible that some of those present responded to Arnold's remarks in this way, it is clear that others picked up on the barbs imbedded in his toast. In fact, years later, prior to Arnold's arrival in the United States for a lecture tour in 1882, a local editorial in the *World* admiringly noted Arnold's insistence on always letting the "fine gentlemen and ladies" know he considered himself to be their superior. Addressing Arnold directly, the writer of the editorial went on: "There is, perhaps, no other man of letters now alive who would have had the intrepidity to make such a speech as you did a couple years ago in returning thanks for the toast of literature at the Academy dinner" (qtd. in Super 478). Thus, if there were those who understood Arnold's toast to be ironic, there were others who saw it as an open attack on those in the audience. Both groups, though, took a common pleasure in rejecting Arnold's claim not to have lived the life of a man of letters.

There are still other explanations for the laughter, of course. Perhaps those present at the banquet followed the intent of Arnold's critique and laughed out of nervousness in hopes of smoothing over a difficult social situation. It is even possible that Arnold's audience understood the toast quite well and laughed out of disdain for Arnold and his circumstances—the vicious laughter that the privileged save for those less well-to-do. What is unlikely, though, is that Arnold was among those laughing; in this crowd, those who didn't *have* to work could afford to have a laugh at the expense of one who did. But Arnold, who at the time of this toast was required to examine every student individually in the schools he inspected, surely had little to laugh about. The disparity in the material conditions of the man giving the toast and those of his auditors is also what allows those assembled to respond, according to the *Times* reporter, with "Cheers and a laugh" when Arnold compared the annual congregation at the Academy to the gathering of a group of Greek expatriates in Italy who "once every year...assembled themselves together at a public festival of their community, and there...reminded one another that they were once Greeks" (374). Again, one can imagine nervous laughter in response to this open display of ridicule. But cheers? How are we to explain those cheers? Is it possible that any of those Barbarians could "hear" what Arnold was saying to them about themselves and the world they had created?

While at one time the effect of Arnold's words could be located somewhere on this spectrum spanning from irony to utter inconsequentiality, it is safe to say that Arnold's words subsequently have taken on a greater weight. Indeed, in his current role as standard-bearer for those committed to studying "the best that has been thought and said in our time," Arnold has assumed a position of central importance in debates about multiculturalism and the mission of English Studies, about the function of criticism, and about the educator's role in social reform. As Chris Baldick has argued so persuasively, this has been Arnold's fate *not* because his approach to literature was unique or because his thoughts about the role of the middle class in revitalizing British culture were particularly innovative. Rather, as Baldick puts it, Arnold's achievement "was to be a kind of prophecy, a reference point for all future combatants in debates over the uses of literary study" (60).[1] And, perhaps because Arnold is now regularly figured as the prophet who fearlessly supported elevated standards and academic excellence against a rising tide of mediocrity, he is also regularly deployed as the negative foundational trope by those interested in launching a critique of English Studies and the status quo. Baldick himself uses Arnold in this way, asserting that Arnold's most lasting and most unfortunate achievement was to create "a new kind of critical discourse which could, by its display of careful extrication from controversy, speak from a privileged standpoint, all other discourses being in some way compromised by partial or partisan considerations" (25). Baldick contends that because everyone who followed Arnold had to take up and respond to this "innocent language," "the title of 'criticism' was usurped by a literary discourse whose entire attitude was at heart uncritical. Criticism in its most important and its most vital sense had been gutted and turned into its very opposite: an ideology" (234).

Edward Said finds Arnold's influence to have been even more nefarious, if possible:

> What is too often overlooked by Arnold's readers is that he views this ambition of culture to reign over society as essentially combative: "the best that is known and thought" must contend with competing ideologies, philosophies, dogmas, notions, and values, and it is Arnold's insight that what is at stake in society is…the assertively achieved and *won* hegemony of an identifiable set of ideas, which Arnold honorifically calls culture, over all other ideas in society. (10, original emphasis)

What is striking about Said's loose rendering of Arnold's definition of culture is that it occurs directly beneath Said's own citation of an extended passage from *Culture and Anarchy*, where Arnold speaks of "the *best* knowledge and thought of the time" (qtd. in Said 10, original emphasis). By truncating and rephrasing the formulation, Said effectively pushes Arnold's concerns into the past and out of the world, a rhetorical move that provides Said with the occasion to call for a new brand of "secular criticism" that would reconsider the relationship between the world, the text, and the critic. The passage cited above comes as Said commences this argument, at the moment when he is establishing Arnold as an example of someone who articulated and authorized a hierarchical definition of culture, one in which culture was understood to move "downward from the height of power and privilege in order to diffuse, disseminate, and expand itself in the widest possible range" (9). Said goes on assert that Arnold shows these commitments most clearly at the conclusion of *Culture and Anarchy*, where in the last (and most telling) instance, Arnold is to be found unequivocally siding with those in power against the powerless and the homeless. In taking this stance, Arnold shows that what is at stake in the combat between culture and society is control over the system of state-imposed exclusions whereby some members of society are marked as insiders — those "at home," those who are "cultured" — and others are deemed outsiders — the homeless, the anarchical, the irrational, the insane, the disenfranchised. In other words, Said argues, to "be for and in culture is to be in and for a State in a compellingly loyal way" (11).

Turning to Macaulay's Minute of 1835 on Indian education, Said then sets out to demonstrate how this notion of a superior, discriminating culture — which assumes something of a benign aspect in Arnold's criticism — had particularly detrimental effects when applied by the British in India. As Said puts it, Macaulay "was speaking from a position of power where he could translate his opinions into the decision to make an entire subcontinent of natives submit to studying in a language not their own" (13). Here again, Said is at pains to establish the urgency of *his own* critical project, which involves the exploration and enactment of a criticism "reducible neither to a doctrine nor to a political position on a particular question,…in the world and self-aware simultaneously," this time by asserting the existence of an affiliative relationship between the Arnoldian mission and the broader project of British imperialism (29). However, by using Arnold in this way, Said appears to have lost sight of two important facts. First, Arnold was thirteen years old when Macaulay's Minute was published, so if anything Arnold stood in a filial relationship to Macaulay's educational ideas rather than the other way around.[2] Second, and more important, Arnold, unlike Macaulay, never occupied a position of power from which he could legislate the actions of others. Indeed, one of Arnold's abiding disappointments was to find himself living in a country where everyone was free to do as he or she pleased. So what Said forgets, in order to make his argument, is that Arnold never was a member of Parliament, nor did he serve on the Supreme Council of India; he was, rather, an inspector of schools. And, as we will see, in this position Arnold exercised very little control over his own working conditions and absolutely no control whatsoever over how the education of the masses was handled in Britain or in its colonies.

This is not to say that Arnold didn't dream of a different world order, one guided not by the machinery of British politics but by the wise council of "aliens" such as he fancied himself to be—those able to take a disinterested approach to problems, those at liberty to allow their minds to play freely over possible solutions without fear of being diverted by partisanship. Indeed, it is well known that Arnold wished he had the authority necessary to squash his opponents if they disagreed with him. Arnold's most open expression of this desire caused such a stir that it was deleted from later editions of *Culture and Anarchy*, thereby depriving future readers of the opportunity to share in Arnold's fond memory of his father's advice about how to rule: "As for rioting, the old Roman way of dealing with that is always the right one; flog the rank and file, and fling the ringleaders from the Tarpeian Rock" (526)![3] And, though Arnold was hardly the model of consistency, his opposition to extending the franchise and his fear of the organizing masses were constant themes for him. To both he unfailingly responded in the spirit of his father's advice: "monster processions in the streets and forcible irruptions into the parks, even in professed support of this good design [of allowing 'an Englishman to be left to do as far as possible what he likes'], ought to be unflinchingly forbidden and repressed" (223). So Arnold certainly wished for radical redistribution of political power in Britain and he unquestionably hoped that the government would become more centralized and more united in its response to those who opposed rule by "sweetness and light." It is too easy to overlook the fact, though, that Arnold was *never* in a position to realize either of these goals.

While Arnold's authoritarian dreams are well known, very little work has been done to document his influence on the material practices of English education in the classroom.[4] This is not to say that Arnold's work as an inspector of schools has gone unnoticed. To the contrary, shortly after Arnold's death in 1888, Sir Francis Sandford edited a collection of Arnold's professional writing, which was published under the title *Reports on Elementary Schools, 1852–1882*. F. S. Marvin followed with a revised edition of these reports in 1908. Sir Joshua Fitch published *Thomas and Matthew Arnold and Their Influence on English Education*, a mixture of biography and reference, in 1897; Leonard Huxley offered a more complete sampling of Arnold's writings on schooling in *Thoughts on Education from Matthew Arnold*, published in 1912. There have even been two book-length studies that focus on Arnold's work as an inspector of schools: W. F. Connell's *Ed-*

ucational Thought and Influence of Matthew Arnold and Fred Walcott's *Origins of Culture and Anarchy: Matthew Arnold and Popular Education in England.* What this incomplete catalogue reveals, then, is that belief in the importance of Arnold's official activities is long-standing: indeed, Raymond Williams, one of the academic community's most thoughtful critics, has argued that *Culture and Anarchy* "needs to be read alongside the reports, minutes, evidence to commissions and specifically educational essays which made up so large a part of Arnold's working life." If this is done, Williams asserts, one can recuperate Arnold on the grounds that his "effort to establish a system of general and humane education was intense and sustained" (*Culture and Society* 119).

As one might expect, those who have worked to preserve Arnold's educational writings and to establish the ongoing relevance of his thinking tend to lapse into hagiographic celebrations of the man and his accomplishments. Connell, for instance, notes that Arnold "was an indefatigable essayist, not voluminous, but reasonably copious, and certainly forthright. It is this characteristic of forthrightness that largely justifies the title of 'Prophet' that has been applied to him by various writers from time to time" (273). And Walcott declares in an ecstatic moment that with some effort one can "perceive about the prophet's [Arnold's] head — within these middle years, at least — the faint, the almost imperceptible aura of the ineffectual angel" (135). While such responses simply judge Arnold as having been "ahead of his time," my concern in what follows is to resituate Arnold's critical writing within the historical context of his civil service career, so that we don't lose sight of the significance of his inability to effect change in his own time. By exacerbating the disjunction between the various ways Arnold has been used to name a kind of otherworldly critical work in English Studies and the ways he actually spent his time while serving as an inspector of schools, I hope to make sense of the anger, annoyance, and disappointment registered in Arnold's toast cited at the opening of this chapter. I hope to suggest, as well, that the ongoing preoccupation in English Studies with Arnold's critical work reflects a disciplinary disinclination to consider how rarely the business of critique has a demonstrable impact on the work that students, teachers, and inspectors actually do in and for the schools.

Arnold Confronts a Student-Teacher:
The Transparent Power of the Paraphrase

In his thirty-five years of service as an inspector of schools, Arnold visited classrooms and examined students and teachers all across England. On three separate occasions, he was sent overseas by his government to collect information on the state of popular education in Europe. He published two book-length reports, *The Popular Education of France* in 1861 and *Schools and Universities on the Continent* in 1867, as well as countless essays touching on educational matters. And yet, so far as I've been able to determine, Arnold refers directly to student work only once in all of this writing. As it turns out, Arnold was unwilling to draw evidence of the failures of Britain's educational system from such an obvious and rich source; in fact, he even avoided speaking directly about student work in the General Reports he was required to write each year as an inspector of schools. As he explained in his General Report for 1874, "I dislike the practice of culling in an official report absurd answers to examination questions in order to amuse the public with them; what I quote will be for the purpose of illustrating the defect of mind to which I have been calling attention, and I shall quote just what is necessary for this purpose and no more" (*Reports*, 177).[5]

It should thus come as no surprise to learn that when student work does make its way into Arnold's writing, its role is to illustrate the failure of the educational system and the student's "defect of mind." The reference that interests me here occurs in the midst of Arnold's debate with T. H. Huxley over the merits of a literary education. In 1880 Huxley asserted in his inaugural address at Sir Josiah Mason's Science College that "for the purpose of attaining real culture, an exclusively scientific education is at least as effectual as an exclusively literary education" (T. Huxley 141). Objecting to Huxley's rendition of his own commitment to "the best that has been thought and said in the world" as merely belletristic, Arnold insists in "Literature and Science" that he had never intended to exclude science from his recommended program of study: "In that best I certainly include what in modern times has been thought and said by the great observers and knowers of nature" (59). However, as Arnold develops his argument with Huxley, it becomes clear that for him the "great observers and knowers of nature" are not scientists at all, but poets and artists. For evidence of the failings of the natural sciences, Arnold refers to Darwin's theory about our ancestral relation to the "hairy quadrupeds," a proposition that he must admit is "interesting" and "important." The problem with men of science, though, is that they resist "the invincible desire to relate this proposition to the sense in us for conduct, and to the sense in us for beauty" (64–65). Poetry and the arts, in contrast, are superior precisely because they respond to the desire for moral rectitude and aesthetic completion.

At this point in the argument, Arnold dramatizes the steep decline in literary education by referring back to a school report he had written in 1876, where he recorded the response a "young man in one of our English training colleges" made to the assignment: "Paraphrase the passage in *Macbeth* beginning, 'Canst thou not minister to a mind diseased?'" To Arnold's dismay, the young man "turned this line into, 'Can you not wait upon the lunatic?'" Arnold does not explain why this response is unacceptable, perhaps because what makes it "bad" is, in his estimation, self-evident. What he does say is this: if he had to choose between working with students who knew the diameter of the moon (his version of scientific knowledge) but who couldn't judge the quality of this paraphrase, and students who were ignorant of the moon's diameter, yet who knew this paraphrase to be "bad," Arnold would prefer to spend his time with the latter group (69).

It's a strange example, serving as it does to undermine the sense that education in either the scientific or the literary realm is particularly important. And, for his part, Arnold quickly abandons it in favor of his next illustration, which is drawn from a speech made in Parliament. But even though Arnold uses the student almost in passing, the example is worth lingering over precisely because it is so puzzling and ineffective. To begin to make sense of why Arnold deems the pupil-teacher's paraphrase unsatisfactory and why he considers paraphrasing the best activity for initiating work with a literary text, we must turn to Arnold's earlier essay, "The Study of Poetry," where he charts out a preliminary rationale for this way of commencing work with poetry:[6]

> Yes; constantly, in reading poetry, a sense for the best, the really excellent, and of the strength and joy to be drawn from it, should be present in our minds and should govern our estimate of what we read. But this real estimate, the only true one, is liable to be superseded, if we are not watchful, by two other kinds of estimate, the historic estimate and the personal estimate, both of which are fallacious. (163)

Given the low premium Arnold places on these other ways of reading, he no doubt approved of the fact that the pupil-teacher in his example was not asked to produce either the historical context of the line from *Macbeth* (even within the limits of the play itself) or a personal response to the line. As far as Arnold can see, such tasks merely distract one from "the enjoyment of the best." What is less readily apparent, though, is how Arnold felt about the examination's failure to ask the pupil-teacher to "estimate" whether the given line of poetry was "really excellent." By withholding this question, the examination Arnold himself has administered appears willfully to deprive the pupil-teacher of the opportunity to participate in the very activity Arnold believes is central to the appreciation of poetry.[7]

From an institutional standpoint, how one resolves to evaluate an act of reading is of critical importance, since this produces the standards to which teachers and students must adhere. Inadvertently, Arnold reveals in "The Study of Poetry" just how unmanageable this issue can be, as he struggles to explain what makes his ten exemplary "touchstones" instances of truly excellent poetry: "if we are urgently pressed to give some critical account of [the touchstones], we may safely, perhaps, venture on laying down, not indeed how and why the characters arise, but where and in what they arise. They are in the matter and substance of the poetry, and they are in its style and manner" (171–72). In other words, Arnold cannot say how or why the touchstones achieve their effect; he can only gesture toward those places where effects are felt. Recognizing that this way of discussing the act of reading produces "but dry generalities" about "the matter and substance" and the "style and manner" of the highest poetry, Arnold proffers a rare piece of concrete advice: it is best if the student of poetry applies the touchstone method on his own, since "made by himself, the application would impress itself upon his mind far more deeply than made by me" (172). And with this observation that one learns to judge poetic quality only by engaging in the act of forming such judgments, the moment of critical "estimation" disappears into a vast and private interiority, far beyond the reach of the examination system.[8]

Given that the moment of estimation was, thus, necessarily unavailable for evaluation, paraphrasing provided the closest approximation of an act of reading that could be tested. In Arnold's example, as we saw, being able to paraphrase is analogous to knowing the diameter of the moon: isolating a single line of poetry produces a discrete object of study comparable to (and perhaps as distant from the reader as) the moon, supplying a similarly contained site for measurement and evaluation. With this in mind, it is worth pausing to consider the line selected from *Macbeth* for the pupil-teacher to paraphrase. The question — "Canst thou not minister to a mind diseased?" — occurs in the act 5, scene 3, just as Macbeth is coming to realize how terribly he has misread the witches' prophecy. Upon receiving intelligence that ten thousand soldiers are descending on his castle, Macbeth turns to the doctor and asks after Lady Macbeth's health, only to be informed that "she is troubled with thick-coming fancies / That keep her from her rest." Macbeth then makes this desperate plea to the doctor:

Canst thou not minister to a mind diseased,
Pluck from the memory a rooted sorrow,
Raze out the written troubles of the brain,
And with some sweet oblivious antidote

Cleanse the stuff'd bosom of that perilous stuff
Which weighs upon the heart? (5.3.40–44)

The "ministering" Macbeth demands for his queen is one of forgetting, an antidote to erase the "written troubles of the brain," a physic that would cure her of her feelings of guilt by "razing" her memory. The doctor's response, which causes Macbeth to curse all medicine and declare he will have "none of it," is that there is nothing a doctor can do for a patient with the symptoms Macbeth has described: "Therein the patient must minister to himself" (5.3.45–46)

Now, if the pupil-teacher's paraphrase "Can you not wait upon the lunatic?" is placed in this context, it does indeed appear clumsy, failing—one can imagine Arnold saying—to fully capture Shakespeare's "matter and substance": glossing Lady Macbeth as a "lunatic" offers a jarring image of Macbeth's feelings for his wife, neutralizing the tension in the play between mental wellness and mental illness and ignoring the role guilt plays in both realms. This, at least, is one way to account for why Arnold judged the paraphrase "bad." It should not go unnoticed, though, that the form of the examination question itself truncates the quote from Shakespeare, removing the train of redactions that provides the specific referents that define what "minister" and "mind diseased" might mean in the cited passage. In other words, the only way to produce a "good" paraphrase of this partial citation is to situate it at least within the full sentence from which it has been drawn, if not the context of the entire play. Based on what Arnold tells us in "Literature and Society," it is impossible to know whether we can reasonably assume that a pupil-teacher would possess the reading skills and the depth of knowledge about Shakespeare's works necessary to perform this task. In fact, in paraphrasing his own General Report of 1876, Arnold has left out the information that would allow one to determine whether the question posed to the pupil-teacher is "fair," for here we are told that the "bad" paraphrase was produced by a "youth who has been two years in a training college, and for the last of the two years has studied *Macbeth*" (*Reports*, 176)!

Had Arnold included this information in "Literature and Science," he not only would have made it easier for his readers to estimate the quality of the pupil-teacher's paraphrase, he also would have been in a position to sharpen his critique of Britain's educational system. He could have argued that given the extended preparation that preceded the student's sitting for this exam and given the results, all would have to agree that the pupil-teacher's training was seriously flawed. Whatever Arnold's reasons may have been for doing such a poor job of paraphrasing his own words, though, there can be no question that he was heavily invested in this particular passage from *Macbeth*. Indeed, as we will see, Arnold quite specifically saw his own social role as "ministering" to the problem of Britain's "diseased mind." In this role, Arnold did not suggest ways to "raze" the problem of popular education from Britain's memory nor did he propose techniques for covering over this problem with "some sweet oblivious antidote." To the contrary, because he fancied himself the doctor qualified to diagnose the nation's ills, Arnold voiced the doctor's response: the only way for Britain to resolve the problems with its educational system was for it to begin to "minister" to itself.

Educating the Populace:
Policy and Practice in Nineteenth-Century England

In *Discipline and Punish*, Foucault issued a challenge: "People write the history of experiments on those born blind, on wolf-children or [on those] under hypnosis. But who will write the more general, more fluid, but also more determinant history of the 'examination' — its rituals, its methods, its characters and their roles, its play of questions and answers, its systems of marking and classification?" (185). Yet after Foucault's work on disciplinarity, it would seem that a history of the examination would contain few surprises, requiring only that one fill in the details of the state's increased interest in surveilling, classifying, and controlling the threat posed by the body politic. Indeed, it would be easy enough to read the events I am about to relate concerning British education in the nineteenth century in exactly these terms. However, because Foucault is not concerned with resistances to the transformation of the schoolroom into a site for expressing disciplinary power, he gives scant attention to the small-scale actions of individuals who were unhappy to find themselves working at the time he rightly characterizes as marking "the beginnings of a pedagogy that functions as a science" (187). Arnold was one of many who worked at this crossroad, where a vast array of contrary instincts and uneasy alliances came into play during the British movement toward popular education.[9] And, I would argue, Arnold warrants our renewed attention precisely because he failed in his efforts to arrest what he termed the increased "mechanization" of the educational process. By understanding the dynamics involved in Arnold's failed attempt to shape public policy and in his response to that failure, we may put ourselves in a position to devise more successful strategies for intervening in the business of educational reform. But in order to place Arnold's work in its historical context, we must first review the events that led up to the British government's direct involvement in educating its poorest citizens.

At the beginning of the nineteenth century, the government had no formal role in educating either the poor or the lower middle class. Instead, it allowed this work to be taken up by two separate private groups: the British and Foreign School Society, established in 1808, which provided nondenominational education, and the National Society, founded in 1811, which was allied with the Church of England and provided both general and religious instruction. Each society offered its services at substantially reduced rates for the poor and at no cost for those entirely without means. Each relied, as well, on the "monitorial" method for delivering its educational product to the most students at the lowest cost. This system, in which a single teacher monitored his or her assistants as they moved through the classroom monitoring the work of the other students in turn, was certainly economically efficient: indeed, Dr. Andrew Bell, the man credited with bringing this pedagogy to England, dreamed of the day when "a single master, who, if able and diligent, could, without difficulty, conduct ten contiguous schools, each consisting of a thousand scholars" (qtd. in Godsen 2). What the single master at the hub of this ideal institution would do "without difficulty" was to issue instructions to the ten thousand students amassed about him. The student monitors would then see to it that the master's or mistress's orders were carried out as they swept through the rows of seated students. It's one version of the bureaucrat's ultimate fantasy, where all is order and obedience, hierarchy and control.[10]

Whatever misgivings government officials might have had about this approach to educating the poor, they were in no position to reform or replace the mode of instruction as long as such work was left up to philanthropic organizations. But as soon as the government began in 1833 to allocate annual grants to both societies for building and maintaining new schools, its fiscal policies drew it deeper and deeper into the work of educating the poor. And, with the ballooning of the amount of time and money devoted to increasing the number of public elementary schools and to addressing the critical shortage in qualified teachers to work in these newly erected schools, there was a growing call for tracking how this money was being spent. All of this activity came to a head in 1839 when Queen Victoria, newly ascended to the throne, had Lord John Russell announce her concern that the government's reports clearly showed "a deficiency in the general Education of the People which is not in accordance with the character of a Civilized and Christian Nation" (qtd. in Maclure 42). The queen then empowered Lord Lansdowne to create the Committee of the Privy Council on Education, which was to directly supervise the distribution and use of the government's grant money, thus discontinuing the policy of turning the money over to the two school societies to parcel out as they saw fit. And thus, in just six years, the government went from leaving the education of the poor to its philanthropic societies to being directly and inextricably involved in the business not only of funding the education of the poor but of formulating educational policy as well.

Although Lansdowne's committee was unable to overcome resistance to establishing a system of Normal Schools for training teachers to meet the demand produced by the construction of the new schools, it did succeed in creating the position of "inspector of schools" in 1840, which would be filled by a corps of civil servants who would evaluate the schools receiving grants from the government. Sir James Kay (later Kay-Shuttleworth), secretary to the committee, informed the inspectors that they were to visit schools in their assigned districts from time to time "in order to ascertain that the grant has in each case been duly applied, and to enable you to furnish accurate information as to the discipline, management, and methods of instruction pursued in such schools" ("Extract from the Minutes" 11). The instructions go on to elaborate the three distinct duties the inspectors were to perform: the inspection of neighborhoods requesting grant money for the erection of new schools; the inspection of schools receiving aid and "an examination of the method and matter of instruction, and the character of the discipline established in them "; and, finally, the inspection of elementary education in particular districts ("Instructions to Inspectors" 12–13). In practice, what this meant was that Her Majesty's inspectors saw the nation's educational machinery working under the least favorable conditions—the poorest students instructed by the least experienced teachers, who depended for their livelihood on a budget always in flux.

And, sure enough, once such inspections began, some of the horrific excesses of the monitorial system did come to light. For example, in an 1844 report, one inspector reported:

> I have visited schools in which a system of signals, communicated by the aid of a semaphore fixed to the master's desk, was substituted for the word of command. The precision with which the boys interpreted and obeyed the instructions telegraphed to them was an interesting spectacle. Any person who might have been induced from it to form a favorable opinion of the efficiency of the instruction, would have been, I fear, in error. (qtd. in Hyndman 18–19)

Another inspector recorded inquiring after why it was taking so long to begin a particular reading lesson, only to find "that the monitors were in the act of placing the finger of each individual boy upon the first word of the lesson to be read" (qtd. in Hyndman 18). In response to reports such as these and further compelled by the shortage of teachers, the committee proposed in its minutes of 1846 a system for training and certifying new teachers that effectively turned each schoolhouse into a potential normal school. Under this new system, only successful *graduates* from elementary school could work as apprentices and pupil-teachers, rather than this work being left to monitors who were themselves still in the process of acquiring an elementary education. The government committed itself to subsidizing this program by offering a series of stipends to the apprentices, pupil-teachers, *and* the schoolmasters and -mistresses.

In its earliest, most ambitious form, the committee's program promised poor students who had excelled in elementary school a better wage for continuing on as pupil-teachers than they could earn in a factory or in the fields. Upon successful completion of three years' service as a pupil-teacher, the candidate was guaranteed employment either in the school system or, if the candidate so chose, in government service. The minutes from 1846 further stipulated that in order to enter this program, the students had to be at least thirteen years old and, among other things, had "to read with fluency, ease and expression" ("Minutes of the Committee" 2). The committee's principal instrument for ensuring the steady replacement of the monitorial system with the pupil-teacher system was none other than the inspector of schools, for it became the inspector's additional responsibility to annually test all pupil-teachers involved in this new program. And it was the fulfillment of this very responsibility that eventually brought Arnold into contact with the unnamed pupil-teacher who produced the "bad" paraphrase discussed earlier in this chapter. It is this task as well that dictated, at least in part, the form of their exchange.

This, then, was how popular education stood at the time Arnold received his appointment in 1851 to serve as an inspector of schools: interest in popular education was uneven, with funding of the nascent venture in this direction neither guided by a consistently thought-out government policy nor supported by any clear constituency. To make matters worse for Arnold in particular, the successful extension of education to Britain's poorest citizens relied heavily on the inspector of schools, whose job it was to determine whether or not the government funds were being well spent, whether the students were learning, whether the teachers were sufficiently challenging, and whether the pupil-teachers were being prepared to take on the increased teaching demands the future promised to provide. Given that the inspector's job entailed this constant and expanding evaluation of schools, teachers, students, and pupil-teachers, the history of British popular education up to this point does, at first, seem to fully illustrate Foucault's assertion that a "relation of surveillance, defined and regulated, is inscribed at the heart of the practice of teaching, not as an additional or adjacent part, but as a mechanism that is inherent to it and which increases its efficiency" (176). The issue that concerns us now, though, is how Arnold worked within and resisted the surveilling tasks required of an inspector of schools. That is, what kind of a surveillant was he? In whose interest was he performing such surveillance and to what end? Or, to put the question another way, when Arnold turned his gaze on the children of the poor to observe them as they were being educated by the state, what did he see?

Arnold and the Newcastle Commission: Placing Hope in the Middle Class

Arnold's first Inspector's Report, written in 1852, comments on the strengths and weaknesses of the new pupil-teacher system. Acknowledging that the system was beneficial in the main, Arnold concludes with these observations about the apprentice teachers:

> But I have been much struck in examining them towards the close of their apprenticeship, when they are generally at least eighteen years old, with the utter disproportion between the great amount of positive information and the low degree of mental culture and intelligence which they exhibit. Young men, whose knowledge of grammar, of the minutest details of geographical and historical facts, and above all of mathematics, is surprising, often cannot paraphrase a plain passage of prose or poetry without totally misapprehending it, or write half a page of composition on any subject without falling into gross blunders of taste and expression. (*Reports* 16)

Although Arnold does not define or provide examples of how "gross blunders of taste and expression" are constituted, he does speculate about the cause of the poor performances in these areas and about their appropriate resolution:

> I cannot but think that, with a body of young men so highly instructed, too little attention has hitherto been paid to this side of education; the side through which it chiefly forms the character.... I am sure that the study of portions of the best English authors, and composition, might with advantage be made a part of their regular course of instruction to a much greater degree than it is at present. Such a training would tend to

elevate and humanize a number of young men, who at present, notwithstanding the vast amount of raw information which they have amassed, are wholly uncultivated; and it would have the great social advantage of tending to bring them into intellectual sympathy with the educated of the upper classes. (16–17)

Arnold's first report thus appears to capture what has since come to be called "the Arnoldian mission" as it moves away from the relatively isolated arena of literary criticism into the much larger space of the classroom. That is, we find Arnold arguing that by improving the reading material presented to the pupil-teachers and introducing them to "the best English authors, and composition," it would be possible to achieve that hegemonic feat politicians alone are unequal to — generating new teachers who are in "intellectual sympathy with the educated of the upper classes."

Before we assess Arnold's position, it is worth recalling that this report was addressed to a parliamentary board whose members certainly would have considered themselves part of the educated upper class. Thus, it is not impossible to suppose that Arnold has adopted a rhetorical strategy that allows him to appeal to the self-interest of the board members while arguing for his own curricular changes. This, at least, is one way to explain why Arnold doesn't elaborate on the connection between high reading and the development of high-class sympathies: there isn't one, but insisting otherwise allows Arnold to promote his own brand of curricular reform. Whatever Arnold's reasons for justifying his proposal along these lines, though, one thing is certain: by the time he published *Culture and Anarchy* in 1869, he had permanently abandoned the idea that the upper classes even had an intellectual life to develop a sympathy for. And once Arnold came to see the upper class as Barbarians in the making, he had to revise his argument about the importance of studying literature.

Signs of Arnold's growing disenchantment with the educated upper class can be readily discerned in the work he performed in 1858 for the Newcastle Commission, whose mission was to "inquire into the present state of Popular Education in England, and to consider and report what Measures, if any, are required for the extension of sound and cheap elementary instruction to all classes of the people" ("Report on Popular Education" 6). To this end, the commission appointed ten assistant commissioners to explore the state of popular education in five specimen districts in England — agricultural, manufacturing, mining, maritime, and metropolitan — two assigned to each district. For comparative purposes, the commission made two additional appointments to study popular education on the Continent:

Mark Pattison was sent to Germany and Arnold was sent to France, French Switzerland, and Holland.[11]

Before leaving for the Continent, Arnold described the appointment to his sister in the following terms: "You know that I have no special interest in the subject of public education, but a mission like this appeals even to the general interest which every educated man cannot help feeling in such a subject. I shall for five months get free from the routine work of it, of which I sometimes get very sick, and be dealing with its history and principles" (*Letters, 1848–1888* 90–91). Within three years he was openly involved in battling the government's plans to revise the system for allocating grants to public schools and declaring to his wife that he would publish his critique of the government's Revised Code even if it meant that he would lose his job: "If thrown on the world I daresay we should be on our legs again before very long. Anyway, I think I owed as much as this to a cause in which I have now a deep interest, and always shall have, even if I cease to serve it officially" (195). Arnold's trip to the Continent was the catalyst that moved him from having "no special interest" in public education to having a "deep interest" in it, proof of which may be seen in his request that the commission allow him to publish his official report at his own expense so that he could make it available to the general public.

Although Arnold misjudged the popular interest in his views on education, his report, published under the title *The Popular Education of France*, has much of interest in it for our purposes. To begin with, Arnold writes admiringly of "the common people" of France, who "seems [sic] to me the soundest part of the French nation. They seem to me more free from the two opposite degradations of the multitudes, brutality and servility, to have a more developed human life, more of what distinguishes elsewhere the cultured classes from the vulgar, than the common people in any other country with which I am acquainted" (9–10). Arnold attributes this elevated status to the quality of the French educational system, which at that time provided an elementary education to a greater percentage of the population, for a longer period of time, and at a lower cost than was available anywhere under the British system. Acknowledging that it would be a "serious misfortune" to lower the salaries of officials and schoolmasters to the levels offered in France, Arnold nonetheless maintained that "there can be no doubt that a certain plainness and cheapness is an indispensable element of a plan of education which is to be very widely extended" (102). One example that Arnold provides to underscore this point also serves to illustrate the level of attention he was required to bring to bear on the minutiae of the educational process: he draws attention to the difference between the length of the inspector's report for individual schools in France and that in Britain, as well as to the significant variation in the quality of the paper used. "These appear insignificant matters; but when you come to provide for the inspection of 65,000 schools, it makes a difference whether you devote to each six sheets and a half of good foolscap [as the British do], or a single sheet of very ordinary note-paper [as the French do]" (103). Building his case on an overwhelming compendium of such details, Arnold thus sets out to demonstrate the benefits of adapting a similarly centralized and cost-efficient approach to education in Britain.

That Arnold's understanding of the mission of popular education with respect to class relations had changed is readily apparent early on in *The Popular Education of France*. Anticipating the inevitable spread of democracy to Britain, Arnold could foresee the aristocracy clipped of its powers; for this reason, he placed his hope in the middle class who, as the "natural educators and initiators" of the lower classes, were in a position to prevent society from "falling into anarchy" (26). While such revolutionary social reform had already occurred in France, Arnold saw Britain's own educational system as standing in the way of a similar cultural revival. Noting, for example, that a greater number of secondary schools were to be found in France than in Britain, Arnold reports:

> Our middle classes are nearly the worst educated in the world. But it is not this only.... It is far more that a great opportunity is missed of fusing all the upper and middle classes into one powerful whole, elevating and refining the middle classes by the contact, and stimulating the upper. In France this is what the system of public education effects; it effaces between the middle and upper classes the sense of social alienation; it raises the middle without dragging down the upper. (88)

The shift in Arnold's position here is significant. It is one thing to have argued for bringing the lower and middle classes into "sympathy" with the educated upper class; it is quite another to say that the upper class was in need of "stimulation" and that the final goal of education ought to be "fusing" the upper and middle classes and effacing social alienation. One need only recall that there were many in Arnold's audience who felt that universal education was neither a right nor a desirable good—many who had a substantial investment in the maintenance of the class system and the perpetuation of social alienation—to realize that Arnold is not rehearsing a familiar or popular argument here. He is, rather, stepping into the ring where a fight over the function and necessity of popular education was in progress. As he says at the opening of his report, he is well aware that in calling for the state to take a much larger role in the education of the nation's citizens, he has "often spoken of the State and its action in such as way as to offend" some of his readers (3).

That the lower classes are absent from Arnold's vision requires explanation. Within the context of the argument made in the passage cited above, the lower classes don't take part in the grand fusing because, quite simply, they never made it into Britain's secondary system of education. Arnold certainly felt this situation should be rectified and, as early as 1853, recorded in his General Reports that "the children of the actually lowest, poorest classes in this country, of what are called the masses, are not, to speak generally, educated" (*Reports* 19). In his report to the Newcastle Commission, he returned again and again to the necessity of providing the lower classes with access to higher education, arguing, for example, that "The French system, having undertaken to put the means of education within its people's reach, has to provide schools and teachers. Here, again, it altogether diverges from ours, which has by no means undertaken to put the means of education within the people's reach, but only to make the best and richest elementary schools better and richer" (*Popular Education* 145). Arnold goes on to make it clear that he is not insisting on free, universal, compulsory education: he understands such a governmental policy to be available only to the wealthiest of countries, like the United States, or to countries where he believes a profound love of knowledge resides, like Greece. Acknowledging Britain's fiscal limitations and dismissing the possibility of the nation's possession of such a preternatural fondness for learning, Arnold nevertheless recommends that something must be done: "What Government can do, is to provide sufficient and proper schools to receive [the rising masses] as they arrive" (149).

To those who felt that such a commitment to education was beyond the government's means and, further, that it was wasted on people who would never rise above their "natural" level no matter how much instruction they received, Arnold responded: "It is sufficient to say to those who hold [this position], that it is vain for them to expect that the lower classes will be kind enough to remain ignorant and unbettered merely for the sake of saving them inconvenience" (159). The import of the "inconvenience" Arnold speaks of here should be clear; the lower classes in France, after all, inconvenienced the upper classes a great deal in 1789. That Arnold saw education as the best means for preventing another such inconvenience is certain: as he put it in *The Popular Education of France*, he saw "the intervention of the State in public education" to be the "matter of a practical institution, designed to meet new social exigencies" (21). (It is also true that Arnold saw the threat of "anarchy" where one of his better-known contemporaries saw the promise of a "proletarian revolution.") Thus, while government officials argued that poor children were better off working in factories than in going to schools and that the extension of universal education was not fiscally feasible, Arnold was willing to entertain the possibility that poor and lower-middle-class children were being deprived of something fundamentally important by policies that declined to make education more readily available to all.[12]

Arnold literally failed to sell this argument to the public when he published *The Popular Education of France* at his own expense, and he also failed figuratively to sell it to the Newcastle Commission, which found more convincing evidence in reports like the one it received from Rev. James Fraser. Fraser rejected both the possibility and the desirability of giving the children of the poor access to the secondary school system, declaring:

> Even if it were possible, I doubt whether it would be desirable, with a view to the real interests of the peasant boy, to keep him at school till he was 14 or 15 years of age. But it is not possible. We must make up our minds to see the last of him, as far as the day school is concerned at 10 or 11. We must frame our system of education upon this hypothesis; and I venture to maintain that it is quite possible to teach a child soundly and thoroughly, in a way that he shall not forget it, all that is necessary for him to possess in the shape of intellectual attainment, by the time that he is 10 years old. If he has been properly looked after in the lower classes, he shall be able to spell correctly the words that he will ordinarily have to use; he shall read a common narrative—the paragraph in the newspaper that he cares to read—with sufficient ease to be a pleasure to himself and to convey information to listeners; if gone to live at a distance from home, he shall write his mother a letter that shall be both legible and intelligible. ("Report on Popular Education" 243)

Fraser goes on to record that if he had ever had hopes for a brighter future for elementary education than those expressed in this melancholy list, what he had seen during his six months' service inspecting schools for the commission had "effectually and for ever dissipated them" (243). Given the choice between Arnold's idealistic vision, on the one hand, where primary and secondary schooling would be made more generally available and where students would read the "best English authors," and Fraser's pragmatic vision of what was "possible," on the other, the commission opted to embrace Fraser's standards for what one could "reasonably" expect a peasant boy to learn in school by the age of ten.

This was the first of a series of failures for Arnold. And because Arnold was unable to generate a counterargument powerful enough to convince his superiors to take a less instrumentalist approach to education, over time his work as an inspector of schools grew increasingly "mechanical"; more important, the content of the education delivered in the primary schools he inspected came to be more fully determined by its potential to produce a measurable product. We can see this in the Newcastle Commission's final recommendations to the Committee of the Privy Council on Education, in which there was no proposal for bolstering secondary education or for increasing the number of elementary schools available to the poor in Britain. Rather, there was a call to simplify the bureaucratic system for allocating funds, which was to be accomplished by making the amount distributed to any given school depend *entirely* on how well students at that particular school performed on a series of exams administered by the inspector. The commission gave its rationale for this proposal, which quickly became known as "payment by results": "Till something like a real examination is introduced into our day schools, good elementary teaching will never be given to half the children who attend them. At present, the temptation of the teachers is to cram the elder classes, and the inspector is too cursory to check the practice, while there are no inducements to make them attend closely to the younger children" (341). From the commission's vantage point, in other words, the best solution to this problem of cramming teachers, crammed students, and cursory inspectors was to increase the surveillance of the teachers, the students, and, through the new reports, the inspectors as well on the assumption that a "real examination" administered to each student individually by the inspector and his assistant examiner would bring everyone back into line. No new infusion of funds was necessary. No new pedagogical approach was called for. No new materials need be made available. The one thing needful, the commission informed the government, was a better system for monitoring and controlling how the government's money was being spent in the nation's primary classrooms.

Once again, the state's principal instrument for accomplishing this additional monitoring and controlling of the disbursement of its funds, the examination of its poorest students, and the assessment of its teachers was to be the inspector of schools. When the Newcastle Commission's suggestions were taken up in the Revised Code, what this came to mean was that the inspector had to examine each student individually in the areas of reading, writing, and arithmetic, since the size of each school grant was made to depend directly on how each student performed on this battery of exams.

Arnold described in his General Report for 1863 how this new method of payment by results had changed his job: under the old system, the inspector served as "an agency for testing and promoting the intellectual force of schools, not [as under the new system] as an agency for testing and promoting their discipline and their good building, fitting, and so on" (*Reports* 91). Rather than exercising an "intellectual force" in the schools, Arnold and all the other inspectors found their work suddenly and completely given over to the activity of "testing" and "discipline," work that fundamentally involved reorganizing the educational environment into what Foucault calls "*tableaux vivants*" — a series of charts, tables, reports, commands, and recommendations that serve to "transform the confused, useless or dangerous multitudes into ordered multiplicities" (148).[13] And, as I will argue in the following sections, Arnold's turn to cultural critique must be understood in relation to his failure to prevent this reorganization of his working conditions.

Arnold and the Revised Code:
The Question of Ascertainable Knowledge

When the Newcastle Commission's Report was published in 1861, the government's annual grant for education was £813,441, up from the £20,000 originally allocated in 1833. Charged with the responsibility of bringing this rampaging expense under control, Robert Lowe, vice-president of the recently established Education Department, proposed consolidating the entire system of grants to schools into a single payment, which would be based on how students in the schools performed on examinations of their abilities in reading, writing, and arithmetic.[14] For each exam passed, one-third of the student's capitation grant would be released to the school, with the full grant being paid for successful work in all three areas. A similar system was to be applied to the apprentices and pupil-teachers, thereby relieving the government of the stipendiary system for underwriting teacher training initiated in 1844. In both cases, Lowe insisted, joining eligibility for funding to the process of examination would help direct the teacher's attention back to the class of students as a whole. Those schools with good teachers would prosper, while those staffed with poor teachers would fail (Walcott 63–64).

In a letter years later to R. Lingen, who had served as secretary for the Committee of the Privy Council from 1849 to 1869, Lowe reflected on the forces that motivated his decision to restrict the examinations to reading, writing, and arithmetic:

As I understand the case,…you and I viewed the three Rs not only or primarily as the exact amount of instruction which ought to be given, but as an amount of knowledge which could be ascertained thoroughly by examination, and upon which we could safely base the Parliamentary grant. It was more a financial than a literary preference. Had there been any other branch of useful knowledge, the possession of which could have been ascertained with equal precision, there was nothing to prevent its admission. But there was not. (qtd. in Connell 210)

As a true Benthamite, Lowe's understanding of this system's virtues rests heavily on terms like "exact amount," "useful knowledge," "precision": they express his overriding interest in seeing education as a "free market" for exchanging practical information. Consequently, Lowe's goal in reforming the examination system was, according to James Winter, "to concentrate authority, to apply to the school system the stimulus of free trade, and to simplify the enormously complicated clerical work at the Privy Council office" (177). Indeed, at the time he introduced these proposed reforms, Lowe proudly announced to the Parliament: "we are about to substitute for the vague and indefinite test which now exists, a definite, clear, and precise test, so that the public may know exactly what consideration they get for their money" (qtd. in Connell 207).

Whether this system ever succeeded in letting "the public" "know exactly" what they were getting for their money is doubtful. But there is no doubt about whether "payment by results" succeeded in reducing government outlays to education. In 1859 the committee distributed £836,920 for constructing new schools, for maintaining already established schools, and for subsidizing salaries for teachers and pupil-teachers. After a revised version of Lowe's proposal was put into effect, the committee's distributions fell to £693,078 in 1865 on their way down to £511,324 in 1869 — a decrease of nearly 40 percent in just ten years. The number of new candidates interested in teaching dropped from 2,513 in 1862 to just 1,478 in 1864, signaling a decline in the applicant pool of more than 40 percent in just two years (Walcott 94–95). This was all just as Lowe had promised during the parliamentary debates over the proposal in 1862: "If [the reform] is not cheap it shall be efficient; if it is not efficient it shall be cheap" (qtd. in Connell 207).

At the time, Lowe's assault on the system's teachers and students must have seemed strange indeed to Arnold. While the government's reading of the Newcastle Report enabled it only to see a problem with *the people* in the system, his work for that same commission had allowed him to see the problems arising from *the system's* low expectations and meager provisions for its students. Thus, for example, in his General Report of 1860, Arnold records that the poor quality of schoolbooks in the French schools had led him "to reflect on the great imperfection exhibited by our [British] school-books also.... [W]hat was wanting [in France], as it is wanting with us, was a good *reading-book*, or course of reading-books. It is not enough remembered in how many cases his reading-book forms the whole literature, except his Bible, of the child attending a primary school" (*Reports* 81, original emphasis). Aware of the consequences of this absence of valuable reading material from the classroom, Arnold goes on in this report to request the development of a set of "well selected and interesting" reading books, a collection that would inspire "a real love for reading and literature" (83). While Arnold fails all too predictably to specify what such literature might be or how it might produce such a "love" for a certain kind of literacy, he does go into some detail over what makes the available reading books unsatisfactory. They are either "dry scientific disquisitions" or anthologies where "far more than half of the poetical extracts were the composition either of the anonymous compilers themselves, or of American writers of the second and third order" (82). Arnold returns to this concern later, in his General Report for 1863, noting a typical sentence from one of the schoolbooks then in vogue: "some time after one meal is digested we feel again the sensation of hunger, which is gratified by again taking food" (97–98). Thus, by virtue of his direct experience as an inspector of schools, Arnold could see what was invisible to Lowe from his perch high atop the Privy Council: examining students on their reading abilities would serve no pedagogical purpose as long as so little attention was paid to the material the students had at their disposal to read.

In "The Twice-Revised Code," the writing in which Arnold most openly engages in politics, he draws on this same wealth of practical experience in the nation's classrooms in an attempt to influence the parliamentary vote on Lowe's proposed reforms. Momentarily accepting the Newcastle Report's assessment that under the current system of education only one student in four successfully learned to "read and write without conscious difficulty, and to perform such arithmetical operations as occur in the ordinary business of life," Arnold argues that reducing educational funding and limiting the scope of the curriculum would not address the root cause of this manifest failure of the school system — namely, the shortness of school life experienced by the poor (215). That is, changing funding and examination practices would not alter the fact that reigning economic conditions compelled working children to leave school at an early age so that they could earn money for their families — a fact, Arnold asserts, any schoolteacher, school manager, or inspector could have presented to the commission or Mr. Lowe had they been asked (220).[15] Arnold goes so far as to predict that the proposed changes would actually exacerbate this problem, since the Revised Code promised to dismantle the one aspect of the educational system that assisted students in escaping their lowly economic conditions—the pupil-teacher stipendiary program.[16]

Having cast the Revised Code's purported benefits into doubt, Arnold then set about dismantling the evidence the code's supporters relied on in making their case for "payment by results." Arnold was particularly interested in the discrepancy between the Newcastle Commission's determination that only one in four students could "read without conscious difficulty" and the inspectors' assessment that three out of five students attained this level of proficiency. Arnold bristled at the allegation—made both in the Newcastle Report and in Lowe's introductory remarks to Parliament concerning the Revised Code—that the discrepancy showed the Inspectors had attempted to conceal the gravity of the educational crisis and the inefficiency of the current system.[17] The discrepancy arose, Arnold explains, because the inspectors and those on the commission had used different standards for evaluating the act of reading. For those on the Newcastle Commission, reading "without conscious difficulty" became, under the rubric of Rev. Fraser's recommended standards, the ability to "read the Bible with intelligence" and "the newspaper with sufficient ease to be a pleasure to [the reader] and to convey information to listeners." Arnold was more than ready to agree that by those standards, no more than one in four of the nation's poorest students achieved reading proficiency. But, Arnold goes on to explain, the inspectors use quite a different standard when evaluating student performance in these schools:

> If, when we speak of a scholar reading fairly or well, we merely mean that reading in his accustomed lesson-book, his provincial tone and accent being allowed for, his want of home-culture and refinement being allowed for, some inevitable interruptions in his school attendance being allowed for, he gets through his task fairly or well, then a much larger proportion of scholars in our inspected schools than the one-fourth assigned by the Royal Commissioners, may be said to read fairly or well. And this is what the inspectors mean when they return scholars as reading fairly or well. (221)

This point *should have been* as obvious to the commission, Arnold asserts, as it was to anyone who worked in the field. As Arnold puts it, all who "are familiar with the poor and their life, and who do not take their standards from the life of the educated classes, [know] that the goodness of a poor child's reading is something relative, that absolute standards are here out of place" (223).

To find Arnold championing *relative* rather than universal standards of evaluation may come as a surprise, given the general thrust of his critical writing, but this is one of the fruitful disjunctions that emerges by turning to practice; for here we see Arnold attempting to apply evaluative criteria that are responsive to local exigencies. In concluding his critique of the Revised Code, Arnold explains why those proposing the reform were blind to these same local constraints: "Concocted in the recesses of the Privy Council Office, with no advice asked from those practically conversant with schools, no notice given to those who largely support schools, this new scheme of the Council Office authorities…has taken alike their friends and enemies by surprise" (232). However surprised the school inspectors were by these proposed reforms, their experientially based counterarguments were powerless before the government's desire to transform "the knowledge ascertained" in the educational process into a fixed and visible object, subject to universal standards of appraisal. Thus, when it came time to vote, Lowe's Revised Code was passed with some slight revisions and payment by results became the law of the land. In the process, the pupil-teacher stipendiary program was shut down and the job of school inspector was effectively reduced to that of exam administrator.

As stunning as this defeat was for Arnold, he nevertheless insisted on declaring it a victory. In his article "The Code out of Danger," published anonymously after the vote, Arnold focused on the fact that in the compromise bill that passed, only *two-thirds* of the state's grant to the schools would depend on the individual examination of the students, with the other third based on attendance. Leaning on this thin reed, Arnold crowed, "In direct contradiction to Mr. Lowe it has been successfully maintained, that to give rewards for proved good reading, writing, and arithmetic is *not* the whole duty of the State toward popular education" (248, original emphasis). In Arnold's subsequent General Reports, however, it clear that this distinction is insignificant: in fact, Arnold's report for 1862 had to be suppressed because it complained openly about the new provision requiring that schools be notified in advance of an inspection (Connell 223).[18] And when Arnold was sent abroad once again—in 1865, this time at the behest of the Taunton Commission, to investigate the handling of the secondary education of the middle class on the Continent—the preface to his subsequent report freely criticized the Revised Code and its effects on the British educational system. Thus, *Schools and Universities on the Continent* begins:

"In England, since the Revised Code, the school-course is more and more confined to the three paying matters, reading, writing, and arithmetic; the inspection tends to concentrate itself on these matters; these matters are the very part of school-teaching which is most mechanical, and a natural danger of the English mind is to make instruction mechanical" (22). Arnold reiterated this point in his General Report for 1867, decrying "In a country where every one is prone to rely too much on mechanical processes, and too little on intelligence, a change in the Education Department's regulations, which, by making two-thirds of the Government grant depend upon a mechanical examination, inevitably gives a mechanical turn to the school teaching, a mechanical turn to the inspection" (*Reports* 112–13). By emphasizing that the code had driven teachers to teach one book over and over throughout the year so that their students would pass the "reading" part of the exam, Arnold wanted to make it clear that he felt this problem would not be solved, as some had suggested, by simply expanding the number of areas of examination: "In the game of mechanical contrivances the teachers will in the end beat us" (115).

Thus, the passage of the Revised Code compelled Arnold to see that the source of Britain's cultural decline lay in its very fascination with "mechanization." In this regard, his critique resonates with Foucault's later assertion that "the examination is the technique by which power, instead of emitting the signs of its potency, instead of imposing its mark on its subjects, holds them in a mechanism of objectification. In this space of domination, disciplinary power manifests its potency, essentially, by arranging objects" (187). Arnold's position was contradictory and conflicted, for as an inspector of schools, his labor time constituted one of the principal sites where this governmental fascination with mechanization expressed itself. But he did not take his defeat in the battle to arrest the growth in the government's "mechanism of objectification" as the occasion to resign himself to the inevitable rise of disciplinary power. Instead, that defeat revealed to him the ways in which his government's policies reflected a national fascination with mechanization. And it is this insight, of course, which Arnold then proceeded to develop into a wholesale critique of British society in *Culture and Anarchy*.

In light of the foregoing discussion, we are now in a position to see that the mechanization of British culture was an issue Arnold knew not in the abstract but rather experienced firsthand in his role as the instrument of the government's educational policy for structuring, controlling, and surveilling the work done by everyone in the nation's poorest classrooms — students, teachers, and inspectors alike. But while *Culture and Anarchy* provides Arnold with a forum to deliberate over the significance of this expansion in the government's powers, it marks as well his retreat from the sphere of direct political action to a safer place where he could identify problems, detect patterns, produce his own loose systems of categorization, and refrain from the brutally disappointing business of proposing actual plans for enacting the reforms he supported. Ultimately, then, Arnold's turn to criticism in *Culture and Anarchy*—coming, as it does, in the wake of his failure to influence the shape of the country's educational policy—must be seen both as an act of despair and as evidence of how overwhelmingly seductive it can be to believe that in a better world, criticism alone would have the power to bring about cultural change. With this in mind, it may be more appropriate to say that Arnold's lasting legacy to the academy is not his argument for "the best that has been said and thought in our time," but rather his inculcation of a habit of mind that seeks refuge from a world gone mad in the comforting activity of producing literary and cultural critique.

Revisiting the Diseased Mind:
Anarchy, Despair, and the Safe Haven of Criticism

Shortly after the successful passage of the Revised Code, Arnold published what is arguably his most influential essay, "The Function of Criticism at the Present Time," where he defines criticism as "*a disinterested endeavor to learn and propagate the best that is known and thought in the world*" (283, original emphasis). Much has been made of Arnold's insistence that in propagating "the best that is known and thought in the world," one must rely on "*force till right is ready*; and till right is ready, force, the existing order of things, is justified" (265–66, original emphasis). If Arnold could have his way, it would seem, he would bring all the force of the state to bear on the project of compelling others to accede to the dictates of Reason— "the legitimate ruler of the world" (266). However chilling this proclamation may be in isolation, when it is read in the context of Arnold's failure to avert the passage of the Revised Code and his inability to control the material conditions of his own employment, it assumes a more desperate tone. It is, I would argue, an example of the plaintive cry made by the structurally dispossessed and the politically impotent when they dream of another world order, one in which the truly meritorious, now inexplicably out of power, would have the means to force others to bend to their wishes. In other words, it is a utopian wish and nothing more, a dream of inverted social relations that Arnold is in no position to bring about—partly because he's an inspector of schools and not a sitting member of Parliament, but also, and more important, because he writes as a polemicist and a critic, and thus traffics in diatribe and distance rather than the arts of the engaged response, of compromise, of multivocalic persuasion.

Arnold, of course, has his reasons for insisting that criticism be removed from the world of practical concerns and consequences. As he puts it: "But criticism, real criticism, is essentially the exercise of [curiosity]. It obeys an instinct prompting it to try to know the best that is known and thought in the world, irrespectively of practice, politics, and everything of the kind; and to value knowledge and thought as they approach this best, without the intrusion of any other considerations whatever" (268). As Arnold understands the workings of the zeitgeist, the production of such criticism is necessary because of the paucity of "true and fresh ideas" in Britain. And from here it is but a small step to realize that Arnold's criticism is itself the expression of all "the force" that is available to him, all that he has to rely on until "right" — that "time of true creative activity" — is ready (269). Thus, what has been lost in all the hand-wringing over Arnold's authoritarian designs is a sense of just how feeble and ineffectual is the force that the critic wields. For his part, Arnold certainly didn't attempt to conceal this weakness. Indeed, he admitted it openly, turning his inability to generate change into a virtue and a structural necessity, given British culture. The aim of such "disinterested" criticism, he declared, was

> Simply to know the best that is known and thought in the world, and by in its turn making this known, to create a current of true and fresh ideas. Its business is to do this with inflexible honesty, with due ability; but its business is to do no more, and to leave alone all questions of practical consequences and applications, questions which will never fail to have due prominence given to them. (270)

The function of criticism, in short, is to be curious and disinterested. And for this to happen, the critic must leave the project of working out the "practical consequences and applications" to other, lesser beings.[19]

And yet, if we return to the events surrounding the passage of the Revised Code, it seems odd that Arnold disdains the business of thinking about the practical consequences of implementing ideas. After all, he himself had eloquently argued on behalf of those who were being sacrificed to *the principle* of "payment by results" and he had stridently opposed the Revised Code on the basis of its practical consequences. He was thus fully taken up with practical considerations and criticized those around him who refused to be deterred by such matters. Arnold wriggles free of these contradictions by arguing that the critic abstains from worrying over the "practical consequences and applications" of creating "a current of true and fresh ideas," of promoting an awareness of "the best that has been thought and said in our time." The critic, in other words, does exactly what Arnold did in his response to the Revised Code: he allows for "a free play of the mind on all subjects which it touches" (270). And this free play consists, primarily and perhaps paradoxically, of looking at the practical consequences of failing to enact policies based on "the best." What it does not do, tellingly, is consider the material constraints that stand in the way of realizing "the best" or the practical consequences that might follow from pursuing "the best."

With regard to the Revised Code, Arnold released his thoughts to play freely over Lowe's proposal in hopes of changing a specific government educational policy in a specific way. In all subsequent cases, he made no attempt to propose practicable alternatives: he had, apparently, learned his lesson. This shift was hardly without consequence, for, as Keating has observed, it caused the rhetorical relationship Arnold established with his readers to become more and more strained. As Keating puts it: "When his middle class readers were slow to respond [to his critique of social relations], he asked them to admit that not only were they narrow-minded, ugly, intolerant, and ignorant, but that their cherished traditions were responsible for their condition. It was not an attractive proposition, and when the awaited response did come it caricatured Arnold as the languid and unpractical aesthete" (222). While Keating prefers to see Arnold's failure to get his readers to embrace his critique of British society as proof that "Arnold's ultimate significance lies elsewhere" (223), I would argue, quite to the contrary, that Arnold's ultimate significance is to be found in his failure to find a way to speak to his target audience, for he transformed his inability to bring about the kinds of social change he desired so fervently into a principled position. This willed impotence, emerging in response to a *single* failure in the political sphere, is surely the central legacy of Arnoldian criticism, for here we find the all-purpose and apparently irresistible justification for the necessity of writing about the world but not acting in it, save through the production of more prose about the failure of the world and the people who live in it to meet one's high expectations.

Seen in this light, *Culture and Anarchy* captures Arnold in his first sustained effort to enact the argument made in "The Function of Criticism in the Present Time." By way of conclusion, I'd like to turn to the moment when Arnold himself silently cites the very same passage from *Macbeth* that the pupil-teacher he was to examine years later would paraphrase so badly. Near the end of the fifth chapter of *Culture and Anarchy*, Arnold catalogues the range of problems threatening Britain: the nation's fascination with mechanization; its general disdain for culture; the triumph of Hebraism over the land; the sorry condition of all of the nation's classes—the Barbarians, Philistines, and the Populace, alike; the dire need for more "*aliens,* if we may so call them,—persons who are mainly led, not by their class spirit, but by a general *humane* spirit" (146, original emphasis). Confronted with this mass of problems, Arnold returns to the language of Macbeth's question to capture the importance of the critic's function:

> We shall say boldly that we do not at all despair of finding some lasting truth to minister to the diseased spirit of our time; but that we have discovered the best way of finding this to be not so much by lending a hand to our friends and countrymen in their actual operations for the removal of certain definite evils, but rather in getting our friends and countrymen to seek culture, to let their consciousness play freely round their present operations and the stock notions on which they are founded, show what these are like, and how related to the intelligible law of things, and auxiliary to true human perfection. (191)

And with this, we find Arnold beating a hasty retreat from the realm of political action, his failure with respect to the Revised Code having taught him that the critic must abstain from the disappointing activity of seeking to remove "certain definite evils." But even as he makes this argument, Arnold maintains that he has not elected to abandon the political sphere or to become suddenly and unequivocally a yes man for the state or even, in reality, to relinquish his commitment to "the removal of certain definite evils." For given the physician's response in *Macbeth,* that "the patient must minister to himself," it seems likely that Arnold would have us believe that he does not abandon the "diseased spirit" of his time but rather, as part of that time, stays above the realm of politics to assist in the process of having the state minister to itself—a ministering that takes the form of allowing the critic's "consciousness to play freely" over the government's operations, determining whether or not such operations lead to "true human perfection."

Arnold begins this ministering work in the closing chapter of *Culture and Anarchy,* titled "Our Liberal Practitioners," where he takes on "stock notions" about how to remove "certain definite evils" with regard to contemporary legislative proposals. Arnold finds that none of these Liberal proposals can reasonably be supported, least of all the system of free trade. As he puts it:

> We must not let the worship of any fetish, any machinery, such as manufactures or population,—which are not, like perfection, absolute goods

in themselves, though we think them so,—create for us such a multitude of miserable, sunken, and ignorant human beings, that to carry them all along with us is impossible, and perforce they must for the most part be left by us in their degradation and wretchedness. (216)

Part of the machinery that Arnold imagined himself fighting against was the machinery of capitalism, machinery that produces "a multitude of miserable, sunken, and ignorant human beings" by fetishizing commodities. Neither a capitalist nor a predictable imperialist, and certainly not a Marxist, Arnold wages his critique of capitalism not in the name of "the people" or the "masses," but in the name of "culture."

It is a contradictory position to occupy and the conclusion to *Culture and Anarchy* collects the contradictions together nicely:

Every one is now boasting of what he has done to educate men's minds and to give things the course they are taking.... We, indeed, pretend to educate no one, for we are still engaged in trying to clear and educate ourselves. But we are sure that the endeavor to reach, through culture, the firm intelligible law of things...is the master-impulse even now of the life of our nation and of humanity,—somewhat obscurely perhaps for this actual moment, but decisively and certainly for the immediate future; and that those who work for this are the sovereign educators. (229)

Renouncing the claim to educate, only to reclaim the larger role of cultural critic and "sovereign educator" who teaches others how to live by "the firm intelligible law of things," Arnold removes himself from the realm of worldly concerns and then insists that in so doing he has actually placed himself at the very heart of those concerns. Thus, Arnold himself may try to conclude *Culture and Anarchy* by leaping into the ethereal realm of the sovereign educator, but such claims must be read against the backdrop of his life as an inspector of schools, where his labor was squarely situated in the worldly realm of the day school educator.

Arnold may claim to be concerned only with educating himself, but he does so after announcing that the goal of learning the firm intelligible law of things is "to get a basis for a less confused action and a more complete perfection than we have at present" (191). He may assume a pose of wanting to "educate no one," but during his working hours he did what little he could to ensure that those children toiling in the factories and fields—children he himself described as "miserable, sunken, and ignorant human beings"—had a better chance to receive, at the very least, an elementary education. Arnold may, in short, cast himself as outside and above the worldly concerns that constrain others, but because he lived the life of an inspector of schools and not that of a man of letters, the only place he could escape the demands of the working world was in the utopian hollow created by his critical project, where his mind could play freely and not have to worry over the bureaucratic detail that filled the hours of his working life.

In commencing my own critical project here with this reassessment of the institutional significance and ramifications of Arnold's work as an inspector of schools, I have returned repeatedly to that single instant when Arnold allowed a voice heard during his labor time to speak in his critical work—Arnold's citation of the student's "bad" paraphrase. By approaching this citation from a number of different perspectives, I have enabled it to tell other stories about the history of the exam in Britain, about the emergence of the pupil-teacher system as a replacement for the monitorial method, about the assumptions informing Arnold's definition and evaluation of the act of reading, and, finally, about the complex and contradictory activity of ministering to a mind diseased when the "mind" in question is understood to be an entire nation and the "ministering" to be the responsibility of this strange, "alien" hybrid of school inspector, literary critic, and poet. What has emerged as a consequence is an image of Arnold as neither visionary prophet nor reactionary renegade. The figure that gets drawn in the ideological space where hegemonic powers battle for the consent of the populace could never function effectively if it ever were so unified: subjects who labor at the site of contradiction and concealment get produced and reproduced in contradiction and concealment.

The contradictions that constrained Arnold are particularly illuminating. Faced with the failure of his initial effort to intervene in the political sphere, Arnold blamed a world unresponsive to the dictates of a disinterested observer. He then withdrew to a rhetorical position of purity, protected by an array of arguments that transformed political quietism into a virtue and that took as proof of their veracity the very fact that others refused to embrace them. In this systematic and sustained solipsism, Arnold found a safe haven from his working conditions, a place where he could imagine himself as exercising a control over his material circumstances that was, in reality, well beyond his reach. To Arnold's credit, what he learned on his travels for the government and through his tours of inspection was the immense complexity of bringing about institutional reform. The availability of suitable reading materials, for instance, was revealed to be intimately related to the allocation of government funds, competing standards of competence, conflicting means of evaluation and levels of expectation, prevalent pedagogical practices, the provision of the means and methods for training teachers, and the laws governing child labor. Given the sheer quantity of variables affecting the form and function of institutionalized education and the resistance to change that was produced by their interaction, Arnold elected, understandably enough, to construct an alternative world, one ruled by "sweetness and light" rather than bureaucratic constraint. In this world, those who objected to change—those, in other words, who refused to follow the dictates of what Arnold termed "the best"—would be forced to accede to his designs until that time when "Reason" overtook them and they could begin to comply of their own volition.[20]

Arnold's flight from the lived realities of a highly bureaucratized state is, no doubt, understandable. Its true significance, though, lies in what it reveals about Arnold's assumptions concerning the instrumentalist interrelationship between the function of education and the function of the critic as the engine for cultural change: within this utopian worldview, the critic produces the "current of true and fresh ideas," the educational system delivers a mass of people ready to be carried along by this current, and the culture's values are elevated. This has become an all-too-familiar model for cultural and institutional reform. Indeed, Arnold's own efforts to defeat the Revised Code reveal this model's woeful inadequacies, since his "current of true and fresh ideas" proved to be no match for the array of forces determined to restrict education to the realm of "ascertainable knowledge." Seen in the best light, Arnold's commitment to the free play of the mind does provide a relatively unrestricted approach for diagnosing shortcomings in institutional policies, if not the means for responding to those diagnoses. But, at the same time, his critical approach is inherently unable to produce useful analyses of social conflict, because it assumes that all who don't ascribe to "the best that has been thought and said in our time" have minds that are diseased in one way or another—minds that are in need of "sweetness and light," of "Hellenism," of Reason, of a desire for true perfection, and so on. The Arnoldian approach, in other words, doesn't acknowledge or contend with competing motivations for acting in ways other than those advocated by "the free play of the mind"; it dismisses and degrades all ways of acting in the world that are more responsive to social conditions and local constraints than to that force which Arnold would like to call Reason. Of course, to attend to the social conditions and local constraints of one's audience is to enter the world of rhetoric, and this requires considering the reasons others act as they do and rejecting that explanation which is always too ready to hand for Arnold and his progeny—namely, that those who don't conform are ignorant, lost, in need of the critic's guidance.

Although Arnold tirelessly proclaimed the dangers posed by a love of machinery, he seems not to have considered the dangers posed by his own highly mechanistic model for engineering cultural reform, perhaps because the production of his criticism was what allowed him to escape the machinery of his own working life. This blindness is all the more striking in light of his work as an inspector of schools, for Arnold had ever before him the consequences of his superiors' efforts to mandate from above changes in the educational system. As one final example of the simultaneity of Arnold's insight and blindness, we have his observations, recorded in the General Report for 1878, on efforts to turn teaching into a science, when instructors were taught a set of first principles that they were then to deploy in their classrooms. Disapproving of this approach as just so much machinery, Arnold declared that the "apparent conformity [of such methods] to some general doctrine apparently true is no guarantee of their soundness. The practical application alone tests this, and often and often a method thus tested reveals unsuspected weakness" (*Reports* 189–90). What is true of pedagogical theories is true of cultural theories as well, though Arnold obviously declined to make such a connection. Nevertheless, by applying Arnold's own critical method to his practical situation, we are able to detect an "unsuspected weakness" at the core of his own "model" for understanding and encouraging the process of cultural and institutional reform. That is, because Arnold's criticism provided him with the means to escape the material conditions of his life—a way to live, however briefly, as a man of letters—and because it rationalized his own attenuated relationship to the world of lived concerns shared by other British citizens, his critical approach was structurally incapable of producing either a rhetorically persuasive argument that resulted in an actual change in his own working conditions or a blueprint for how to bring about broader social reforms.

Thus, while no one would deny that Arnold's writing has since exercised an immense influence over the form and function of literary criticism in the academy, it is much harder to trace or verify how this influence has played itself out in terms of shaping concrete institutional practices or determining the educational experiences of actual students. Though Arnold did leave behind a remarkable amount of writing about the social world, there is little evidence to suggest that he effected any material change in how the business of education was carried out in that world. While the reformers discussed in the chapters that follow all share something of Arnold's faith in the power of education to produce and underwrite cultural change, their various efforts in educational reform forced them into those same murky waters that Arnold refused to enter and refrained from acknowledging in his own critical work—that world of working relations where one is intimately involved in the creation and administration of actual educational programs, as well as the development of the machinery meant to ensure that the institution preserves and reproduces such programs. As we will see, when these educators entered the sphere of practice that Arnold came to disdain on principle, they were compelled to develop other strategies for generating viable and sustainable educational communities beyond declaring a commitment to "the best that has been known and thought in our time."

3 "Education for Everybody"

Great Books and the Democratic Ideal

On its face, current debate about the merits of a canonical education has become a pretty predictable affair, with the opposing sides regularly convening either to decry the resilience of "the standard Great Books
course" or to lament its passing. Given this context, it may be surprising to
learn that the initiative to establish a wider readership for the Great Books
has received some of its harshest criticism not from anyone committed to
multiculturalism, feminist theory, or postcolonial studies, but rather from
one of the earliest architects of the Great Books program. Indeed, Scott
Buchanan, considered "the father of St. John's College's new program of instruction" devoted to the study of canonical texts (Charles Nelson i), con-
demned the approach after he resigned as dean of the college in 1946. As
Buchanan put it in a letter to the college's president, John Keiffer:

> The aim of the [Great Books] program, altho[ugh] good in itself, in-
> volves a revolution, the courage, energy, and wisdom for which [are] not
> existent or at least not forthcoming. It should be put on the shelf and
> forgotten. It is not even a pattern to be laid up in heaven and beheld, if
> the educational house is to be put in order. It is in fact a poison corrupt-
> ing a household at St. John's, and because it is at St. John's it will become
> poison wherever it is tried. (SBC 6/8/48)[1]

The logic behind Buchanan's critique is obscure, but the thrust of his argument is not: those involved in trying to put together a coherent liberal arts
program had created a monster, "a poison," that now needed to be de-
stroyed. Obviously, since St. John's continues to offer its "New Program" at
its campuses in Annapolis and in Santa Fe to this day, Buchanan's recom-

mendation that the approach be "put on the shelf and forgotten" was ignored. Nevertheless, it is worth considering what led Buchanan to disown both the college he had helped refound and the Great Books curriculum that he himself had designed, just as it is important to understand the significance of the college's having felt it unnecessary to heed the advice of its founding father.

While Buchanan's rejection of the Great Books program is admittedly extreme, it does show that the community of educators, scholars, and critics interested in the Great Books is not necessarily unified in its sense of the virtues and the perils of this curricular initiative. In fact, there is considerable disagreement in this community about who should read the Great Books and how these works should be read. Thus, though one might have expected Allan Bloom and Mortimer Adler to be natural allies in the battle to salvage the liberal arts, Adler assessed Bloom's analysis of what ails the academy in *The Closing of the American Mind* as "inaccurate and inadequate," insisting that his "slight effort to propose a cure falls far short of what must be done to make our schools responsive to democracy's needs and to enable our colleges to open the minds of [our] students to the truth" (*Reforming Education* xix). In the midst of this criticism, Adler asks the following startling question: "can any reader of *The Closing of the American Mind* fail to detect the strong strain of elitism in Bloom's own thinking, as evidenced by his devotion to Plato, Rousseau, and Nietzsche, and by his advocacy of reading the great books by relatively few in the student population, certainly not by all?" (xxiv–xxv). Adler's own efforts to promote the Great Books are designed to counter this elitist impulse, he argues, and to rectify the lack of "a truly democratic system of public schooling or institutions of higher learning that are concerned with making good citizens of those who attend our colleges" (xxv).

To further complicate this issue of whether the Great Books ought to be considered a "poison" or an antidote to "elitism," Adler's own effort to assign a "democratic" impulse to his use of the Great Books has been openly ridiculed by another member of this group of devoted readers, Dwight Macdonald. Macdonald lambasted the Encyclopaedia Britannica's fifty-four-volume set, *Great Books of the Western World*, edited by Adler, Robert Maynard Hutchins, and others, for its inclusions and exclusions, for the low quality of its translations, for the absence of supporting materials to explicate the scientific and mathematical treatises, and even for the size of its typeface. But Macdonald's gravest reservations concerned the very *idea* of putting together such a collection and marketing it to the masses: as far as Macdonald was concerned, the real motivation behind the series was "hieratic rather than practical—not to make the books accessible to the public (which they mostly already were) but to fix the canon of the Sacred Texts by printing them in a special edition" (257). Thus, far from seeing Adler and Hutchins's series as the extension of a democratic effort to disseminate to the general public the best that has been thought and said, Macdonald understood the Great Books project to be the brainchild of a group of economically motivated cultural hucksters who were preying on the public's sense that it was more important to own these books than it was to read them.

If these scuffles between the various factions of the Great Books community have been of little material consequence,[2] institutional responses to the Great Books curriculum have had considerable effect on what courses are made available to students, as we will see. To give a brief example: when Lawrence Kimpton was selected to succeed Robert Maynard Hutchins as chancellor of the University of Chicago in 1951, it was apparently with the understanding that he would not "undo Hutchins" by dismantling his predecessor's initiatives that established a unified, core curriculum for undergraduates, grounded in the study of the Great Books (Ashmore 309–10). And yet, whatever assurances he may have made prior to taking control of the university, it became clear once Kimpton assumed power that his commitment to Hutchins's curriculum was actually quite weak. As Kimpton explained years later, his own sense was that

> Every queer and unusual student who disliked athletics and the normal outlets of younger people was attracted to the Hutchins College.... The Great Books course was a joke, and Hutchins knew it was. When I used to kid him about it, how superficial and shallow it was, he would say, "Well, it's better than getting drunk," and I think that's a pretty good summary of it. It certainly made no intellectual contribution. (qtd. in Ashmore 308, original ellipsis)

Given this disparaging assessment of the "Hutchins College" and this familiar demonization of those attracted to sustained work in the liberal arts (the "queer" versus the "normal," athletically inclined student), it is not surprising that the speaker of these words quickly committed himself to returning the university to what might be termed curricular normalcy.[3]

As these examples have been meant to suggest, the discursive world of the Great Books is actually a rather disorienting place, where, instead of homogeneity and general agreement, one finds confusion about who is friend and who is foe. This confusion is produced, in part, by lumping together a number of different educational initiatives under the general rubric

"Great Books," a conflation that explains how it has come about that Bloom, advocating a return to the Great Books, is accused of being an "elitist" by Adler, who has spent his entire professional life promoting the study of the Great Books. However comical such disagreements may be, they reveal the tensions that reside at the heart of the Great Books rhetoric, as claims of a democratic intent and elitist commitments work with and against one another. Since such tensions get worked out in very different ways at the level of local institutional practice, in what follows I shift attention to the history of efforts to institutionalize the evolving Great Books curriculum. After a preliminary discussion of John Erskine's General Honors course at Columbia in 1919, I will consider Hutchins's efforts to redefine the mission of the University of Chicago in light of his own experiences teaching a course modeled on Erskine's. I will conclude with an investigation of Stringfellow Barr and Scott Buchanan's successful establishment of a Great Books program at St. John's College in 1937.

Throughout, I am concerned with an allied set of questions: Who was meant to benefit from this series of initiatives? What pedagogical, institutional, political, and polemical needs were understood to be met by these curricular changes? And how was pedagogical practice itself configured as both the object and agent of these reforms? In pursuing this line of inquiry, I will only briefly touch on matters pertaining to the method for selecting the Great Books and on the exclusionary nature of this process: the critique regarding the absence of women and of racial and ethnic minorities from this curriculum is already well known and need not be rehearsed here.[4] Rather, I will focus on a number of crucial historical points that have been all but forgotten in the ongoing debate about the purportedly hegemonic power of the Great Books. Thus, I will show that initial efforts to establish an entire undergraduate curriculum grounded in the Great Books met with sustained opposition long before the advent of multiculturalism, feminist theory, and postcolonial studies; that resistance to the Great Books approach as a *pedagogical* rather than a *curricular* reform has been, in almost all cases, an unqualified success; and that, over time, the rhetoric used to support this approach has frequently claimed for itself a commitment not to elitism but to the project of producing citizens fully able to participate in a democracy. By historicizing the development of the Great Books approach in this way, I will delineate the range of forces that enabled and restricted efforts to institutionalize this contradictory idea, which sought to unite an "aristocratic" content with a "democratic" teaching practice in order to provide, as Hutchins put it, "education for everybody" (*Higher Learning* 62).

"The Best Sellers of Ancient Times": Erskine's Initial Formulation at Columbia University

In *The Memory of Certain Persons*, John Erskine has recorded the faculty's response to his proposal, in 1919, that a two-year honors course in the Great Books be offered to juniors and seniors at Columbia:

> How often was I told by angry colleagues that a great book couldn't be read in a week, not intelligently! And how often have I retorted, with my own degree of heat, that when the great books were first published, they were popular, which was the first step toward their permanent fame, and the public who first liked them read them quickly, perhaps overnight, without waiting to hear scholarly lectures about them. I wanted the boys to read great books, the best sellers of ancient times, as spontaneously and humanly as they would read current best sellers, and having read the books, I wanted them to form their opinions at once in a free-for-all discussion. (342–43)

Erskine, a poet and novelist as well as a college professor, had little patience for the classicists, philologists, and his other colleagues in the English department who argued against allowing "the boys to read great books" on the grounds, first, that "the boys" weren't adequately prepared for the encounter and, second, that in any event, such attempts should only be made in the text's original language. As Erskine conceived it, the purpose of *his* course was to wrest control of the Great Books from the clutches of these scholarly specialists so that the reading public might use the books as they pleased. In arguing for such a course of instruction, Erskine did not maintain, as others have since, that he was restoring a more traditional curriculum in the liberal arts, one that had been lost with the advent of the elective system of education. To the contrary, Erskine rejected efforts to recall the halcyon days of a past that never was: while his colleagues contented themselves with complaining about how general knowledge of the Great Books had declined since they had attended college, Erskine admits that he "doubted whether the elders in general, even among college professors, spent much more time than the youngsters reading world classics" (*My Life* 165).

Despite the nostalgic longings of these colleagues, Erskine's proposal ran into trouble precisely because it assumed that everyone would agree on what constituted a "great book." He reports that during the ensuing faculty debate on the matter, it "immediately became clear that the faculty could not define a great book; at least they couldn't agree on a definition. Worn out by futile talk, the Committee abandoned the task and told me to go ahead in my own way. The permission was granted in a tone which seemed to say, 'And may God have mercy on your soul!' " (168). In the semesters that followed the eventual introduction of the General Honors course into Columbia's curriculum in 1921, Erskine was left to his own devices to generate a satisfactory definition of a Great Book and to determine what pedagogical practice was best suited to bring students into contact with such books for the first time. In the process of trying out a set of books and a discussion method that would allow students to engage with the Great Books as they would with any contemporary best-seller, Erskine settled on the following working definition and justification for the approach: "A great book is one that has meaning and continues to have meaning, for a variety of people over a long period of time. The world chooses its great books by a social process. I wanted the boys to study great books by the same social process—by reading them simultaneously and by exchanging opinions about them" (168–69). Thus Erskine decided books that attracted "only readers and admirers of a certain temperament" did not qualify as Great Books and were, therefore, best encountered in a lecture hall rather than in the social setting of the discussion group (his examples, tellingly, are of "two extremely interesting women writers"—Amy Lowell and Gertrude Stein [169]). Those books that did qualify, though, were assigned in the honors seminars, where thirty students met one evening a week to have a "free-for-all discussion" with two instructors "selected for their disposition to disagree with each other" (170). Erskine's relative silence about the content of these discussions is a characteristic feature found in nearly all future arguments for this approach: from the very outset, it was understood that what was said mattered much less than the fact that the discussions were taking place.[5] Indeed, because Erskine felt that the discussions made available to the students "perhaps for the first time the basis of an intellectual life in common" (169), he apparently assumed that their basic content would be known to all who have already embarked upon such a life. Erskine was far from reticent, however, regarding the topic of who should participate in these "free-for-alls." Aside from making sure the groups had leaders "who can keep the talk going in a profitable direction," Erskine recommended "that these discussion groups should be homogeneous, with all the members on approximately the same cultural level" (173).[6] Furthermore, as Erskine saw it, the best teachers of the course looked "forward hungrily to the next opportunity to read" the Great Books and had, in addition, "a personal philosophy." That is, "at the very least he must believe in a spiritual life, he must assume in every human being a soul. This minimum faith may have a Catholic background, a Protestant, or a Jewish." Under no circumstances should the discussion to be led by someone who believed in the "impoverished philosophies which define man as a biological or chemical accident, or as the by-product of economic forces" (171).

Obviously, the "free-for-all" discussions were, in practice, neither "free" nor "for all," apparently functioning best when a homogenous group of male students from a prestigious university was led by a male teacher who would ensure that certain godless approaches would not intrude on the seminar's discussion of the male-authored texts. It is important to recognize, however, that neither were these prejudices inherent to this pedagogical approach nor were they its inevitable by-product. Rather, they were expressions of larger, nationally shared institutional policies excluding women and racial and ethnic minorities from higher education, as present in the other disciplines as they were in the English department at Columbia. While this does not excuse the criteria recommended by Erskine, it should make it possible to see that within an avowedly racist and sexist system, the Great Books approach offered a small, select group of students at the university direct access to some of the texts most revered by the academy. In so doing, within the context of the university system at the time, Erskine's—perhaps minor—pedagogical and curricular intervention was seen as a clear threat to the status quo. By placing important texts in the hands of students, by providing students a social space to work out their responses to the books with each other, and by asking teachers to speak *with* the students rather than lecture *to* them, the approach disturbed, however briefly, the most fundamental assumptions about what being a student and being a teacher entailed at the university level, disrupting in the process the academy's most familiar pathways for circulating both knowledge and texts.

With this in mind, we may find it particularly ironic that Columbia temporarily dropped Erskine's General Honors course from its curriculum in 1929 on the grounds that it "provided specialized study for an Honors 'aristocracy' " and thus was seen to be "invidious and remote in spirit from the noncompetitive atmosphere which the [university's] new elective system encouraged" (Buchler 72). Odd as it may seem that an Ivy League university would have misgivings about making "invidious" distinctions among the student populace, Columbia did find a way around this problem when, in 1937, it made another version of Erskine's course, Humanities A, a requirement for all entering students (73–75).[7] This action effectively removed the charge that the course serviced only an "aristocracy" of honors students and, simultaneously, ensured that the approach taken in the course would not spread throughout the university. It was this latter, more radically invasive version of curricular reform that was to be pursued at the University of Chicago, where Mortimer Adler, a former student and then instructor in

Erskine's General Honors course, introduced the university's new president, Robert Maynard Hutchins, to the allure of an undergraduate education *entirely* grounded in the Great Books.

"To Initiate the Education of Hutchins":
Great Books and General Education at the University of Chicago

Before discussing the migration of Columbia's General Honors course to the University of Chicago, I must first describe the curricular reforms that were already well underway before Hutchins assumed the presidency in 1929. Since the founding of the university in 1891, its presidents had been plagued by the question of what role the undergraduate college was supposed to play at a major research institution.[8] Conceding that proposals to eliminate the college entirely or to move it across the Midway were not feasible, Charles Mason, Hutchins's immediate predecessor, convened the Senate Committee on the Undergraduate Colleges to decide what to do about the undergraduate curriculum. Then, the day before the faculty was to vote on the committee's proposal to establish a general education curriculum for all undergraduates, Mason resigned and consideration of the curricular reforms was tabled until a new president could be found.[9]

Mason's senate committee, chaired by the dean of the colleges, Chauncey Boucher, had determined that two central problems confronted the college. First, the elective system had reduced the undergraduate degree to signifying little more than the successful fulfillment of "the bookkeeping and adding-machine requirement in terms of semester-hours or course-credits," producing in the process "an academic record sheet that should now be considered worthy of a place in a museum of educational monstrosities" (Boucher 2, 14). Second, because the elective system was so easily abused, it "resulted not infrequently in a pronounced case of intellectual anemia or jaundice for the student," who graduated only to discover that he or she had "nothing in common in intellectual experience, background, or outlook" with other graduates (26). The committee's solution, known first as "the New Plan" and then, eventually, as "the Chicago Plan," attacked both the elective system and the intellectual contagion it released by instituting a set of core courses in the junior college that would constitute a "general education" shared by all students in the college, regardless of which area of specialization they hoped to pursue in the senior college. The committee further recommended that attendance at the core courses be optional and that progress in each area be measured through the administration of uniform, comprehensive exams applied to *all* students. Optional attendance, the committee argued in its report, would "give the student an opportunity, which he will gladly seize, to assume more responsibility for his own education" (qtd. in Boucher 5). The anonymously scored comprehensive exams would guarantee that at least in the future, the possession of a bachelor's degree from the University of Chicago would signify that all its bearers had performed comparable amounts of work, measured and approved by the same reliable, objective methods.

In short, the project to reform the undergraduate curriculum at the university was well under way prior to Hutchins's arrival. In fact, Hutchins's initial contribution to this ongoing process was purely administrative: after approving the committee's report, Hutchins suggested that all departments in the university be collected into five divisions. There would be the college, whose work would conclude at the end of the sophomore year, and there would be the four upper divisions — the biological sciences, the humanities, the physical sciences, and the social sciences (Boucher 8).[10] Obviously, at this early stage the Great Books played no role in the movement toward general education at the university. Rather, the New Plan to reform the actual *content* of the undergraduate curriculum at the university was motivated by a number of other distinct concerns: getting the students to "assume more responsibility" for their education; promoting "general" as opposed to specialized education; making undergraduate education more cost-effective by delivering core courses to large numbers of students; and, finally, replacing the arbitrariness of individually designed exams with a series of uniform, comprehensive exams in order to establish an equivalence among those who were granted degrees. Within this initial cluster of concerns, then, the students were understood to be "assuming authority" by determining whether or not they would go to class rather than, as under the elective system, which classes they would take.

While the New Plan trumpeted the virtues of receiving a general education in the fundamental concepts governing the major areas of knowledge, once the plan was implemented, its supporters went on to praise its ability to attract anything but the "general" or average student. For instance, Joseph Humphreys's analysis of the New Plan noted that 13.5 percent of the students failed under the new curriculum, while only 2 percent failed under the elective system, a fact Humphreys then marshaled as evidence to support his conclusion that "a student body of distinctly higher mental ability is required by new-plan conditions" (139). And Dr. Dudley Reed, director of Health Services at the university, had this happy report for Dean Boucher after he and his staff had interviewed the entering class in 1934: "we feel that we are getting a much finer type of student in the main than we used to, our observations being based on evidences of personal hygiene as well as on those of alertness, intelligence, and good family training which appear in our contacts with students" (qtd. in Boucher 133). Finally, William McNeill reproduces the university's own way of speaking about these changes in his retrospective assessment that what "had seemed to many a very risky venture of treating undergraduates as grown-ups actually had the effect of selecting for Chicago a group of students who were in fact able to handle the freedom and responsibility the New Plan gave them" (52). In sum, by providing an educational system where students had to act as "grown-ups," the university attracted a clientele "able to handle the freedom and responsibility" demanded by the New Plan: that is, students who could monitor their own learning and hygiene and, when the time came, were able to respond correctly on multiple-choice or short-answer exams.

As these examples suggest, the rhetoric that surrounds the project of general education implies, but does not flatly state, that the project's intellectual rigor promotes "clean" social behaviors along with its self-monitoring reading practice. Hutchins's contribution to this discussion was to openly insist that pursuing this project would help produce citizens better able to handle their responsibilities in a democracy. Hutchins did not, however, arrive at the University of Chicago with this conviction about the importance of a general education. Rather, his thoughts about the form and function of undergraduate education were greatly influenced by Mortimer Adler, whom he had met while dean of the Yale Law School and had subsequently appointed to the law, philosophy, and psychology departments at the University of Chicago.[11] As Adler tells it, Hutchins confessed early on that "he had never given much thought to the subject of education. He found this somewhat embarrassing now that he was president of a major university. I had never ever given much thought to the subject either" (*Philosopher at Large* 128–29). In their discussions on the matter, Adler described Erskine's General Honors course and Hutchins, enthralled by the vision of a course that centered on open discussion of the Great Books, came to see that he himself needed to take the cure. Subsequently, Hutchins decided that starting in the fall of 1930, he and Adler would run a two-year seminar modeled on Erskine's course for twenty randomly selected honors students in the college. Although the course ended up having much greater significance, according to Adler in the beginning it "was originally designed to initiate the education of Hutchins and continue the education of Adler" (129).

Thus, the Great Books honors course joined the University of Chicago's curriculum not in response to the perceived needs of the student populace, but rather because the president sensed his training at Yale had been inadequate and projected his needs onto the university community at large.[12] To make matters worse, the introduction of such an honors course into the undergraduate curriculum ran completely counter to the reforms just approved in the New Plan, since Hutchins and Adler were proposing to offer a college-level course that was *not* open to all students, that *required* regular attendance, and that was *not* readily amenable to the strictures of an independently administered comprehensive exam. And yet, despite these significant problems with the course, there was nothing anyone on the faculty could do if the president chose to proceed in this manner.[13]

Accounts of the seminar show that Adler and Hutchins understood the pedagogical task of leading a discussion in significantly different ways. Adler records that Hutchins "was a witty interrogator of the students, catching them on vague or airy statements about the readings" — so witty, in fact, that the course gained a certain national notoriety and had "a constant stream of visitors," including Lillian Gish, Ethel Barrymore, and Orson Welles (*Philosopher at Large* 138). While Adler's description suggests the seminar had been transformed into something of a spectacle, Edward Shils tempers this view somewhat in his laudatory essay on Hutchins's tenure at the university. Shils records that he witnessed Hutchins display "a Socratic gift for raising questions that made students aware that what was visible on the surface of their minds was insufficient. He could question without causing discomfiture, he would persist in his questions without causing embarrassment" (189). On the other side of the table, one observer noted that during her visit to the seminar, "Adler slapped the table and badgered students. He pushed the students to see the 'errors' in the books and the contradictions between different authors' claims to truth" (qtd. in Dzuback 102–3). Shils confirmed this account in an unpublished earlier draft of his essay on Hutchins, where he described seeing "as harsh a piece of brow-beating of a student as [he had] witnessed, carried out by Mortimer Adler" (qtd. in Ashmore 102). It appears that in leading their discussions of the Great Books, Hutchins and Adler together played, in effect, a version of good cop/bad cop, oscillating between the extremes of charming conversation and ruthless interrogation.

Though it is unclear exactly what students were meant to gain from this pedagogical approach, there is no question that leading these discussions transformed Hutchins: they led him to conceive of a new mission for the university, one that linked "general education" with the Great Books curriculum. Hutchins's developing argument for a general education in the Great Books crystallized in his polemical essay *The Higher Learning in America*, published in 1936. Here, the case that Hutchins makes for the New Plan differs from the one made by Dean Boucher and others in two significant ways: first, the threatening world outside the academy figures prominently as evidence of the necessity of reform and, second, the study of Great Books becomes the foundation on which a general education program is to be built. Hutchins begins *Higher Learning* with the observation that while education had been held in high esteem prior to the Great Depression, "the magic of the name [education] is gone and...we must now present a defensible program if we wish to preserve whatever we have that is of value. Our people, as the last few years have shown, will strike out blindly under economic pressure; they will destroy the best and preserve the worst unless we make the distinction between the two somewhat clearer to them" (3–4). He does not specify exactly how or where "our people" have been striking out blindly, but the threat "they" pose is clear. Like the protestors at that other Hyde Park, Hutchins's masses threaten to bring down the civilized world. And to counter this threat, Hutchins's "we," an ill-defined group of knowing educators committed to the study of metaphysics, must "make the distinction" between what is best and what is worst clearer to "the people."

Although representing those outside the university as motivated by a mixture of ignorance and economic necessity is hardly unprecedented, it is surprising that Hutchins offers a general education in the Great Books as the *best* way to address the threat posed by this unsettled citizenry. In fact, by his own estimation, it is "the people's" understanding of the function of education that is the strongest impediment to significant reform: "This is the position of the higher learning in America. The universities are dependent on the people. The people love money and think that education is a way of getting it. They think too that democracy means that every child should be permitted to acquire the educational insignia that will be helpful in making money. They do not believe in the cultivation of the intellect for its own sake" (31). Whatever it is that the people may want, Hutchins argues that the university should not be the place where "vocational training" occurs, nor should it be the home for technical and applied research: it is only the people's love of money that has forced the university to sully itself with such practical activities.

To rescue "the higher learning" from this degradation, Hutchins proposes taking the university out of the people's grasp and placing it in some realm beyond the economic, where it would be free from the daily turbulence of the marketplace and its members could devote themselves fully to matters of the mind. Though this seems designed to ensure that higher education would remain the preserve of those in a position to ignore daily economic demands, Hutchins insists that his intentions lie elsewhere: "The scheme that I advance is based on the notion that general education is education for everybody, whether he goes on to the university or not. It will be useful to him in the university; it will be equally useful if he never goes there" (62).

Hutchins's "everybody" is somewhat misleading, of course, for within his scheme "everybody" comes to mean "everybody who can learn from books"—which, by his rough estimate, constitutes about two-thirds of the students in high school (77, 61). Thus, under Hutchins's plan, students who demonstrated an ability to learn from books would leave high school in their junior year and enter the college system. There, they would receive a general education grounded in the Great Books, which, Hutchins reminds us, are "contemporary in every age" and "cover every department of knowledge" (78, 81). Upon completing four years of general education at the college level, these students would receive their bachelor's degrees and most would move out into the world to pursue their careers, in which they would receive on-the-job training. Others, who wished to continue their education, would then move into the upper divisions at the university and begin to specialize in a given field or profession. Meanwhile, those high school students who had been deemed unable to learn from books would have received vocational training beginning in their junior year in high school and would already be well into their working lives. With these students siphoned off to the working world, Hutchins argues that higher education will be better off: "in a university like this it should be possible to get an education; it is possible to get one in no other way, for in no other way can the world of thought be presented as a comprehensible whole" (108).

It is not just the host of unworthy, laboring students who stand in the way of this project to present the world of thought as a "comprehensible whole," however. As Hutchins makes quite clear, the academy itself houses many factions opposed to this project: the vocationalists, the specialists, the representatives of the textbook industry, the relativist sociologists and cultural anthropologists, and those who believe in scientific progress. Dismissing research in the modern and social sciences, technical and professional training, and physical education with the assertion that "we have excluded body building and character building. We have excluded the social graces and the tricks of the trades" (77), Hutchins offers the study of the Great Books as the antidote to the social and curricular ills that beset society. As long as we pursue a general education that seeks after the metaphysical principles in order to unite all the fields of knowledge, Hutchins feels there is cause to be cautiously optimistic about the future of the nation: "It may be that we can outgrow the love of money, that we can get a saner conception of democracy, and that we can even understand the purposes of education" (118–19).

While Erskine's Great Books course briefly irritated his colleagues, its small scale and modest ambitions did not warrant much of an organized response, beyond a certain scowling in the halls. Hutchins's proposal, in contrast, incited the faculty both at Chicago and at universities around the country to question the politics that lay behind his commitment to "society rationally ordered" and his desire to produce citizens who "prefer intelligible organization to the chaos that we mistake for liberty" (119). John Dewey, for instance, questioned Hutchins's insistence on the existence of ultimate first principles:

> Doubtless much may be said for selecting Aristotle and St. Thomas as competent promulgators of first truths. But it took the authority of a powerful ecclesiastic organization to secure their wide recognition. Others may prefer Hegel, or Karl Marx, or even Mussolini as the seers of first truths; and there are those who prefer Nazism. As far as I can see, President Hutchins has completely evaded the problem of who is to determine the definite truths that constitute the hierarchy. (104)

Closer to home, Harry Gideonse, one of Hutchins's own faculty members, penned *The Higher Learning in a Democracy* in order to show that this commitment to metaphysics as the principal concern of the university was "essentially a claim to intellectual dictatorship" and that Hutchins's proposal had been "conceived and born in authoritarianism and absolutism, twin enemies of a free and democratic society" (30, 33). Most important, though, Gideonse wanted to assure his readers that the program Hutchins described in his tract was *not* the program of general education then offered at the University of Chicago, where the contributions of modern science were, in fact, readily acknowledged, where research and empirical work continued to be pursued, and where all departments retained their relative autonomy and determined their own disciplinary "truths." And this, Gideonse averred, was exactly as it should be: "The unfettered competition of truths—which is 'confusing' and 'disorderly'—is at the same time the very essence of a democratic society" (25).

Thus, to underscore a point that has escaped the attention of those fighting the culture wars, when Hutchins proposed a general education based in the Great Books he was accused, *in his own time*, of being fascistic, authoritarian, dictatorial, and opposed to the free flow of thought in the unregulated, democratic marketplace of ideas.[14] Furthermore, once Hutchins linked the Great Books approach to general education, resistance to both projects *increased* dramatically, not so much because of the content of the Great Books or because of the pedagogical approach used in their instruction, but because this effort to overhaul the entire curriculum was seen to deny students and faculty access to the "fundamentally democratic" elective system and to reject the institutional model of professionalism and expertise. In other words, what made the Great Books approach so threatening in this instance was both its broad *inclusiveness* and its insistence on the ultimate integration of all knowledge, goals that, if pursued, would require the institution of general requirements for all students and the disintegration of disciplinary specialties. When Hutchins took up the Great Books as his concern, the perceived problem with the approach ceased to be restricting access to "the cultural goods" to an "aristocracy" of honors students and became, instead, requiring all members of the university community to consume those goods.

This battle over the form and function of the curriculum at the University of Chicago, variously called "the Chicago Fight" and the "facts versus ideas debate," was intensely waged, with the faculty more often than not represented as the enemies of change, clinging to their privileges within the current system, reluctant to move out of their safely protected disciplinary niches.[15] For our purposes, the most critical moment in this struggle occurred the same year that Hutchins published *The Higher Learning in America*, for in 1936 Hutchins also formed the Committee on Liberal Arts, whose charter was to consider the place of the liberal arts in modern education. The committee's ten members, handpicked by the president, included Adler, Richard McKeon (whom Hutchins had brought to the university in 1934), and Scott Buchanan and Stringfellow Barr (both of whom had been lured from the University of Virginia where they, too, had been involved in designing a curriculum based on the Great Books). While the minutes from the committee's first meeting show that the members charged themselves with a modest three-year assignment to produce "a list of a hundred books, combining the Columbia list and the Virginia list" (HL, "Minutes," 10/3/36), suspicion among the faculty ran high that the committee's real purpose was to provide Hutchins with a blueprint for sneaking his cronies and his curriculum in the back door of the university. It became clear soon enough, though, that the faculty had little to fear from this committee: in their only report to the president, the committee members stated that they had "no intention of considering *at any time* questions of organization or administration. We are concerned with subject-matter and methods of study" (HL, 3/25/37, emphasis added). Their conclusion was even less ambiguous about what the committee was willing to do: "We wish to devote ourselves exclusively to this project and do not wish to be diverted by teaching, administrative, or departmental obligations."

What these reassuring words about the committee's harmless intentions conceal is the remarkable fact that the catastrophic internal difficulties experienced during its first meeting effectively neutralized its ability to function at all. That is, although the committee members had been selected on the basis of their belief in a liberal arts curriculum grounded in the Great Books, by all accounts the participants displayed such animosity for one another that they quickly splintered into factions and abandoned their communal project entirely. In a letter to Hutchins, Buchanan explained, "These meetings were discontinued when it appeared that civil conversation to say nothing of intellectual discussion and reading of texts was impossible" (HL, 2/12/37). Adler's description is blunter: "After a few meetings of the group as a whole, in which we could not agree about what books to read or how to read them, the committee blew apart" (*Philosopher at Large* 176).

Explanations for why the committee could not hold vary. Adler casts the central conflict as being between himself and McKeon over how one should read the Great Books; while he came "down flatly in favor of certain propositions as true, rejecting their contraries or contradictories as false," McKeon was willing to "accommodate, or even to attempt to reconcile, conflicting points of view" (175).[16] Buchanan saw the battle as being between three different positions—his own, McKeon's, and Adler's—which "separately had absorbed and accumulated the energies of our associates." When these positions came into contact, "heat and light became thunder and lightning. There was never another general meeting of the whole committee. We agreed to disagree and to pursue our separate courses" (13). Harry Ashmore has it that Adler felt work should begin with Aquinas, Buchanan preferred Aristotle, and McKeon wanted an initial investigation of liberal arts in the present (139). William McNeill notes only that Barr and Buchanan, as newcomers to the university, "began by quarrelling and ended by sulking" (71). And J. Winfree Smith asserts that McKeon, Adler, and Buchanan actually attempted to read one of Aristotle's works together, but had to stop because there quickly ensued "vehement accusations of distortion of the text" (20). Regardless of the specifics of what happened behind those closed doors, the end result was that the various factions went their separate ways and the committee failed utterly to fulfill whatever role it was to have had in advancing curricular reform at the university. As Buchanan explained it to Hutchins, once Adler and McKeon abandoned the committee, the rest of the group was left to discuss the Virginia list "in the hope that either Adler or McKeon or both would be induced to join later when time and inclination would permit, but that hope gradually disappeared" (HL, 2/12/37).

The spectacle created by this congregation of specialists opposed to specialization—these men utterly devoted to sustaining "the great conversation" but wholly incapable of speaking to one another[17]—is more than just comical. It is also evidence of the unresolved pedagogical and theoretical contradictions that lie at the heart of this movement. Though defenders of this curriculum could imagine arguments as occurring between books' authors, though they could maintain that the Great Books were best studied through discussion, and though they could insist that such discussion provided the foundation for the production of good citizens in a democracy, they could not, in fact, provide a constructive way for members of the academy to participate in such conversations nor could they provide a record of or a model for what such a democratic exchange might be. Thus, from the outset, the attempt to establish a Great Books curriculum at the university level was hobbled *from within* by questions like "Great to whom?" and "A conversation about what? beginning where? and to what end?" When such questions could not be raised even among friends and fellow believers, it seemed clear to all concerned that the expanded Great Books curriculum had no lasting future, at least not at the University of Chicago.

But as fate would have it, with the threat of the United States' entry into World War II, opposition to Hutchins's reforms temporarily declined as a result of faculty enlistment and the science faculty's involvement with the war effort. Consequently, Hutchins was able to force a version of his curricular program through the Faculty Senate. Yet while a version of Hutchins's four-year general education curriculum based on the Great Books was offered for a few years at the university, in the end Hutchins didn't succeed in converting a significant portion of the faculty to what he himself had termed an "evangelistic movement" (*Higher Learning* 87), nor did he leave behind a system of reforms secure enough to survive his own departure. In assessing his twenty-year reign at the university, he concluded that "the triumphs of natural science and technology have convinced everybody that they are important. The Great Books program is convincing some people, I believe, that understanding the ends of human life and social organization and sharing in the highest aspirations of the human spirit are undertakings quite as significant as prolonging life and improving the material conditions of existence" (*State of the University* 34). But whoever those people convinced by the Great Books approach were, they certainly did not comprise the majority of faculty members at the University of Chicago, for within two years of Hutchins's resignation in 1951, the reforms he had shepherded through the institution began to be dismantled. The awarding of the bachelor's degree by the college at the completion of the sophomore year was rescinded; the independent board of examiners was disbanded and comprehensive exams as a substitute for course credit were revoked; most of the large, introductory general education courses were dissolved; and, under the command of Hutchins's successor, Lawrence Kimpton, the university came more and more to resemble its East Coast rivals (Ashmore 299–310).

While it is undoubtedly true that students enrolled at the college during the short time it approached Hutchins's ideal were afforded a unique educational experience, from an institutional vantage point it is impossible to judge Hutchins's attempt to establish a unified undergraduate curriculum grounded in the Great Books as anything other than a complete failure. Incapable of reproducing itself, unable to convert resident institutional resistances into support for the program, powerless to combat the successes of the sciences, Hutchins's version of the Great Books approach proved, in the end, to be no match for the established model of undergraduate education provided by the university system. However complete this defeat was at the university level, though, outside the academy the approach prospered. Hutchins and Adler's Great Books seminars for members of the business community eventually led to the creation of the Great Books Foundation in 1947, which continues to this day to offer Great Books curricula to public schools and adult education discussion groups alike. *Great Books of the Western World*, the fifty-four-volume set edited by Hutchins, Adler, Barr, Buchanan, Erskine, and others, originally published in 1952, has since been expanded and is still marketed alongside the *Encyclopaedia Britannica*.[18] And, finally, Adler himself has devoted considerable energy since leaving the academy to devising and promoting his Paideia Proposal, his own version of a Great Books program for children in public schools. In each of these instances, the Great Books approach has been presented as a fundamentally democratic venture, intent on making the best reading material available to "the people" for their consideration. The Great Books approach has also survived in the academy, most notably at St. John's College in Annapolis, Maryland, and at its sister campus in Santa Fe, New Mexico. How the approach found a home at this institution will be the next focus of discussion.

"The Common Intelligible Way of Learning for Both Good and Mediocre Minds": Barr and Buchanan Reinvent St. John's College

When Hutchins's Liberal Arts Committee collapsed in disarray in 1936, Scott Buchanan turned his attention to writing a series of position papers for the president, which he titled "The Classics and the Liberal Arts." In the first of these papers, he set out to establish that "the only available medium which is adequate to the intellectual salvation (education) of the American student is the great European tradition" (HL, "Number 1" 1). Drawing on T. S. Eliot's argument in "Tradition and the Individual Talent," Buchanan saw this salvation as being achieved by an educational system that sought to "understand and organize the whole, literally the whole, of European history and bring it to bear on each individual in a single proper way and order" (5–6). With this vision of the educational mission in mind, Buchanan then argued against Hutchins's implicit position that such salvation should be extended only to the nation's "intellectual aristocracy":

> I doubt if there can be an American intellectual aristocracy unless the whole mass is somehow brought a little higher than it is being brought by our public education. I can think of no more effective or fit way to accomplish this preliminary task than the general reading of the classics with as much of the liberal arts as can be recovered and made effective at present. I am here following the parallel with the sacraments. They are the minimum of discipline and they are for everybody. (9–10)

Buchanan's contorted logic here might best be read as evidence that he was still very much in the process of deciding who should read the Great Books and why. At this stage in his thinking, he saw disseminating the texts widely as making an "American intellectual aristocracy" possible.

Buchanan retained this missionary imagery in his second position paper, where he informed Hutchins:

> Most of the classics were written for ordinary people, not for the academic world only. They are in some sense a basic language about everything, and if they are chosen for their excellence as fine arts as well as for their excellence as liberal arts, they will have an immediate intelligibility for anything that they are saying. They are like the sacraments in that; they talk about water, wine, bread, and oil in such a way that the incarnation and transubstantiation are conveyed. Grace is infinite, therefore sufficient for your needs. (HL, "Number 2" 18)

Here, the texts are reconceived as a sort of secular sacrament, available to "everybody," to all "ordinary people." And though, or perhaps because, they constitute "a basic language about everything," they are "sufficient" to the task of providing one's intellectual salvation. It is, obviously, an odd analogy, for within ecclesiastical traditions, sacraments certainly are not for "everybody." However, the analogy succeeds in capturing Buchanan's sense that these texts, in themselves, could redeem the nation's fallen educational system.

Even though the Committee on Liberal Arts had declared that it had "no intention of considering at any time questions of organization or administration," Buchanan soon found himself deeply mired in such work, when the Board of St. John's College in Annapolis, Maryland, invited Stringfellow Barr to become the college's president and Barr, in turn, recommended that Buchanan be appointed dean.[19] Perhaps the board was moved to this action by their favorable assessment of the intellectual merits of Barr and Buchanan's proposal to establish a "Great Books College," but they were also driven by desperation: the college, teetering on the edge of bankruptcy, had lost its accreditation in 1936 when it was disclosed that the president had awarded a degree to a student who hadn't successfully met the requirements for graduation (J. Smith 7). In fact, the dire financial and academic state of the college actually served Barr and Buchanan well, for it provided them with a warrant to implement sweeping changes in the curriculum and among the remaining personnel. Although Barr was frankly surprised, on assuming the presidency, to learn of the magnitude of the college's problems, he confessed to Hutchins: "My only consolation is that had the College not been in this desperate condition, its Board would never have turned to so drastic an educational solution as ours. I have also felt that the alternative to Saint John's was either a similarly run-down college or starting a new college at much greater cost" (BC, 7/30/38). Thus, by assuming control of a college near collapse, Barr and Buchanan were at liberty to build their liberal arts program from scratch, bringing onto the faculty like-minded colleagues from the defunct Committee on Liberal Arts, Catesby Taliaferro and Charles Glenn Wallis, converting resident instructors to their approach, and firing the rest.[20]

Provided with the college's physical plant and the freedom to do as they pleased, Barr and Buchanan did not have to worry about being hounded by the kind of organized, institutionally structured resistance that had confronted Hutchins and Adler at Chicago. Without a resident tenured faculty to deal with or cadres of preeminent scholars and scientific researchers to appease, Barr and Buchanan were, by comparison, relatively free to redefine who the "real" teachers and who the "real" students were in the program. As Buchanan put it in the college's 1939 catalogue: "the real original and ultimate teachers at St. John's are the authors of some hundred of the greatest books of European and American thought.... These are the real teachers, but we also have a secondary faculty of tutors and fellows who act as auxiliary intermediaries between the books and the students" (*St. John's College Catalogue* 24). This reconceptualization of where the students' attention ought to be focused meant in turn that the more familiar pedagogical relationships had to be reworked in the new curriculum. Thus, from the advent of the New Program, it was understood that students and tutors alike would come to the college to learn from the "ultimate teachers," the authors of the Great Books.[21] In addition to requiring this reconfiguration of the student-teacher relationship, Barr and Buchanan also insisted that the program at St. John's was "not conceived as only for the better students, but rather as the common intelligible way of learning for both good and mediocre minds" (qtd. in J. Smith 23).

It is certainly true that a financially imperiled institution, without accreditation, would stand to benefit by assuming such a principled position, since opening the program to all comers would serve to increase the number of potential consumers of the educational product. It is also true, however, that this position allowed the college to begin to act on its fundamental belief that all who cared to read the books could participate in the conversation: while Hutchins talked about the approach as "education for everybody," St. John's has, from the outset, admitted most students who applied to the program (and in the early days, to be sure, there weren't many).[22] But whatever the ultimate motivations were for admitting students with "good and mediocre minds," the goal "of the teaching and learning [in the New Program] is," according to the college catalogue of 1939, "the production of good intellectual and moral habits which provide the basis for human freedom" (*St. John's College Catalogue* 28–29).

In practice, the route to this "human freedom" was through a curriculum that offered the students no electives: throughout their four years, all students in the New Program were required to attend seminars in the Great Books; tutorials in mathematics, the language arts, and laboratory; and a weekly lecture. In each area, the students were expected to work through the relevant Great Books chronologically, starting with the Greeks freshman year and finishing with the German philosophers senior year, because, as the catalogue explained:

> Although each book must tell its own independent story, it is an important fact, which we regularly exploit, that one great book talks about the others, both those that came before, and, by anticipation of doctrine, those that come after. Each book in a list of classics is introduced, supported, and criticized by all the other books in the list. It thus gains pedagogical power and critical correction from its context. (26)

In order to ensure that the students actively participate in this dialogue between the Great Books, classes are kept small (annual attendance since the seventies has hovered around four hundred students; during the forties, the college struggled to keep its enrollment above one hundred students) and the instruction is discussion-centered. Although students are graded for their work, this type of evaluation is understood to be a necessity forced on the college by outside accrediting agencies: the "real" assessment of student work occurs at the end of each semester, when each student's tutors come together to give the student an oral evaluation of his or her performance during the term.

Although this structure has been tinkered with over the years, St. John's College still adheres to Buchanan's basic curricular design. There is much to admire about the pedagogical practice that resides at the heart of this structure: the curriculum presents students with the occasion to work with some of the most revered texts in the academy; the college provides an environment where talk about those texts, both inside and outside of class, is valued and encouraged; the seminars and tutorials are resolutely student-centered, focusing on the students' engagement with and evolving understanding of a remarkably various set of materials; the sequence of core courses in the intimate college setting produces for the students a sense of community—what Erskine called "an intellectual life in common"—that is simply unavailable within the elective system or on a university campus; the requirement that tutors teach throughout the curriculum enacts an alternative model of mastery to what is found within traditional fields, where specialization receives the highest valuation. In fact, this list of the admirable aspects of the curriculum and its pedagogy makes Buchanan's repudiation of the program, cited at the opening of this chapter, all the more mysterious. How is it that he came to see the program as a "poison corrupting a household at St. John's"? Why did he and Barr resign so precipitously in 1946, wishing, as Buchanan put it in a letter to Alexander Meiklejohn, to sever all ties to the college "in spite of the feeling we all have that we have parental responsibilities to the College we have smashed in Annapolis" (HL, 1/3/47)?

Finding the answers to these questions is not an easy matter, in part because the questions touch on an embarrassing chapter in the college's history that the community itself would rather forget. Indeed, at a recent alumni homecoming at the college, all was forgiven: Barr and Buchanan were celebrated as "buccaneers, boarding academic ships in distress, saving what they wanted and throwing overboard the rest" (J. Van Doren 10); Buchanan was posthumously made a member of the class of 1944 (Barr had been inducted into the class of 1949 years before); and plans were announced to name the new library after the New Program's founding fathers. The function of alumni fund-raising events is, of course, to generate sanitized versions of the alma mater's institutional past that, in turn, foster nostalgic yearnings. Unfortunately, the sole effort to provide an historical account of Barr and Buchanan's tenure at St. John's is similarly hamstrung by the author's close ties to the institution. While Barr himself had intended one day to write a history of the college, as did his successor, John Keiffer, the job ultimately fell to J. Winfree Smith, who studied under Barr and Buchanan at the University of Virginia and subsequently became one of the college's most respected tutors. Smith himself concedes, in his preface to *A Search for the Liberal College*, that some feared he "might be partial to the curriculum and to the men who had most to do with starting and establishing it," but, he assures the reader, he has done his best just "to stick to the facts" (vii). While Smith does provide a remarkably detailed description of the events leading up to the founders' resignation, he ends up skirting the issue of why Barr and Buchanan became so disillusioned with the college. As a consequence, Smith celebrates the very fact I want to puzzle over—namely, how is it that the college survived the efforts of its founders to "smash" it? Answering this question will reveal how the success of the Great Books curriculum at St. John's was the result of a linked set of historical contingencies and local institutional constraints that, as Barr and Buchanan discovered too late, could not be replicated elsewhere.

In order to track Buchanan's growing dissatisfaction with the institutionalization of the Great Books approach, we must first consider the effect that the United States' entry into World War II had on the college. As we have seen in the preceding discussion, the war had an immediate impact on student enrollment and faculty retention nationwide. St. John's, because of its small size, was particularly vulnerable to shifts in its personnel: thus, though the size of the student body remained relatively constant immediately after the bombing of Pearl Harbor, by the following academic year the college had only forty-two students enrolled in the three upper classes (J. Smith 61). Forced to find bodies to fill their courses, Barr and Buchanan resorted to admitting fifteen-year-old high school students in September 1943 and then added a summer session so that the new students could complete their work for the degree prior to being eligible for the draft (62). While this attracted enough students to keep the college open, Barr and Buchanan also had to respond to another unforeseen problem precipitated by the war—the effort by the United States Naval Academy, located across the street from the college in Annapolis, to seize the college's property under "eminent domain." Although the navy's plans for the property were never terribly clear, Secretary of the Navy James Forrestal began negotiating with the Board of Visitors and Governors in June 1945 to determine a reasonable cost for moving the college to another location so that the navy could take over the land. Preparation for these negotiations produced a flurry of activity at the college: Buchanan made notes estimating the cost of moving and reestablishing the program elsewhere, deciding on a figure near four million dollars (HL, 7/5/45). These calculations were reworked in a draft of a policy statement and then abandoned altogether in the final version, as the board broke off the discussions with the navy, declaring that "further negotiations under circumstances that imply sharing by the Board of the responsibility for unjustified damage to the College are impossible" (HL, "A Restatement of the Policy of the Board of Visitors and Governors," 7/21/45).

What happened next is more than a little bizarre. Although the board's statement made clear its commitment to keeping the college in Annapolis and to having its case heard by the courts, Buchanan responded by threatening to resign from the board as a vote of no confidence in its actions. Apparently, though Buchanan himself drew up the figures to determine the value of the campus and the curriculum, he appears, on reflection, to have had a change of heart: as he put it in a memo titled "St. John's versus the Navy," "the moral and legal right of the Government to destroy or move institutions of learning is in question" (HL, "St. John's versus the Navy" 6). Focusing on this matter of principle, Buchanan declared in his statement resigning from the board that accepting the navy's argument without going to court would be to sacrifice

> the integrity of the institution and [the Board's] right to be trusted further with a campus or a curriculum, neither of which is worth very much without the other. As holders of property we shall have lost our rights because we didn't know them or our duties with respect to them. As promulgators of a curriculum we will turn out to be exploiters of an old college for publicity and fake reform. This will be so even if some of us think that our educational function would be more effective elsewhere. We cannot honorably move without an unmistakable mandate from the sovereign. (HL, "Resignation Statement" 6)

In effect, this battle with the navy over the fate of the college forced Buchanan to confront the institutional and legal realities of the college's existence not simply as the embodiment of a set of curricular ideas but as a set of buildings, a plot of land, and a chartered agreement dating back to the seventeenth century.

Suddenly, Buchanan was waist deep in the very kind of administrative and practical matters that years before he had said held no interest for him: now, in the face of the navy's efforts, he was compelled to meditate on what the relationship between the college and the state was, what status a college had as a legal entity, what fiduciary responsibilities a college's board could reasonably be expected to perform, and how and where one could locate the "value" of an educational system. Does the value of an educational institution reside in its students? its faculty? its buildings? its location? its curriculum? Buchanan taunted the board with this last possibility by praising the New Program in terms of its

> high publicity value, its high doctrine, its major controversial character. After eight years of startling public success, all out of proportion to its real effectiveness, it has gone through a year of the hottest kind of debunking criticism from rather unscrupulous enemies. At this juncture we get the Navy to move us and endow us. We look like clever fellows and some of us think we are. We ought to use the money to set up a big advertising firm. The whole thing has been a publicity stunt. (7)

The problem with this "publicity stunt," as Buchanan saw it, was that it failed to recognize that the campus itself ought to be considered to be a kind of fixed endowment, for "it is by its nature unique and incomparable, therefore not replaceable" (9). In fact, because the value of the campus continues to improve over time, to "sell out without the highest justification [is] ... in effect destroying an infinite endowment" (9)!

What makes this interchange bizarre, aside from the thunderous and contorted rhetoric, is that Buchanan is arguing with a board that is apparently in total agreement with him. That is, at the time Buchanan was composing his resignation statement, the board had already stated unequivocally that it was unwilling to continue negotiations with the navy. And should there be any lingering doubt about the board's position, the members announced at a meeting on October 2, 1945, that they "would not willingly sell the historic campus at any price." Then, when no decision about the matter was seen to be forthcoming from Washington, the members declared on November 21, 1945, that they regarded "the unfortunate episode as concluded, and trust that the Naval Academy and St. John's are now free to proceed in mutual respect and harmony, as neighbors, to get on with their respective functions" (qtd. in J. Smith 78). Although the mystery surrounding Buchanan's response to the board may never be fully explained, it is safe to say his dissatisfaction with this conclusion arose because he wanted to see the issue of whether or not it was in the nation's interest to preserve and protect liberal education resolved through rational argumentation, rather than through the machinations of politicians and the local business community. Indeed, Buchanan became fixated on the issue of how one could disprove the notion that it lay in the "national interest" to condemn and reclaim property on which the business of educating the nation's citizenry was conducted.

Buchanan started to work out the details of this insight in a "Dean's Statement," to which he gave the preliminary title "In Search of the Authority for Teaching." A meditation on what Buchanan had learned as a result of the battle to save St. John's, this essay argues that the college must be seen as a "corporate body, whose properties are nonetheless immortality and individuality" (HL, "Dean's Statement" 1). Buchanan then goes on to observe that "as teaching has made the curriculum blossom and bear fruit, so has administration progressively uncovered and revealed the character and soul of this artificial body" (2). It was this dawning understanding of "the character and soul" of the artificial, bureaucratic body of higher education that threatened to shatter Buchanan's sense that teaching and learning could be "free human activities." What the fight with the navy showed Buchanan, instead, was that imagining the college as a space governed by academic freedom

> ignores the institutional problem of responsibility, and at the same time implies and imposes an impossible burden of protection upon the corporate entity. It asks the institution to guarantee the individual freedom of its members against all interference from within or from without, but it does not provide either the authority or the power to fulfill its duty. Spirit is everywhere free, but body, including artificial bodies like institutions, are everywhere limited by power. (2–3)

In effect, Buchanan recognized that the ongoing existence of a college interested in sustaining the "great conversation" would always be contingent upon a compliant power structure and, for this very reason, such a college would never be able to guarantee its members the freedom necessary to pursue *any* open educational venture. To see that institutions "are everywhere limited by power" is to acknowledge, however fleetingly, that Reason will never rule. It is also to see that one's job as an administrator in an educational institution is not to pursue reasoned debates—for example, about what constitutes "national interest"—but rather to be locked in a constant war of position, where rhetoric and capital are one's only resources for keeping one's home institution open for business. As it happened, though, Buchanan never worked this insight out, nor did he distribute this statement to the college community: instead, his deliberations about the "authority of teaching" stop just at the point where he was to consider the ways financial constraints influence decisions about teaching. Perhaps these fiscal, political, and bureaucratic realities were something he just couldn't bear to think about.

The skirmish with the navy came to a similarly abrupt and inconclusive end, precipitated by events that were wholly outside the control of the college or the Naval Academy: with the conclusion of World War II, the navy's argument that it was in the nation's best interest to move the college elsewhere at such great expense ultimately couldn't be credibly maintained. Though many in the Annapolis business community were bitterly disappointed when they learned of the House Naval Affairs Committee's decision on May 22, 1946, to quash the navy's plan to acquire the campus, the governor of Maryland, Herbert O'Conor, went so far as to issue a statement requesting the navy to announce that it would abandon "permanently the move for the acquisition of St. John's"—a request to which the navy never formally responded (HL). As if to confirm Buchanan's greatest misgivings about the ways decisions about educational matters are inextricably woven into a web of political power, the governor went on to explain that the state had much to gain from keeping the college in Maryland: "the educational institutions of the state, as well as throughout the country, are overcrowded and thousands of returning veterans and others are desirous of taking advantage of higher educational opportunities." In short, inasmuch as the college generated revenue for the state, it warranted the governor's protection: and so, in effect, the governor's statement of open support actually served to underscore the college's precarious reliance on the kindness of strangers for its continued existence.

There are, then, many reasons that might explain why Buchanan failed to be satisfied with the college's apparent complete triumph over the navy: the victory was inconclusive because the legal status of the argument regarding "national interest" was never settled in court; the Naval Academy never formally renounced its claims on the college and thus the threat was never completely put to rest; and finally, and perhaps most important, the very contingency of the victory challenged the central assumption upon which the Great Books curriculum rests, that ideas are understood to exercise power outside of and over historical circumstance. To elaborate on this last possibility, it is worth considering Smith's explanation of the role that the study of history is meant to play in the Great Books curriculum: "Teachers and students have no interest in studying the past as past. They have an interest in reading certain books that were written in the past because those books raise important perennial questions, questions which are always live and present questions if we let our thought get hold of them" (54). Given this understanding, it is not hard to see how the historically contingent solution to the "perennial" question of the state's relationship to education would gall someone who took the notion of the great conversation seriously. For the battle with the Naval Academy showed with startling clarity that what mattered most, in the world of material relationships, was not who had the best argument but who had the power to make the decisions that others had to abide by. The battle showed, in other words, that the fate of the college would always rest in the hands of others. In realizing this, Buchanan saw, however briefly, that teaching can never be "free"; it can only be made to appear so through the maintenance of a willed blindness to the administrative, institutional, and national structures that make teaching possible in the first place.

There were other forces besides the failure to resolve the intellectual issue of "national interest," however, that motivated Buchanan's rapid withdrawal from St. John's, which began when he took a year's leave of absence in June of 1946 and culminated in his resignation six months later. To start with, in the midst of the fight with the navy there emerged a real alternative to going on with the project in Annapolis, an alternative that appeared to offer Barr and Buchanan a way to escape all the problems involved with running an institution that had a preexisting charter, a resident Board of Governors and Visitors, a newly settled faculty, and an administrative and curricular structure already tending toward rigidity. It took the form of Paul Mellon's instruction to the Old Dominion Foundation that they distribute $125,000 annually to develop "the type of education now carried on at St. John's College" (HL, letter from Mellon to Barr, 4/16/46). Mellon, who had attended St. John's briefly in 1940,[23] had developed a commitment to the idea of the program and to Barr and Buchanan while there. In light of this experience, he informed the trustees at the foundation that they were to rely strictly on Barr's "personal judgment as to whether St. John's can be expected to preserve its campus, or whether some other college [Barr] may designate will better carry out my intention and thereby become the beneficiary of these funds." This offer, in combination with the announcement that the navy's plans had been disapproved just a month later, would seem to have provided Barr and Buchanan with ample reason to believe that the venture in Annapolis was secure.

And yet, much to the board's astonishment, Barr decided that it would be best if the funds from the Old Dominion Foundation went to some other institution! As Buchanan laid out the rational for this decision in "The Dean's Nine Year Report," the project of liberal education had to be expanded beyond what was possible at the college: to revitalize the project would demand "the rebirth and completion of a true university whose other parts are, first, a school of liberal arts for adults ... and, second, a graduate school devoted to the search for the unity of knowledge and wisdom, which would continually discuss and revise what all men should know" (SBC, 7/31/46, 1). It is more than ironic that Buchanan proposes to replicate the very system of specialization the Great Books curriculum had from its inception explicitly set itself against: for here, as Buchanan begins to spin a fantasy about ways to promote the program's "colonization" of the uncivilized world, what emerges is a plan to provide an institutional home for a core of liberal arts specialists who would engage in ongoing research into what should be studied by others. Attached to this liberal arts research center would be two schools, one to disseminate the research findings to the undergraduates and the other to pass it on to adults in continuing education.

When this vision of the program's future was formally offered to the board as an appealing alternative to life in the shadow of the Naval Academy, the board declined Barr and Buchanan's invitation to join them on this next journey, as did the faculty at the college. Although accounts of the specific reasons for rejecting this proposal are not readily available, it is not hard to imagine why the board and the faculty would have decided to stay put. To remain at the college was evidence of a commitment both to the program and to the students; and it was, as well, the safest bet that one was going to keep being paid for services rendered. Buchanan met with a series of similarly stunning and unambiguous defeats from his old friends when he tried to drum up interest in the colonizing ventures of the corporate entity he and Barr had formed, "Liberal Arts, Incorporated." In a letter to Adler, Buchanan describes his plan for a new university and then issues what might be read as either a threat or an invitation: "The Chicago–St. John's axis has got to be abolished. You have either got to join us or be suppressed. We need what you've got and can give us, and you need what the new venture can give you" (HL, 8/14/46). Buchanan then proceeded to denounce the Encyclopaedia Britannica's *Great Books of the Western World* project, which Adler and Hutchins had commenced: "I am now quite horrified at the job of selecting books that we did, and wish I had stuck to my resignation [from the series' editorial board].... [The encyclopedia's] money has corrupted and stolen good members of our faculty, and has made all of us look like go-getters to ourselves. The burden of selling the books has given your activities in adult education a fever that also horrifies me." Using this rhetorical approach, in turn, on Adler, Hutchins, McKeon, and Mark Van Doren, Buchanan found that none of his fellow believers were willing to follow him to the farm Liberal Arts, Inc., had purchased just outside of Stockbridge, Massachusetts, to create a new institute for studying liberal education.

Buchanan's pleas to his longtime friends reveals yet another facet of his dissatisfaction with the form that education had assumed at St. John's: in addition to the college's proximity to the Naval Academy, the legal and philosophical issues raised by this proximity, and his dawning sense that an institution's history brings with it certain inescapably confining and constraining fiduciary responsibilities, Buchanan felt quite strongly that something had gone awry with the New Program at St. John's. While Smith repeatedly cites Buchanan's negative assessment of the program as contradicting Buchanan's own assertion that the college had experienced "eight years of startling success" (J. Smith 76, 81, 85), Smith's elision in the material he cites is itself responsible for the apparent contradiction. As we've seen, Buchanan asserted that the college had had "eight years of startling *public* success," but he also observed that this success was "all out of proportion to [the New Program's] *real* effectiveness" (HL, "Resignation Statement" 7, emphasis added). Buchanan elaborates on this point in a letter to Hutchins: noting that the initial effort at St. John's did succeed in getting "some liberal arts into motion within a framework of the Great Books," Buchanan concedes that it "is clear now that we don't know what it is that we are teaching and studying, and it is also more than clear that we ought to find out" (HL, 12/5/46). And in a letter to A. W. Schmidt of Liberal Arts, Inc., Buchanan develops this idea further still, explaining that the goal of the new project in Massachusetts is to rework the relationship between mathematics and language in order to rethink all the subject matter in the sciences and the humanities:

> If we're going to find out what every man should know, we've got to make some knowledge that will dissolve present subject matters, courses and departments and re-crystallize them as vitamins for our whole culture. This calls for nothing less than the sacrifice on the part of natural scientists and teachers of humanities of their stock-in-trade and an all out effort to acquire by learning and relearning something that is worth teaching. (HL, 3/13/47)

In short, whatever the public perception was of the program's relative merits, and however the faculty and the board at St. John's assessed the program's success, Buchanan was firm in his conviction that much more important work remained to be done not only on the curriculum but also on the very way knowledge was constructed and categorized in the modern world. In fact, years later Buchanan confessed that as far as he was concerned, there was nothing magical about the Great Books themselves: "I'm not stuck on the classics at all.... The classics are important, but I was immediately embarrassed when we got to be exclusively connected with the classics and the classical tradition [at St. John's]" (qtd. in Wofford 157).

Long after Liberal Arts, Inc., had folded and its assets had been liquidated, Buchanan clung to this sense that the curriculum at St. John's had failed because it had neither determined what it was that students should learn nor what it was that was worth teaching. When Buchanan was invited back to St. John's to participate in a three-day colloquium on the state of liberal arts education more than twenty years after his resignation, he made it clear that his assessment of the college had changed little. Asserting that the goal of the curriculum ought to have been sustaining an investigation into "what a liberal arts college ought to be," Buchanan concluded with this bleak assessment of the outcome of this search at St. John's:

> We never found out, and haven't yet, I take it from all the signs, what we're teaching. We have all the conditions for teaching, but we've never decided what we're teaching and therefore have never been able to revise the program. ...I'm not talking about a doctrine. I'm talking about a subject matter, a direction, an intention. I suppose the best word for it is the truth. ...And I think we have to find out in the contemporary world just where we find our truth. (SBC, 1/25/68, 84–85)

It is here, perhaps, that we find the source of Buchanan's assessment that the New Program at St. John's was "a poison"—its very institutional and curricular stability implied that the search for a liberal education in the Great Books had come to an end. This final critique of the program suggests that in the end, Buchanan may also have been disillusioned with the discussion-oriented pedagogical approach that underwrote the curriculum, an approach that had failed to produce "truth" and instead had only allowed the great conversation to roil on endlessly. This, at any rate, was the conclusion that McKeon had reached, as he explained to Buchanan in a letter turning aside the invitation to join the project in Stockbridge:

> I am inclined more and more, since the visit in Annapolis, to the conclusion that if you are out of the project [at St. John's], the project as we have been talking about it for some twenty years is not feasible, and I shall not get into the new version of it [in Massachusetts] either. I am losing faith in the effectiveness of the dialectical process: it may give another fellow a good subject matter for dialogue, but it seems to be designed for a hemlock ending. (SBC, 2/9/46)

"A hemlock ending" of another order awaited Barr and Buchanan once they left St. John's and commenced their efforts in earnest to establish their "true university" in Massachusetts. Aside from failing utterly to attract others to their project, Barr and Buchanan quickly realized that the funds allocated by the Old Dominion Foundation were wholly insufficient to the task of building a college from scratch: they just didn't have enough money to establish a library, stock laboratories, convert existing buildings to dormitories, build a dining hall, attract faculty, and so on. Thus, in less than six months, it was clear to everyone involved that the former president and the former dean of St. John's College were in over their heads and that the project needed to be terminated as quickly and as tidily as possible. In desperation and suddenly bereft of any institutional affiliation, Barr and Buchanan asked Mellon to authorize the Old Dominion Foundation to distribute the funds to Liberal Arts, Inc., anyway. Mellon was unequivocal in rejecting this plan:

> As an alternative [to the failed plan in Massachusetts], you have requested Old Dominion Foundation, through me, to release the entire benefits of the endowment fund to Liberal Arts, Inc. (which I have always understood to be a temporary legal vehicle for the purchase of land and to obtain a Massachusetts charter for an undergraduate college) for purposes which seem to me extremely vague and which you have not expressed in any definite or detailed form, either verbally or in writing. I now gather that Mr. Quirico [a lawyer involved in the process] feels that it would be unwise to express them. (HL, letter from Mellon to Barr, 6/24/47)

Although Mellon remained committed to the project of advancing the study of the Great Books, Barr's refusal to state openly his intentions for the monies left Mellon with no alternative but to authorize "the abandonment of the entire project on the ground that it has been practically impossible to carry out under the legal terms of the letters of agreement, or in compliance with the real intentions of the principal individuals involved." And so, by the end of 1947, the funds and the attendant endowment of some four million dollars reverted to St. John's College and Barr and Buchanan were left to fend for themselves.

To imagine Buchanan as the tragic figure in all this is, I believe, a mistake, for what the preceding analysis of the trajectory of the Great Books approach has shown is that Buchanan, like Hutchins before him, had failed utterly to understand that the attractiveness of any curricular reform depends not on "a reasoned assessment" of the virtues of the reform but on the social, cultural, and economic benefits that accrue to those who will be influenced by the reform. And, as we've seen, the perceived merits of the Great Books curriculum vary wildly at the extreme poles of an established research university and a small, financially imperiled liberal arts college. At the University of Chicago, the effort to reconstruct the undergraduate curriculum was eagerly embraced by those few intellectuals who were new to the community and who had the most to gain from the program's success—

as specialists in general education, the designers of the Great Books curriculum and their followers stood to become the new experts in the university system, while those hired under different terms with different teaching expectations would have to retool if they hoped to have a future in the new university. However, those elements of institutionalized education designed to ensure that the academic status quo and its values are preserved—the tenure system, the division of knowledge into discrete fields of expertise, the accreditation system—all worked as required, with the result that the university flexed enough to accommodate the demands of its nonconformist president and then constricted at the first opportunity, returning to a form roughly homologous with that of its peer institutions. At St. John's, Barr and Buchanan faced a significantly different situation; by doing such a good job of handling adversity, they established a community that has long outlived its abandonment by its founders. Though Barr and Buchanan may have dreamed of producing a rootless community of scholars, students, and board members willing to move at their command to continue the search for truth, they discovered that their successful introduction of a curriculum into an institutional vacuum at St. John's had reinvigorated a corporate body they could neither control nor terminate.

"Overestimating the Average Ability of Students": The Great Books as Content and as Pedagogical Practice

In looking at these linked efforts to develop a liberal arts curriculum grounded in the Great Books, we have seen that the sense of who should receive such an education and what the fruits of such an education should be has varied over time.[24] With his modest goal of getting upper-level honors students to engage in "free-for-all" discussions of the Great Books, Erskine set out to unite a popular reading practice (consuming best-sellers) with texts revered by the academy, all in the hopes that the combination would bring the books to life for the students. This marginal venture was transformed into a central concern when it was combined with general education at the University of Chicago, where the Great Books approach took on an open contempt for vocational training and utility. Defining higher education in opposition to the prime reasons motivating students to continue their studies (a better job, increased earning potential, the acquisition of know-how), at Chicago Hutchins purposefully created a program at odds with traditional students and their teachers, turning a deaf ear to economic concerns and refusing to entertain the possibility that contemporary work in philosophy, sociology, cultural anthropology, educational theory, or the sciences had anything of value to contribute to the great conversation. With its contempt for money and all things of this world, Hutchins's initiative was never able to build a strong enough following to survive the departure of its high priest. The initiative at St. John's, in contrast, succeeded where Hutchins's had failed, partly because the college's desperate circumstances made it possible for Barr and Buchanan to, in a sense, wipe out the institution's immediate past, removing all employees who did not fit the needs of the New Program, while implementing curricular reforms designed for a small student populace — those with "both good and mediocre minds" — who had specifically elected to pursue the approach.

Throughout this discussion, the world outside the walls of the academy has had a shadowy, if increasingly threatening, presence — it has been figured as a space one gestures toward in order to justify a set of educational initiatives principally concerned with dismantling the influence of relativism and reinstating the reign of Reason within a democracy. Yet despite these vaunted goals, it would be difficult, given the events recounted here, to represent either Erskine's General Honors course or the curricular reforms realized for such a brief time at the University of Chicago or even the successful installation of the Great Books approach at St. John's as having traced out a trajectory of institutional dominance. And, though there can be little doubt that the Great Books continue to appear on the syllabi of literature courses across the nation,[25] the *pedagogical* approach advocated by Erskine, Adler, Hutchins, Barr, and Buchanan has found few places where it is welcome: the small classes, the discussion-based format, and the redefinition of mastery all require material resources and a commitment to revising standard teaching practices that remain in short supply at our institutions of higher learning.

But while resistance to the Great Books curriculum extends back to its inception at Columbia in the twenties, it is important to recognize that the grounds of contestation have shifted in the present moment. For our purposes, the most important shift is this: whereas the approach initially was accused of being "elitist" because access to the Great Books was restricted to a handful of students and of being "antidemocratic" because the goal of *the pedagogy* was to establish a unified body of metaphysical principles, it is now *the list itself* that is understood to be elitist and antidemocratic because it excludes women and minorities and because it tacitly celebrates a tradition of Western domination. Adler's position on such charges perfectly illustrates the limited effect this line of criticism has had on those promoting the great conversation. As he sees it, "the fact that, in the Western tradition until the nineteenth century, there simply were no great books written by women, blacks, or non-Europeans, does not make those that were written by white males in the earlier centuries any less great" (*Reforming Education* 334). In short, although the critique mounted against the Great Books curriculum has shifted from the question of who should be allowed to read the books on the list to that of which authors should appear on the list, the participants in the great conversation still aren't listening to what those on the outside have to say.

What tends to get misplaced in these debates about the Great Books as a kind of content is the potentially empowering pedagogical project that resides at the heart of the Great Books approach. Although the preceding discussion has shown the variability with which "the student" can be constructed within this curricular regime, it has also shown that the early history of this approach records an evolving commitment to the image of the student of the Great Books as an ordinary, common reader who can nonetheless establish a meaningful and productive relationship with a wide range of immensely complex texts. This flies in the face of prevailing assumptions about average students, who are regularly constructed by the textbook industry and by the professoriate at large as needing to start small, slow, and easy, and who are somehow never seen to be quite ready to fully participate in or understand discussions about ideas, great or otherwise. Thus, there is a fundamental and fruitful contradiction between the "aristocratic" arguments for pursuing the study of the Great Books and the "democratic" impulse in the approach's pedagogical assumptions about the average reader. This disjunction unquestionably constrains who can participate in the discussion and what can be discussed. But, at the same time, it also allows those who enter such a program of study the opportunity to generate and test their own interpretations, to work across disciplinary boundaries, languages, and historical periods, and to study in an institutional community that self-consciously seeks to produce a shared body of literate experience. We will see, in the following chapter, how this disjunction between the promotion of privileged cultural material and the provision of a comparatively democratic pedagogical practice gets reversed at Britain's Open University, where the university's reliance on technology to deliver distance education has given it access to a wider audience while, at the same time, greatly constraining the interactions of the course designers and their students.

4 Cultural Studies for the Masses

Distance Education and the

Open University's Ideal Student

In the fall of 1968, students in the Du Bois' Club at the City University of New York issued a petition demanding, among other things, "that the racial composition of future entering classes reflect [the racial composition] of the high school graduating classes in the city" (qtd. in Lavin, Alba, and Silberstein 9). Shortly thereafter, the Black and Puerto Rican Student Community (BPRSC) picked up these concerns and spearheaded the effort that eventually led to the occupation of buildings on City College's South Campus on April 22, 1969.[1] Declaring the establishment of the "University of Harlem," these students and others who joined their cause renewed the demand that the administration address disparities in the racial composition of the student body, that it commit itself to equitable admissions across disciplines and majors, and that it establish a separate school for Black and Puerto Rican studies (10). After two weeks of negotiations, the students agreed to leave the buildings; but when the college reopened on May 6, what had been a relatively peaceful protest turned violent. Unable to quell the troubles, President Buell Gallagher called in the police on May 8 and that afternoon, amid the fistfights and bottle throwing, the auditorium at the college's main student center was set on fire. The final decision to commit the CUNY system to open admissions was not made for another two months, but there can be little doubt that this apocalyptic scene profoundly influenced that deliberative process. Seymour Hyman, deputy chancellor, described his reaction to seeing smoke billowing from the student center: "The only question in my mind was, How can we save City College? And the only answer was, Hell, let everybody in" (qtd. in Lavin, Alba, and Silberstein 13).[2]

At the same time officials from CUNY were facing student insurrection and the threat that one of their campuses might be burned to the ground, across the Atlantic officials from Britain's newly founded Open University were confronted with what can only seem, in comparison, to be a comical set of obstacles. As Walker Perry, the OU's first vice-chancellor, has described it, there was considerable discussion about where best to hold the inaugural ceremony for a university with plans to rely on the mass media of radio and television to transmit its lessons. That is, how does one install a chancellor at a university that aims to transform every living room in the nation into one of its classrooms? at a university that is meant to be everywhere and nowhere at the same time? And, more important, what does one wear to the ceremony? Should the chancellor and those in attendance don traditional academic garb? Or would such trappings simply serve to symbolically resituate the university within the very hierarchical tradition that its open admissions policy was specifically designed to disrupt? If the university was really meant to be open, wouldn't a show of pomp and circumstance at its inception send the message that the only thing *really* different about this university was its reliance on distance education (Perry 46–47)?

On the one hand, then, we have the events at City College, where curricular and administrative change was both prompted and accelerated "from below" and where the definition of "open admissions" was immediately and clearly linked to issues of racial and economic inequities. On the other hand, we have the peaceful founding of Britain's Open University, which from its originary moment was committed to allowing anyone over twenty-one years old to enroll in its courses and pursue a degree, regardless of the applicant's previous academic performance. With this preliminary juxtaposition in mind, I would like to consider the range of institutional, discursive, and disciplinary forces that simultaneously enabled and constricted the pedagogical encounter with the OU student. In order to do this, I will focus specifically on the OU's influential interdisciplinary course on popular culture, U203. I have chosen to discuss this course for a number of reasons. First, it was, according to Sean Cubitt, "the largest undergraduate take-up for any cultural studies course in the United Kingdom," reaching over 6,000 students during the period it was offered at the OU from 1982 to 1987 (90). Second, the team who created this course was headed by Tony Bennett and included many other writers and consultants who, like Bennett, already had made or would soon make significant contributions to the emergent fields of cultural and media studies: Stuart Hall, Paul Willis, David Morley, Janet Woollacott, and James Donald, to name only the most prominent members.[3] And, finally, because the course delivered such a large audience to this group of cutting-edge thinkers committed to recognizing the cultural and political significance of the working class, U203 provides a unique opportunity to examine intellectuals at work in the academy. In many ways, the combination of the popular course topic, the dedicated teaching staff, the nontraditional student body, and the institutional apparatus seems perfect for creating an environment where dominant academic relations might be reworked and a transformative pedagogical practice enacted—a moment, in short, when cultural studies' potentially empowering critical approaches and materials might be disseminated to the disenfranchised at little or no cost. What could be better?

My aim in concentrating on this moment—when work in British cultural studies, moving out of the Centre for Contemporary Cultural Studies at Birmingham, and work on film and media studies, moving away from the British Film Institute, coalesced and began anew at the Open University—is not to chart the inevitable decline of some pure, originary project. Rather, my overarching interest is to consider cultural studies not as a set of ideas or theories, but as an intellectual practice located in and influenced by historical conditions. It has, of course, been useful for the discipline that "cultural studies" has effloresced into an umbrella term under which many different agendas can meet and converse. But this very utility has impeded efforts to historicize the emergence of the discipline, since reference to any given version of a cultural studies project as it was understood by a specific set of scholars working on a specific course at a specific institutional location at a specific time can be discounted on the grounds that it is not the *ideal* cultural studies project. By pursuing just such a local history here, I mean to argue that no given version can be anything more than the conglomeration of a set of contingencies that includes but is not limited to the scholars engaged in the project, the institutional location where that project is realized, the students who partake in the project, the discursive preoccupations of the profession at the time, and the prevailing political and economic climate during which the project is pursued. With this in mind, we will see in what follows that U203, like all courses, is best understood as the end result of sustained efforts to negotiate such contingencies, a brokered solution forged in the midst of the always-already bureaucratized encounter between the teaching apparatus and the target population.

U203 in Institutional Context:
The Interlocking Paradoxes of the
Open University's Educational Mission

While open admissions at CUNY rose up from the smoldering ashes of the student auditorium, at the Open University open admissions was officially brought into being before the approving eyes of Prime Minister Harold Wilson and a host of vice-chancellors from competing British universities in July of 1969 at the ceremony installing the OU's first chancellor, Lord Geoffrey Crowther. In the end, it was decided that those officially in attendance should appear in full academic regalia because, as Vice-Chancellor Perry put it, there was a strong sense that "the students themselves would come to demand just the same sort of ceremonial as was provided by any other university" (47). And so, with no students to speak for themselves, university officials had to construct a student body for whom they could then ventriloquize a set of desires. At this founding moment, the official response, both telling and seemingly inevitable, was to construct a student body desirous of conformity, official trappings, public rituals.

While this version of the OU student emphasizes a continuity of tradition between the Open University and its rivals at the face-to-face universities, another version, which stressed the uniqueness of the university's mission and its target population, surfaced at the OU's first graduation ceremony. Here, officials self-consciously put forth the image of the university as fulfilling the radical educational mission of serving the oppressed, the downtrodden, the marginal. To this end, the OU conferred honorary degrees on Paulo Freire and Richard Hoggart, figures who metonymically stand in for, respectively, liberatory pedagogical practice and the hidden potential of the working class. And, to further emphasize the university's commitment to serving students shut out from pursuing a higher education elsewhere within the British system, "Fanfare for the Common Man" was selected to accompany the student processional. It must have been an odd experience—all these students who went to school at home and studied lessons conveyed over the radio and the television, getting together for the first time to receive their credentials en masse.

The tension between these two versions of the OU student is, in fact, one of the fundamental structuring relationships that allows the OU to compete as a legitimate educational institution, for the university constantly evokes the nontraditional students who are the purported targets of its courses and, simultaneously, insists that these students have the same quotidian desires one would expect to find among students at any university.

The 1983 film *Educating Rita* captures this tension nicely: at the center of this retelling of the Pygmalion story is Susan Rita White, a twenty-six-year-old married woman from the working class who has, as she puts it, "been realizing for ages [that she was] slightly out of step" with her peers. Rita's love of reading brings her to study literature at the OU, where her course tutor, a bitter drunk who has lost faith in the virtues of education, helps her transform herself from an irreverent respondent into a successful student who says just what's expected of her. Thus, as the film depicts it, the university does, in fact, serve a certain sector of the working class; but it does so by engaging those students willing and able to abandon their home cultures in exchange for more "universal pleasures," which the film defines as reading Yeats. As Rita succinctly defines her position early on in the film, "The masses — it's not their fault, but sometimes I hate them."

We find a similar tension between the educational mission imagined for the university and the students it was thought might be drawn to such an education in accounts of the university's conception. As Harold Wilson, who launched the project when he became prime minister, describes the evolution of his idea for a university that would use the mass media to deliver an affordable education to the working classes,

> The decision to create the Open University, then known as the "University of the Air," was a political act. It was announced as a firm commitment of the incoming Labor Government on 8 September, 1963; the text and outline proposals had been written out by hand in less than an hour after church on the previous Easter Sunday morning. It was never party policy, nor did it feature in Labor's election manifesto. (Wilson vii)

This story is almost too good to be true, for in it the OU emerges from impeccable lineage, the scion of Labor government concerns and Easter Sunday reveries, a utopian dream that would provide for the salvation of the working class by means of an act that was "political" without ever being "party policy." In his alternative account, Brian MacArthur asserts that Wilson had, in fact, been thinking about a university that drew on the powers of the mass media for some time prior to that fateful Easter Sunday in 1963. Those thoughts were spurred on, in part, by his having learned during his frequent trips to the Soviet Union that 60 percent of Soviet engineering graduates got their degrees through a program that combined correspondence courses and university attendance (3). After one such trip, Wilson visited Senator William Benton in Chicago, who arranged for him to see some of the Encyclopaedia Britannica films that were used in the Chicago College of the Air. It was, in all likelihood, the combination of Wilson's experience in Chicago and his awareness of the great success of the Soviet system that led him to propose his own "University of the Air."

Obviously, there's no way of knowing when or why, "exactly," this idea was born. For our purposes, it suffices to note the differences between these divergent efforts to locate the university's origin on the one hand within the nexus of concerns represented by the Labor Party and Easter Sunday and, on the other, as a response to prevailing fears about recent Soviet successes in space. While there is no arguing the fact that Wilson's election as prime minister in 1964 paved the way for establishing the OU, it is also true that when the Conservatives were voted in after the elections of 1970, the new prime minister, Edward Heath, could easily have done away with the university before it had ever admitted a single student. Indeed, Heath's first chancellor of the exchequer, Iain McLeod, had specifically targeted the OU for budgetary extinction, saying that this "great socialist opportunity for the part-time student" had to go (qtd. in Young 69). But, as fate would have it, McLeod died after just one month in office, and Heath's minister of education was thereafter able to successfully defend the university's place on the governmental budget. That the OU's savior at this moment of fiscal crises and political upheaval was none other than Margaret Thatcher should make it perfectly clear that the university's mission and its target audience cannot be constructed as, in any way, intrinsically allied with or predisposed to a political project meant to facilitate the resurrection of the Labor Party or of socialism more generally. To the contrary, according to George Gardiner, one of Thatcher's first biographers, the woman who came to be known as the "Iron Lady" was able to support the OU because she understood its mission to be "giving educational opportunity to those prepared to work for it" (qtd. in Young 69).

It would also be a mistake to read Thatcher's insistence that the university be reserved for those students "prepared to work" as a Conservative shift in the university's mission. In fact, as early as 1966, the Open University's Planning Committee was hard at work assuring everyone concerned that although the university would rely on new teaching methods to reach a new student populace, OU students would have the same "rigorous and demanding" experience provided by other universities (qtd. in MacArthur 8). Indeed, the committee went so far as to argue that supporting distance education amounted to a kind of fiscal patriotism: "At a time when scarce capital resources must, in the national interest, be allocated with the greatest prudence, an open university could provide higher and further education for those unable to take advantage of courses in existing colleges and universities. And it could do so without requiring vast capital sums to be spent on bricks and mortar" (qtd. in MacArthur 9). In short, long before

Thatcher appeared on the scene, the Planning Committee was hard at work silencing fears that their efforts to redistribute educational opportunities to people previously excluded from the system might have profoundly disruptive social, cultural, and institutional repercussions. The OU wasn't trying to restructure class relations in Britain; it was simply promising to deliver the same high-quality educational product available at other British universities, for a fraction of the cost, to those students willing and able to make up for lost time. And what reasonable person could object to this?

When Lord Crowther stood to deliver his acceptance speech in 1969, he offered a similarly unobjectionable image of the university's mission by defining the many ways in which the new institution would be worthy of its name. Crowther asserted that by virtue of its admissions policy, it would be "open, first, as to *people*" and, because of its reliance on the media for mass communications, it would also be "open as to *places*." That is, with its campus to consist of little more than a block of offices and printing and production facilities, Crowther pictured the university with its toe touching ground in its home base of Milton Keynes, while the rest of the enterprise would be "disembodied and airborne." And in order to disseminate its lessons to the largest number of students across the widest possible area, Crowther insisted that the university would also be "open as to *methods*." "Every new form of human communication will be examined," he promised, "to see how it can be used to raise and broaden the level of human understanding." Finally, Crowther said, the university would be "open as to *ideas*," approaching the "human mind as a vessel of varying capacity" into which knowledge needs to be poured, and "as a fire that has to be set alight and blown with the divine afflatus" (qtd. in J. Ferguson 19–20). His remarkable speech captures the ambitious and optimistic spirit of this educational endeavor. But if we recall the contemporaneous events at CUNY, it shouldn't escape our notice that at this originary moment the student for whom this university imagined itself opening its doors was assumed to be a deracinated, locationless, disembodied being who had slipped through the gaps in an otherwise laudable system.

However necessary it was at the rhetorical level to evoke such a student, at the bureaucratic level one of the most acute challenges that confronted the original planners at the OU was how to design courses for the geographically bound, historically situated, fully embodied students who were scheduled to begin "attending" the university in the fall of 1971. This challenge was particularly daunting for two reasons. First, the teaching apparatus called for in this context was an enormous, unwieldy bureaucratic mechanism that could only be controlled by coordinating the actions of a large number of educators and technicians working simultaneously on different parts of the course. (U203, for instance, had twenty-five "authors" and ten other members involved as editors, BBC producers, or advisors from the OU's Institute of Educational Technology.) Each course team had to divide up the labor of writing the course books and putting them into "blocks" that could be sent through the mail at an affordable rate; designing texts that were "student active," which would engage nontraditional students and prepare them to do well in the course; producing television and radio broadcasts that complemented the material presented in the course books; collecting and publishing "set books," which contained additional required reading in the course; collecting and publishing supplemental material to reinforce and restate the concerns of the course in greater detail; when necessary (as was the case in U203), providing cassette tapes of recorded material discussed in the course books; planning a meaningful series of lectures and activities for the required two weeks of face-to-face meetings at summer school; designing the final exam and a series of other exams and/or Tutor Marked Assignments to be administered through-out the course to measure student progress; and, finally, in courses like U203, which required written responses from the students, providing explicit directions to the students on how to prepare the assignments and to the course tutors on how to evaluate the students' responses. If coordinating all of this work weren't daunting enough, course designers had the further complication of having to anticipate the needs and abilities of the kind of students it was assumed *might* enroll at the OU. And since the expense and the labor required to revise a course once it had been produced was prohibitive, given that the courses were designed to run from four to six years, it was vitally important that the course team pitch the material at the right level and in the right way. For if the course team imagined the wrong kind of student—if it aimed too high, or too low, or in the wrong direction altogether—it was a mistake the university (or, more accurately, the students enrolled in the university's course) would have to live with for a long time.[4]

For these reasons, then, one of the OU's highest priorities has been to track what kinds of students actually enroll in its courses. The OU's Institute of Educational Technology (IET) provides a steady stream of statistical information regarding the students and their assessments of the OU courses, but the value of such data continues to be the subject of debate within the OU community itself. According to David Harris, as educational funds tightened up in the mid-seventies, the OU's Regional Tutorial Services (RTS), who employed the course tutors, found themselves competing with the IET for space in the OU's budget. Consequently, those working for the IET tried to establish the "face-to-face elements [of OU's program] as the least justifiable area" in the budget, arguing that the RTS was only necessary for remediating the poorest of students (Harris 52). RTS responded by drawing attention to the unreliable and inscrutable material gathered by the IET, observing that a "very low pass rate could be interpreted as an indication of ineffectiveness of the course, but equally as an indication of the unsuitability of the students" (55). Thus, although a great deal of information about the OU's student body has been collected, there has also been substantial disagreement over how to interpret that information, as the "hard" science of market analysis at the IET has contended with the "soft" science of firsthand experience at RTS.

This aspect of the OU's bureaucratic structure, which seems to ensure that the needs and concerns of the OU's target population are ultimately displaced, is reinforced by the OU's reliance on advanced technology to deliver its educational product. To begin with, the very "openness" of the university means that its professors cannot close their classroom doors and teach "in private." Because the lectures are broadcast over the radio and television, the course team never knows which experts in the field might be checking up on their colleagues over at the OU. While this feature of the OU was celebrated by Raymond Williams, who, in an early review, praised the televised lectures for making "some aspects of the real work of universities...available for direct public observation" ("Open Teaching" 139), the drawbacks of having classes taught in this version of the panopticon soon became obvious to everyone involved: the course textbooks appeared to be written at a level to thrill the course team's colleagues rather than to instruct the nontraditional student population thought to be taking the courses for credit. Although this apparent discrepancy between the pitch of the course materials and the students' abilities might be seen as an unintended by-product of distance education, the following internal memo written by a social science professor at the OU, commenting on the weakness in a colleague's course, suggests that this disjunction was considered a necessary part of OU's pedagogical practice: "It seems to me you have made serious strategic mistakes.... In particular in making the course too easy.... Personally, I think the right answer is to bash them with something difficult, although the main justification for that is simple academic credibility...and it might be as well to think of the kind of attacks you might get [from other academics] in the educational journals and magazines" (qtd. in Harris 124 n. 13, original ellipses and brackets). Beyond impressing their colleagues in the field, there was another very good reason why the course team might feel it was necessary to "bash" their students with particularly difficult material. In the early days, the OU faced the challenging task of convincing the academic community that a degree achieved through distance education would ever be comparable to a degree earned at one of Britain's better-known universities. While no "correspondence school" in the United States has successfully waged this battle for legitimacy, John Verduin and Thomas Clark argue in their study of distance education that the OU has succeeded where others have failed, in part because it has made its courses challenging in the ways described above and in part through its "association in the public mind with the British Broadcasting Corporation and its quality programming, the involvement of top-caliber authors and academics, political sponsorship by Lord Perry, representation on national educational and governmental committees, receipt of national research awards, and an international reputation" (113–14). Thus, the "bashing" of students by "top-caliber authors and academics" in such a public and respected arena may ultimately have helped to allay fears that the education provided at the OU significantly differed from that offered elsewhere in Britain.

The difficulty of getting direct access to the students enrolled at the OU, the disagreement about how to interpret the results of student evaluations, the ready availability of course materials to people outside the OU, and the importance of the OU's establishing itself as a viable, competitive university—these bureaucratic realities militated against the course designers focusing too much attention on the institution's pedagogical approach. And so, in effect, the interplay between the OU's institutional position and its reliance on technology meant that the student *had to be* factored out of the educational equation if the system was to run smoothly and achieve parity with the other British universities. I do not intend to imply that the OU is "uninterested" in its students, whatever that would mean. To the contrary, the OU created the IET to generate a profile of the needs and concerns of "the OU student." Having allowed 25,000 students to register for the first term in 1971, the university was particularly interested in learning more about the 20,000 students who stayed on to start the courses. Based on their original assumptions about what kind of skills and abilities the new students would bring with them to the OU, university officials had estimated that somewhere between 10 and 20 percent of the original class would end up getting a degree. However, much to the administration's surprise and delight, over 75 percent of the students in the initial batch successfully completed their first course for credit and, by 1975, 42.5 percent of the entering class had already graduated (McIntosh, with Calder and Swift 264).[5] While officials were initially baffled by this completion rate (after all, if its students *really* were nonstandard adult learners and the OU *really* was offering a degree on par with its competitors, how could so many of its students be making it through the system?), ongoing research by McIntosh and others began to unravel the mystery of the OU's incredible success: on further analysis, the data revealed that the university was not, in fact, attracting people who had been shut out of the educational system so much as it was reaching a special sector of the population already committed to upward social mobility.

In a preliminary study, McIntosh provided this composite portrait of the "typical" student in this class: "The typical Open University student is a man, in his thirties, in a white-collar job; although he is now apparently middle-class, his parents were probably working-class and he himself may well still call himself working-class. He has clearly already been involved in a lot of study, either 'full' or 'part-time,' and thus has been able to move on to a different sort of job from his parents" (54). After further evaluation of the statistical data available, McIntosh, Calder, and Swift were compelled to conclude that the vast majority of the students in the initial class had not actually suffered "great educational deprivation at school" (123). And, by charting the inter- and intragenerational class mobility experienced by these students, they found as well that these OU students were "clearly atypical of their peers in one critical way—in their propensity to learn" (133). Thus, as pleased as University officials were with their students' successes, these revelations about the actual attributes of the OU's student body raised some disturbing questions. Why wasn't the OU reaching more women? Why was it that less than 5 percent of the entering class were classified as having come from the working class? Why was it that the university was attracting so many teachers interested in improving their credentials and so few disenfranchised members of the broader population?

At the time this information began to come out, Vice-Chancellor Perry's first line of defense was to argue that "the original objectives [for the university]…make no explicit mention of any special provision for the deprived adult" (Perry 144). He then insisted that it "was much better to have as our first students a large number of school teachers who were motivated, well prepared and with time for study," rather than students from the working class, "many of whom would have been ill-prepared," because the presence of qualified teachers allowed the university to "polish" its methods and to achieve the kind of academic recognition that was so vital to its survival (144). Finally, Perry had McIntosh retally her numbers, putting students not in their self-declared class but in the classes their fathers occupied, which immediately produced a much more satisfying picture of the student body: depending on your source, it appeared that anywhere from 60 percent to 85 percent of the student body could be said to have come from the working class (McIntosh 60–61; Perry 144). With these results in hand, Perry could safely crow that the system of education provided by the Open University had not lowered standards to attract nontraditional students, but rather had put together "the most difficult way of getting a degree yet invented by the wit of man" (167)![6]

As the paradoxes produced by the OU's complex social mission pile up, they also begin to resolve one another. Although the Open University admits students on a first-come-first-served basis, it ends up not with a sampling of what many thought was its target population but with a mass of relatively well-prepared, upwardly mobile, largely male students—people, in short, rushing to be the first in line. The presence of students with this profile explains why the OU's commitment to delivering a competitive educational product did not result in high failure rates but in a flood of newly credentialed graduates. The success of these highly committed students was further assisted by the course team's production of study materials designed for two very different "ideal students." As Harris explains:

> In the case of the student activities in the units, "the student" is someone who wants to stop reading to reflect and pursue implications and then compare his or her thoughts with the author's, to pursue his or her "own" interests further with extra reading in more depth, to engage critically with the material he or she encounters in the text, even to seize upon assumptions or flaws in the unit itself.... The student of the supplementary materials is rather different. He or she has limited time and has to "cut corners," he or she wants the core of the argument rather than having to read any unduly "difficult" material, and he or she has a well-organized and rather calculating approach to assignments. (108)

This writing strategy provides the course team with a reasonable enough solution to the problems produced by the necessity of teaching "out in the open." It allows them to showcase the "good" student in the most public course materials, thus promoting the image of the OU's high seriousness and academic rigor. And it also permits them to reach out to the "resourceful" student with its supplementary materials, where all the information necessary to pass the course is presented in a more readily digestible mode, thus providing the students with another avenue to success.

By performing a small ethnographic survey of students enrolled in an education course at the OU, Harris was able to trace out the degree to which actual students used the course materials in the ways imagined by the course designers. To no one's surprise, he discovered a general pattern of "selective neglect" with regard to how students responded to the demands of the course, a pattern perhaps best exemplified by a "Mr. Wavendon," who paid little attention to the course's structure or content, doing just enough to pass and get credit toward his degree (113). What is intriguing about Harris's work is the relationship he sees between this kind of "student instrumentalism" and the business of distance education.

> Both approaches have the effect of reducing academic materials to objects which are organized according to largely strategic considerations; both pursue an "efficient" approach to their given ends; both operate with an indifference to anything that cannot be operationalized as a means to those ends. Student instrumentalism as an orientation is thus a kind of deep conformity to the logic of the system after all. Far from being deviant, it is almost openly encouraged by the study guides as a necessary approach for survival in the teaching system, and is often implicit in discussions of "study skills." It is a complement to the official ideology of course production, rather than a deviant response. (118)

Thus, within a system that downplays (and in some respects actively seeks to remove) the view of education as interactive, the students themselves reject interacting with the assigned material in their courses in favor of readily conforming to the systemic demand that they produce the easily evaluated, regulated, and monitored responses solicited for credit. In other words, the system has not failed when it confers its credentials of distinction on those students primarily concerned with getting the assigned material to divulge the "right" answers. What has happened, rather, is that the system has fully realized its own internal logic, ensuring that only those students, in Thatcher's words, "prepared to work" within this instrumentalist mode can continue the advance toward their degrees.

Thus, despite its rhetoric of "openness," the OU can be seen to be fully implicated in higher education's fundamentally conservative agenda; but what about U203 and its seemingly radical course content? Could such a course, on the basis of its subject matter alone, bypass the historical, structural, and technological constraints of the OU in the late seventies and early eighties to provide an oppositional education experience? To answer this question—indeed, to see if this is even the right question to pose—we need first to consider what other resources the course team members were able to draw on in their efforts to address the institutional necessity of commodifying both students and knowledge. That is, if, at some level, the OU required an instrumentalist pedagogy, then we should determine how the question of the relationship between pedagogical practice and institutional mission was being handled in the larger community of those involved in film, media, and cultural studies. Did the thinking in these areas work with or against the model of pedagogical practice adopted at the media-oriented

Open University? As it so happens, in the years just before the creation of U203, the two media journals, *Screen* and *Screen Education*, carried on a set of heated debates about the importance of pedagogical concerns to the business of producing and disseminating critical knowledge. It is to those debates that we must next turn our attention.

U203 in Discursive Context:
Arguing for the Sake of Theory at *Screen* and *Screen Education*

In 1971, the same year the OU's first courses were broadcast, the Society for Education in Film and Television (SEFT) began publishing *Screen Education Notes* as an adjunct to *Screen*, its journal devoted to scholarly work on film and television studies. The earliest issues of *Screen Education Notes* provided a place for teachers developing courses in the emergent fields of film and media studies to discuss the practical problems involved in bringing the examination of the visual media into the classroom: the journal's articles disseminated information about available material, where it was to be found, and how to get access to it; they included sample syllabi for other teachers to model; they suggested ways to evaluate student film productions and to establish equivalences between such "practical work," as it was called, and the more traditional work of student essays; and they offered strategies for addressing the problems of administering examinations given the scarcity of materials and — these being the days prior to the proliferation of VCRs — the impossibility of re-viewing the films.[7] All of this curricular work was crucial for beginning the battle to open an independent institutional space for the study of visual media. If this battle was to be won, however, more had to be done than produce imaginary syllabi and possible examination policies: if the new area was to justify its existence, it had to constitute for itself an object of study and an array of analytic skills not adequately covered by the other academic disciplines.

With just such a goal in mind, Tom Ryall argued, in his 1973 *Screen Education Notes* editorial, for the necessity of establishing a discipline that "attempts to develop student's visual literacy, their ability to make their own 'reading' of a film" (2). Ryall's proposal, which imagined the new discipline's job as developing abilities the students already possessed, differs considerably from the one staked out by Manuel Alvarado and Richard Collins in their editorial, which declared a new mission for the newly titled *Screen Education* in 1975: "The ambit that we are defining for ourselves in this issue and for future work is a large one — consideration of the relations between mass communications, particularly TV, and their containing culture — the social and political relations they constitute, reinforce or inhibit" (2). Although Alvarado and Collins were careful to avoid the term "visual literacy," their new project for the journal assumed that being "literate" in the media requires an ability to read the relationship between the image as broadcast and the image's "containing culture." This way of describing the object to be studied shifts attention away from working directly with how students make sense of the media onto the new terrain of structural and ideological critique. And, as Alvarado and Collins readily acknowledged, such a shift was not without its difficulties: "Only fairly recently has a concern with film analysis as part of a more general concern with ideology and social relations reached the agenda — and then expensively armored with a tough theoretical carapace" (3). These editorials, separated by just two years, capture the journal's dual, and perhaps irreconcilable, commitments to something that sounds as rudimentary as "visual literacy," on the one hand, and to something as seemingly daunting as theories about the interplay of ideology, psychoanalysis, and social relations, on the other.[8]

In the following issue, the editors at *Screen Education* took the remarkable step of acknowledging that "many gaps, confusions, and contradictions underlie the range of articles that we have published over the last 15 months" (Alvarado, Bazalgette, and Hillier 1). To throw some light on the journal's conflicting inclinations, the editors invited an educational sociologist to write an article evaluating the state of *Screen Education* and of media studies more generally. Nell Keddie's analysis, titled "What Are the Criteria for Relevance?" located a fundamental contradiction in the emergent discipline's effort to express "a radical social philosophy within an education system committed to traditional liberal values" (5). This contradiction manifests itself most clearly, Keddie asserted, in the journal's general reluctance to publish articles that argued for the emergent discipline on the grounds of its relevance to students' lives. Keddie explained the source of this reluctance as follows:

> Such a claim may involve opting for low academic status on the one hand and for a commitment to the status quo on the other.... [Thus w]hen it is argued that film should not be relegated to a place as illustrative material in Social Studies or English, the rejection of its superficial social relevance is made to suggest a more serious and fundamental relevance. Analysis of the constituent images of film in terms of coding, where the codes are situated in terms of interests arising from control of the means of production, involves serious political education. (10)

Keddie's diagnosis helps explain the eventual failure of "screen education" to name the new field of study, of "visual literacy" to name what those engaged in it acquire, and, finally, of "practical work" to name what takes place in that field.[9] In each case, the term in question drew the emergent discipline in the direction of what Keddie describes as "low-status work for the less able" (10), a place, apparently, where those committed to "serious political education" would not be in a position to achieve their larger political goals.[10]

Insisting that films are, first and foremost, "moving and exciting experiences," Keddie closes with a warning about the potentially alienating aspects of the emergent discipline's methodology:

> It strikes me that very little attention is given to the quality of this experience in the accounts of film teaching that I have read. . . . What bothers me is that the notion that film is not to be treated as transparent might lead to a premature formal analysis of a film before the student has had time to become aware of the nature of his own response which has been characterized as "intuitive." It would be folly to exchange knowingness for response. If you concentrate on the 70 odd changes of camera angle in the 45 seconds of the shower murder in *Psycho*, you effectively alienate yourself from the horror of the killing. (11)

As it turns out, Keddie was not alone in fearing that the analytical tools brought to bear on the media might effectively remove the student's response from the classroom and therefore undermine the new field's stated commitment to truly "serious, political education." In fact, just a few months after Keddie's article appeared, at a time when the editors and writers for *Screen Education* were forging ahead with their efforts to acquire the "tough, expensively armored carapace" that would enable them to participate in discussions about the ideological powers of the media, a curious thing happened: the editorial board at *Screen*, SEFT's theoretically oriented journal, found itself unable to contain an internal disagreement about what role theory should play in the study of media.

The problems on *Screen*'s editorial board surfaced publicly at the end of 1975, when four of its members — Edward Buscombe, Christopher Gledhill, Alan Lovell, and Christopher Williams — coauthored an essay published in the journal that was highly critical of the influence that psychoanalytic theory exercised generally over film and media studies and over the articles in *Screen*, in particular. Specifically, they argued that the Lacanian and Freudian psychoanalytic paradigms had been uncritically accepted by most of the film and media studies community, that many of the applications of these psychoanalytic models to film were unintelligible, and, finally, that the validity of such applications had not been satisfactorily determined ("State-ment" 119). Asserting that the journal was in danger of losing its readers ac-tively involved in education because of its heavy reliance on such shoddy intellectual work, the coauthors predicted a near-certain future, when the journal "would drift into a cultural void and become a conventional acade-mic magazine with a 'leftist' coloring and no political situation in which it can specifically engage" (123). Concluding with a call for a reconsideration of the power of psychoanalytic criticism to disable the educational process, the coauthors suggested that Lacan should serve as a starting point for such an examination since they "believe[d] that no socialist educationalist could be happy with Lacan's authoritarian account of the learning process" (130).

When it became clear that no official response to this critique was forth-coming, the four quickly penned another article, straightforwardly titled "Why We Have Resigned from the Board of *Screen*." While they were ready to concede that SEFT's original project in establishing the journal had never been to provide a forum for work that could be "immediately applied" to the classroom, the coauthors nonetheless insisted that the society certainly had intended that "the question of the relationship between work on film theory and the concerns of teachers should always be present in the mind of the board and should inflect its work" ("Why" 107). That *Screen* had failed to keep this relationship in mind was evident, they felt, in three ways: the journal was "*unnecessarily obscure and inaccessible*"; its reliance on "*politico-cultural analysis*...[was] *intellectually unsound and unproductive*"; and, finally, the journal had "*no serious interest in educational matters*" (107–8, original emphasis). In expanding this critique, they made it clear that they felt the journal's failings extended beyond the heavy reliance on psychoan-alytic theory into the overall engagement in "politico-cultural analysis," which manifested itself in the journal's general reliance on "Althusserian Marxism, semiology, psychoanalysis and avant-gardism" (109). And, as far as the resignation signatories were concerned, the turn to this brand of the-ory had become an excuse for ignoring the question of what place "educa-tional matters" should have in the emergent disciplines of film, media, and cultural studies.

In their seven-page rejoinder to the resignation article, the remaining members of *Screen*'s editorial board allowed but one paragraph of response to this final charge.[11] They "categorically refused" this accusation on the grounds that they were "not ignorant of educational theory but *deeply crit-ical of it in its present forms*" (Brewster et al. 116, original emphasis). That the board declined to engage this charge is, perhaps, understandable. After all, given their colleagues' suspicions, how could they provide evidence of a "serious interest in educational matters"? And yet, it is not so easy to understand the board's outright refusal to consider ways of articulating a more readily discernible position with regard to education: that is, why did they remain silent about how their theoretical work had been or could be of estimable use to teachers?[12] However the board might have responded to this question, it was clear enough from their extended rebuttals of the other two charges that they were not about to see the journal abandon its work with psychoanalysis, semiotics, ideological critique, or linguistics in favor of work more overtly linked with what the resigning editors had termed "the concerns of teachers."

As stark as this breakdown in communication was, it would be a mistake, I believe, to read this editorial rift as *the* defining moment in the history of the disciplinary formation of film and media studies—that moment when theory and practice broke contact and went their separate ways. Indeed, one of the remaining board members at *Screen*, Colin MacCabe, has stated that at the time, the project of transforming the journal into a "theoretical magazine" was seen to be a "pressing necessity for teachers" who found themselves faced with the "problems of reconciling film with traditional conceptions of art" (4). *Screen* helped such teachers, MacCabe argues, because it equipped them with a theoretical basis and a practical program for "revitalizing and redefining the socialist project for society," which was accomplished by uniting Lacanian psychoanalysis with Brecht's notion of the epic theater (5). Such theoretical work, with its focus on films that broke with dominant narrative and cinematic codes, was seen to be useful to teachers in two ways: it provided them with a new aesthetic for discussing film and it allowed them a way to define their work as assisting in the production of new, counterhegemonic subjects ready to participate in the resurrection of the socialist project for society.

As exciting as MacCabe found such work at the time, in retrospect he has conceded that it ultimately ended up serving to revalorize the avant-garde and thus roundly failed to assist teachers in the ways it had promised: "For those teachers who had looked to film theory to break out of the high art enclave, [the linkage of Lacan and Brecht] had led firmly back there, albeit in a highly politicized version" (11). According to MacCabe, it was "this pattern of evaluation of the cinema [i.e., valorizing the avant-garde and denigrating the works from Hollywood] which provided the most important area of disagreement when, in 1976, four of the board members most closely associated with secondary education chose both to resign from the magazine and to fight a campaign to gain control of [SEFT]" (11). And yet, despite observing that the journal failed to deliver on its pedagogical promises, MacCabe then devotes the remainder of his account of the events to recasting and responding to the debate over psychoanalysis, never once mentioning that fully a third of the resigning board members' critique concerned the question of what educational role the journal was meant to play. MacCabe's silence here does more than simply replay the silence that this part of the critique received a decade before: it dramatizes the lasting incommensurability of these two divergent understandings of how *Screen* could best meet the educational needs and demands of teachers in the field.

Nevertheless, MacCabe's essay also provides a candid insider's assessment of what the loss of the dissenting board members meant to the theoretical and intellectual vitality of the journal. For, according to MacCabe, not only did the board at *Screen* lose "its balance both in relation to those engaged in secondary education and those committed to Hollywood," it also found itself in the years immediately following the resignation "locked into bitter internal debate," with much of its "original energy and excitement...refound in the society's new magazine *Screen Education* where concerns both with secondary teaching and popular culture were very much to the fore" (12). Thus, MacCabe's account suggests that this editorial disagreement at *Screen* did not signal a watershed event where theorists and practitioners went their separate ways. Rather, it marked a moment in the history of the emergent disciplines of film, media, and cultural studies when two different definitions of theory sought to part company—with politicized readings of films ending up at *Screen* and work on popular culture and education finding a temporary home at *Screen Education*.[13]

Before concluding my discussion of *Screen Education*, I would like to briefly consider the journal at the moment of its evanescence, just before it was merged into *Screen* in 1982—the very year that U203 made its initial appearance on TV screens and in mail boxes across Britain. *Screen Education*'s editorial mission changed frequently after 1976, and by the spring of 1981 the journal saw fit to devote an entire issue to "Pedagogics: Practices and Problems" because, as Angela McRobbie put it, "recent, even radical pedagogic discourses" had neglected to discuss the role of the teacher and the "play for power" in the classroom (2). Included in this issue is Bob Ferguson's essay "Practical Work and Pedagogy," which delineates the problems that arise when the means of production, in this case video cameras, are placed in the students' hands. Noting that most students, when left to their own devices, simply point the cameras and begin filming, Ferguson takes some time to discuss one of his student's efforts to put together a sort of video talk show about skateboarding. Although Ferguson found the video itself visually uninteresting, he nevertheless insists that the halting, stumbling narrative that accompanied it captured a moment when *writing* took on a new meaning for the working-class student: "I would venture to suggest that the script was probably the first piece of purposeful writing the student had ever undertaken. He actually *needed* it in order to facilitate a piece of communication" (52–53, original emphasis). By making his students' material and his own way of reading that material available for discussion, Ferguson provided a version of "critical pedagogy" that had, up to that point, received little attention in either *Screen* or *Screen Education*. That is, by opening the door on his classroom so that his readers could see how he theorized his practice and how he practiced his theory, Ferguson occupied a position less easily read as either just the place of practice (discussions of syllabi, examination procedures, "teaching tips") or just the place of theory (discussions of intervention, struggle, radical politics).

It's hard to say how Ferguson's article was received. The only evidence available is the one response it elicited in the journal: Andrew Bethell's sarcastic riposte, in reference to Ferguson's discussion of the video on skateboarding, that "apparently, this boy's fumbling attempts to sound like Robert Robinson [a popular sportscaster] is what real Media Studies and English teaching should be about" (77). Bethell went on to assert that only an "ill-informed and somewhat arrogant assumption" about the primacy of Standard English would allow a teacher to praise this working-class student's efforts to use a language other than his own (77). And thus, for a brief moment, Ferguson's work provided the occasion for a concrete examination of how ideology informs the evaluative process in the classroom. But whether or not this interchange helped to shift the focus of discussion toward the problems involved in soliciting, reading, and evaluating student work, it was a direction the journal or its readers were unable to pursue: Bethell's reply appeared in the journal's final issue. In 1982, the economic recession "forced SEFT to reconsider its publication strategy," as *Screen* editor Mark Nash put it (6). As a result, *Screen Education* was merged into *Screen* and the editors of the resultant hybrid, clumsily titled *Screen Incorporating Screen Education*, have allowed pedagogical concerns to quietly recede from the journal's pages.[14] Thus, just as the largest course ever to be taught on popular culture in Britain was about to be broadcast out of the Open University and across the British airwaves for the first time—at a time, in other words, when student work on the visual media was being solicited and responded to on a scale never before imagined—the journal devoted to providing a forum for discussing issues related to screen education flatlined.

However great the symbolic irony may be, we should not allow the irony or the coincidence of these events to seduce us into believing that all discussion of pedagogical issues in relation to media studies came to an abrupt end. Rather, I have staged *Screen Education*'s disappearance in this way simply to highlight the discursive conflicts and collapses that accompanied the emergence of the disciplines of film, media, and cultural studies during the time that immediately preceded and then followed the initial offering of U203. I have also meant to suggest that the problematic positioning of pedagogy at the OU was reinforced and replicated at the discursive level in the debates at *Screen* and *Screen Education*, for at both journals, as at the university, one finds considerable discomfort over what role to accord educational concerns in emergent work with and on the media. As we have seen, the discussions at these two journals circulated around the question of what kind of study of the visual media ought to be legitimated: Althusser and ideology or Lacan and psychoanalysis? "visual literacy" or that "tough, expensively armored carapace" of theory? And the two journals were concerned, as well, with the question of whether the relevance of such study should be understood in terms of its immediate accessibility or in terms of its ability to deliver a "serious political education." These are the central terms, figures, oppositions, and options that marked the terrain of film, media, and cultural studies when the OU began broadcasting U203 in 1982.[15] And now, having traced the borders of one of U203's discursive contexts and having considered the ways in which U203's home institution shaped the encounter between the students and the course, we are in a position to consider the course itself as both the product of and a response to these institutional and discursive forces.

The Teaching Machine at Work:
Studying Popular Culture at the Open University

The following "advertisement" for U203 appeared in the OU's house newspaper, *Sesame*, in June of 1981, hyping the course prior to its initial offering in 1982: "*Popular Culture* will offer you the opportunity of standing back from your day-to-day familiarity with popular culture in order to think critically about the ways in which it influences your thoughts and feelings as well as about its broader social and political significance" (T. Bennett, "Stand Back"). Because the course was "U-designated," signifying that it was part of the OU's new interdisciplinary area, it was particularly important that course team leader Tony Bennett make the course sound fun and attractive. Thus, although Bennett tells the students that they can expect to be taught "to think critically" about their experiences with popular culture, he concludes on an upbeat note: "I'm no doubt biased, but if I was in your shoes I'd regard [U203] as a *must*. It's got everything. Its subject matter is intrinsically interesting. It's just the sort of course the OU was designed for, opening up new areas of knowledge as well as making full use of the multi-media teaching system. And you'll find it intellectually challenging and rewarding" (original emphasis). It seems like a perfect fit: a course on popular culture taught by a team of educators implicitly predisposed, through their affiliation with cultural and media studies, to view education itself as one of the principle sites where the struggle for hegemony is waged. Would they be able to overcome, through strength of will or intellectual commitment, the conservative forces of OU's institutional structure and mount an oppositional educational experience?

The course that emerged from this collaborative effort consisted of seven "blocks" — the first offering a general overview of the themes and issues involved in the study of popular culture, the second providing a view of the historical development of popular culture in Britain, and the remaining blocks connecting popular culture to everyday life, politics and ideology, science and technology, and the state. There was also a middle block that considered the formal analysis of popular culture. The blocks were subdivided into units authored by various members of the course team and the readings in these units were then further supplemented by all the materials previously discussed — televised lectures, radio broadcasts, cassette recordings for the musical sections, meetings with course tutors, and the assignment of additional articles from the "set" books. It was, without question, the largest undertaking of its kind and, as we will see, one not without its problems.

To begin with, "exit polls" measuring students' response to the course suggest that they felt that there was a considerable disparity between the product they had been promised and the one they actually received. In summarizing the students' evaluations of the course as a whole during its first year, Bob Womphrey and Robin Mason of the OU's IET Survey Research Department record that just 36 percent of those students who completed the course found its content and only 16 percent found the approach similar to what they had expected. A full 86 percent of those polled found the course, in general, more difficult than they had anticipated. And when the students were further queried on how they felt about the content and the approach of the course, regardless of their initial expectations, 69 percent of those who completed the course had either a negative or neutral response to its approach and 45 percent recorded a negative or neutral response to its content (Womphrey and Mason 2). While these final evaluations, like all such assessments, are hardly definitive, it is certainly clear that the course did not enjoy anything like a high level of "popularity" during its first year. What happened? Why was it that so many students found this course on popular culture so profoundly unpalatable?[16] Was the course "falsely advertised," as Gerry and Pat O'Brien, two of the original U203 students, charged in a letter to *Sesame*? Had the course team really promised, as these students claimed, to deliver "a light, interesting course" and then served up the findings of a bunch of "crazed Marxists" who were bent on showing that "inside the body of a popular TV series was hidden a structural linguist, ready to destroy any human he met with his deadly jargon and impenetrable phrases" (O'Brien and O'Brien)?

Although the O'Briens seemed to have missed this point, it is safe to say that one of the central projects of U203 was to problematize assumptions like theirs that popular culture is best thought of as the space of pure, innocent fun where success is measured in terms of the size and volume of the audience's response. In fact, the principal difficulty that confronted the course team as it began to put U203 together was how to respond to such efforts to strip popular culture of its larger political significance. In his essay "Popular Culture: 'A Teaching Object,'" which appeared in *Screen Education* in 1980, Tony Bennett explained that the course team rejected definitions of popular culture as either something "liked by a lot of people" or as a kind of folk, alternative culture opposed to mass culture; they preferred instead to think of popular culture as an "area of exchange" and "a network of relationships" where the dominant class' struggle for hegemony is waged (25). Reading popular culture in terms of Gramsci's conception of hegemony, Bennett maintained, had the advantage of enabling one to see popular culture as "one of the primary sites upon which the ideological struggle for the construction of class alliances or the production of consent, active or passive, is conducted" (26). While this approach to popular culture has since become a central premise of much work in cultural studies, what is striking about its appearance here is that Bennett argues for appropriating the Gramscian paradigm on *pedagogical* grounds: in Bennett's terms, this approach "puts one—directly and immediately—into the business of teaching processes, relationships and transactions and to doing so historically" (28).

With this claim in mind, it seems best to approach the course itself as just such an "area of exchange" and to consider the "network of relations" internal to the course that constrained and controlled the kind of exchanges that could occur between U203's course designers and their students. As we've already seen, Bennett felt that the course should set itself over against "commonsense" definitions of popular culture that students themselves would bring to it. Bennett has subsequently stated that the course team's thoughts about how best to approach the study of popular culture were considerably influenced by the writings of Stuart Hall, the former director of the Centre for Contemporary Cultural Studies in Birmingham, who joined the faculty at the OU and served as an advisor to the U203 course team ("Out in the Open" 137).[17] And in "Notes on Deconstructing 'The Popular,'" we get a glimpse of how Hall justified devoting his attention to popular culture:

> Popular culture is one of the sites where this struggle for and against a culture of the powerful is engaged: it is also the stake to be won or lost *in* that struggle. It is the arena of consent and resistance. It is partly where hegemony arises, and where it is secured. It is not a sphere where socialism, a socialist culture—already fully formed—might be simply "expressed." But it is one of the places where socialism might be constituted. That is why "popular culture" matters. Otherwise, to tell you the truth, I don't give a damn about it. (239, original emphasis)

One cannot help but wonder what might have happened if such sentiments had been openly expressed in the advertisement for the course. Although Bennett himself has gone on record as regretting that Hall allowed this final sentiment to appear in the printed version of his talk, since it was "clearly a throwaway line made in the context of the cut-and-thrust of debate" ("Out in the Open" 137), the truth of the matter, as we will see, is that many students and reviewers of U203 sensed that such political sentiments rested at the course's core. Thus, those students who had enrolled in U203 because they, too, found "the subject matter...intrinsically interesting," were undoubtedly in for a surprise, for what awaited them was a course that, in the main, didn't "give a damn" about popular culture except as a site "where socialism might be constituted."

This particular disjunction between the desires of some of U203's course planners and the interests of many of the course's potential students was picked up on in reviews of the course as it was going into production and during the time it was broadcast. Iain Chambers argued that Bennett appeared "to be arranging the potential definitions of 'popular culture' around an assumed—we might even say taken-for-granted—measure: working class culture" (113). John Thompson, reviewing the set books for the course, noted a generally negative assessment of the products and the social function of popular culture and warned that students were in for a long bout with some "strangely colorless and solemn writing" (52). Sean

Cubitt, in his failed attempt to rally support for the course in 1987, had to acknowledge "the highly structured, if at times patronizing, way in which the materials are presented" (91). And finally, once the course had been canceled, Alan O'Shea and Bill Schwartz commented on U203's "overly rationalistic ambition," its "dedication to an integrated and totalizing theory," and the fact that its "students found the work heavy going—often far removed from their own experiences of popular culture" (105).[18] That so many scholars felt compelled to comment on the course's content and approach is a testament to U203's larger importance in the media, film, and cultural studies communities. But the gist of these comments attests to a general perception about the stance the course team had adopted toward its object of study and its students: that is, these reviewers seem to agree that the course team tended to perceive popular culture and its consumers in a negative light, that popular culture was equated with working-class culture, and that the course carried out its discussion of these matters in a manner that was alternately turgid and dogmatic.

It wasn't only fellow scholars who perceived this marked disparity between the possible courses that might have been produced on popular culture and the actual course students ended up taking in U203. Indeed, as we have seen, as soon as the course began, students started registering their surprise and dismay at both its content and approach. In the evaluations of the course's first block, where two units on how Christmas is celebrated around the world were followed by Bennett's unit on "Popular Culture: History and Theory," students had a great deal to say. With regard to the television broadcasts, one student wrote: "They related well to Tony Bennett's approach to the course. The subtle brainwashing has started" (Womphrey, "Feedback Block 1" 7). Another wrote about the first block as a whole: "Course is not what I expected or looked forward to. Do not like patronizing, faintly disapproving almost puritanical attitude—the implication that if something is popular it must either a) have something wrong with it or b) have been imposed by 'The Media' " (33). And another student, commenting on the second block, which offered a more "traditional" account of the historical development of popular culture in Britain, had this to say: "I welcomed a more sensible explanation to 19th c. pop. cult. I loathed the bias & heavy going involved in Unit 3, the 'red' set book and the Intro to Block 2" (Womphrey, "Feedback Block 2" 46).

The appearance of these predictable responses—as they surely must be for any teacher who has sought to introduce concepts such as hegemony, ideology, and patriarchy into the classroom—represents another force constraining the kind of exchanges possible in the course: the team's reliance on a mode of presentation that was incapable of addressing the ready resistance students were bound to produce in response to the course's overarching political agenda. For it is truly a problem when a classroom is so structured that students are not allowed to do work that either they or their teachers would be likely to value. Yet these student comments could just as well be dismissed as the words of those who had not done their homework or who had done it poorly. Indeed, one could say that these comments prove how strongly the dominant ideology interpellates its subjects and, thus, that they demonstrate the urgency of making oppositional material of this kind more generally available. As with all student evaluations, it is hard to know just how much weight to give the impressions voiced by those who stand outside the system or how to use those impressions in assessing the strategies, goals, successes, and failures of the course designers. The students' responses in themselves don't provide an unmediated picture of what the course was *really* like: rather, the problems involved in interpreting these comments are the same as for any other reception data.

If the student comments are read alongside the course materials, however, it is possible to get a better sense of what work the course designers thought the students *ought* to engage in. As we have already seen, the unique structure of the OU's course team format required that authors with potentially divergent disciplinary, political, and pedagogical commitments work together to produce a unified and coherent course. This was particularly true of U203, because its status as an "interdisciplinary" course meant that the designers "had to draw on the expertise of as many as possible of the University's six Faculties—Arts, Education, Social Sciences, Science, Technology, and Mathematics" (T. Bennett, "Out in the Open" 138). And, as the course materials amply show, there was considerable disagreement among U203's course team members over what status to accord Gramsci's notion of hegemony. Evidence of Gramsci's influence on the course first appears when Bennett argues, in the concluding unit to the first block, that the concept of hegemony shows one "how to understand the ways in which the cultures and ideologies of different classes are related to one another within any given social and historical situation" ("Popular Culture: History and Theory" 29). Applying the concept of hegemony to popular culture, Bennett goes on to explain, thus allows one to escape the bind of seeing popular culture as either simply imposed "from above" or spontaneously emerging "from below," revealing it to be, instead, a historically produced and ideologically invested area of struggle. That there were others on the course team who did not share Bennett's enthusiasm for Gramsci is made clear in Bennett's introduction to block 5, "Politics, Ideology, and Popular Culture," where he notes that the authors in block 2 "sought either to criticize or qualify the concept of hegemony in various ways" and that the authors of the third block "criticized the focus on class implied by the concept of hegemony in arguing that other social groupings—those based on age or gender, for instance—are relevant to the analysis of popular culture, and in arguing for a more pluralist conception of the make-up of society" (Introduction 3). Bennett's response to these criticisms is telling: he devoted his unit in block 5 to refining the definition of hegemony—here it becomes an area of "*unequal exchange*"—and to insisting that events in Britain after 1966 are best read as exemplifying a contemporary crisis in hegemony (15, original emphasis).

That there was disagreement among the various camps on the course team is clear enough, but what isn't clear is what the students were supposed to do with the skirmishes that were taking place between these blocks. In a way, the answer to this question is as straightforward as it is unfortunate: the students weren't supposed to "do" anything with these debates at all. That is, since the seven Tutor Marked Assignments (TMAs) administered during the year respected the boundaries of the course's seven blocks, the examination system itself prevented students from entering the fray, as it were, to address the substantially different ways in which popular culture was being constituted and studied at various points in the course. In fact, the TMAs restricted the students to reiterating the information proffered in each individual block, a situation the students commented on repeatedly in their evaluations of the course, regardless of whether the TMA in question concerned a Gramscian or a liberal-pluralist take on popular culture. In response to the TMAs in block 3, for instance, one student observed: "I have found that the wording of questions + student notes tends too much to define the parameters, at least in the mind of the tutor, within which the questions are to be answered, leaving little room for manoeuver. Suggested approaches within the student notes turn out to be the required approach and 'helpful' background readings turn out to be indispensable" (Womphrey, "Feedback Block 3" 18). And another remarked: "As with previous TMA's on U203 I feel that all the alternatives required little independent thought but required mainly a selective precis of the relevant unit. I find this quite unstimulating and find it difficult to motivate myself into writing the TMA's" (22). Even the more positive assessments of these assignments signaled that something was amiss with this aspect of the course: "Enjoyed doing [the TMA], however it does just regurgitate the main themes in the course, i.e. concepts of Marxism" (Womphrey, "Feedback Block 2" 37).

There is nothing unusual about having students devote a lot of time to mastering the central texts and concepts in the given field of study, of course: indeed, this is a constraint that is felt in any content-based class. If the TMAs thus served as the place where the students' acquisition of the course's "main ideas" was monitored, did the course team require or allow any other kind of response from the students? Was there a moment, for instance, where the students were invited to apply the various theories about cultural production and reception to objects of their own choosing? Such work might have been initiated elsewhere in the course,[19] but it certainly wasn't encouraged on the final exam. Perhaps the best way to represent the exam's shortcomings is by first considering the student who has spent an entire year working through disagreements about whether or not Gramsci's notion of hegemony provides the most useful approach to popular culture. Next, imagine that student sitting down for a three-hour written final exam composed of seventeen questions (none of which is more than two sentences long), from which the student is to select three to answer. It is the institution of the OU that brings the student to this evaluative moment, but it is the course team that provides the student with such questions as "What historical and narrative factors led to James Bond becoming a popular hero?"; "In what ways did radio broadcasting become more 'popular' during the Second World War, and why?"; and "What are the characteristics of the classic realist text?" ("Second Level Course Examination" 2). The few questions that venture beyond asking the students to restate the facts and arguments of the course verbatim run into other problems. When the student is asked to "analyze the construction of images of the nation in at least two popular cultural texts," the directions stipulate that the student "*must* refer to the cassettes, television programs (including those shown at Summer School) and radio programs for the course" (2, original emphasis). In short, none of the questions asks the students to apply the approaches learned in the course to material not specifically discussed in the course. Not once are the students asked to wander somewhere beyond the landmarks and approved positions already clearly staked out in the readings, for to solicit such a response would be to invite the students to produce material much less susceptible to the standardized protocols for assessment. Thus, the examination system played a powerful role in shaping the students' encounter with the course material, ensuring that the course itself served as one of the more familiar areas of "unequal exchange."

The course books themselves reveal a similar antipathy about inviting students to make connections between their work in U203 and their interactions with popular culture outside the course. Bennett's unit on hegemony in postwar Britain, for example, concludes with the assignment of Stuart Hall's seminal essay on the two paradigms of cultural studies. In the accompanying instructions, the students are first told that they "should particularly concentrate on... [Hall's] assessment of the relative strengths and weaknesses of culturalism and structuralism" ("Popular Culture and Hegemony" 28). Just below the questions for this reading assignment, these instructions are rescinded: "While it's not important that you should be concerned with the relations between 'culturalism' and 'structuralism' in a detailed way in this block, I have thought it useful to remind you of these considerations at this point so that you might be aware of, and be on the look-out for, the different directions from which particular arguments are coming" (28). Then, the "Checklist of study objectives" for the unit, which *immediately* follows this passage, reinstates the initial instructions, listing as its third objective the hope that the students will have acquired a "deeper and more finely nuanced understanding of the relationships between 'culturalism' and 'structuralism' " (29). This series of contradictory directions might be read as a sign of the course team's anxiety over ensuring that their students successfully acquired the central terms of Hall's essay. Or the contradictory instructions might be seen as evidence of the consequences of a production schedule that cannot allow time for worrying over the finer details of the course's instructional apparatus. In either case, from the students' perspective the end result is the same: little thought seems to have been given to the question of what kind of reading and writing assignments might be most productive for students just beginning work in cultural studies.

This is one more instance of the general inattention to the place of student work in U203 that we are now in a position to see pervaded the course, the surrounding institution, and the larger discursive context. Thus, by this point, it should be clear it is no accident that the course team begins to issue contradictory orders at the very moment it contemplates the possibility that students might actually *apply* the material they have studied rather than simply respeak the words they've read. Or, perhaps, it might be better to say that the course team's failure to reimagine the form and content of student work within this course was overdetermined, the seemingly inevitable by-product of the overlapping contexts with which I have been concerned throughout this chapter.[20] First, we have the institutional context of the Open University, which provided the team with the blueprint for designing a course that fit into the OU's curricular and assessment structure. That structure explains why the TMAs, final exams, and textually embedded reading assignments demanded nothing more from the students than the simple repetition of the course's main tenets: this was the mode of examination most ready to hand at the OU, one that helped maintain the enabling fiction that the student work produced in these courses, though solicited from all over the country, was ultimately subject to the same, relatively stable, standardized and objective system of evaluation. As we have also seen, the discursive context at this moment served to reinforce these institutional pressures, providing an intellectual environment predisposed to favor a transmission-based model of pedagogy. And within this discursive context, there was considerable debate about the importance of theorizing cultural studies relative to the work of providing the students with an alternative educational experience. By the time U203 was being created, the debate appeared to have been so clearly won by those with exclusively theoretical commitments that pedagogical concerns were effectively tabled. For, as we've seen in this section, the course team's stance toward popular culture and its reliance on the pedagogical apparatus provided by the OU combined to ensure the delivery of an educational product whose primary features were its theoretical sophistication and the antagonism it provoked from the students.

Putting It All Together: Taking It All Apart

It would be a mistake, I believe, to accord *all* of the pedagogical problems evident in U203 to the overlapping institutional, discursive, and disciplinary pressures that so powerfully influenced the shape of the course. In fact, to do so would be to rely on a notion of determinism that cultural studies has been particularly intent on problematizing through its appropriation of the notion of "hegemony." Thus, acknowledging the collusion of these constraints in determining how the course had to be taught, which students ended up in the course, and what those students were expected to produce does not sufficiently explain the apparent failure of U203's course team to offer any significant resistance to these constraints. That is, if we think for a moment of the institutional structure of the OU as representing the forces of hegemony, then where in the popular culture course is "the struggle for and against a culture of the powerful...engaged," to use Stuart Hall's evocative phrase? Where is the struggle? And between which parties is it occurring?

That I have searched for resistance of this kind within the course team's pedagogical practice rather than in the "knowledge" disseminated in the course team's materials speaks to my own interested position in pursuing this research. Focusing on cultural studies as it has been taught rather than as it has been theorized has led me to work with a set of documents currently at the margins of cultural studies' institutional history: course textbooks, examinations, student evaluations, school newspapers, and working papers on pedagogical practice. And though I have been at pains to locate the shortcomings of U203's pedagogical project within a set of local institutional, discursive, and disciplinary constraints, the critique I have mounted may well appear to imply that there exists a critical pedagogical practice that both should and could have meshed much more neatly with the overarching political commitments of cultural studies, regardless of any given individual program's institutional location. Although we have reached some understanding about why this particular course turned out the way it did, we have not seen sufficient evidence to conclude that this course was so completely determined that *no* other outcome was possible. Rather, I would argue that from a pedagogical standpoint, this moment when a group of dedicated scholars designed a course on popular culture for a technological system able to bring the insights of cultural studies to large numbers of people normally excluded from such investigations has shown itself to be a richly instructive lost opportunity. For despite cultural studies' apparent a priori commitment to "the people," and despite the tangible successes during the early days at the Centre for Contemporary Cultural Studies (CCCS) when, in Hall's words, everyone involved in the cultural studies project was forced to abandon "the normal pedagogical relations where the teacher is supposed as the keeper of wisdom and students respond to the question 'This is so, is it not?' with that kind of compulsive drive that requires them to say, 'Of course, of course' " ("Emergence" 17),[21] nevertheless at the time U203 was drawn up, the course members found themselves interacting with a set of constraining forces that discouraged them from seeing pedagogy as a place where theories might be tested, practice reimagined, and institutional structures and relationships renegotiated. Indeed, Bennett is unequivocal on this issue: "At no point . . . did Hall and I, or any other members of the course-team or core planning group, discuss or see ourselves as trying to transplant the Birmingham experiment of 'disrupting' normal pedagogical relations to the Open University context" ("Out in the Open" 139). As far as Bennett is concerned, such experimentation is best reserved, as it was at Birmingham, for the graduate seminar; there, he explains, "the divisions between teachers and taught are *supposed* to weaken, and . . . collaborative endeavors across this divide resulting in joint working papers, publications, seminars and the like are *supposed* to happen" (141, original emphasis).

When we keep in mind Bennett's declaration of the necessity of reserving collaborative, interactive work for those seeking to enter the profession, we see more readily that U203's course team was fashioning pedagogical solutions out of materials that were not entirely of their own making—that they, too, were controlled by the educational commonplaces and conventions of their historical moment. Of course, this insight into the dialectical tension between a people's aspirations and extant institutional constraints, which is the very foundation of Marxist thought, has yet to make itself felt either in the many calls now being made for the broad adoption of the cultural studies project or, more generally, in the ongoing celebrations of cultural studies' "critical pedagogies." As Bennett himself has recently remarked, "more interesting and more serviceable accounts [of cultural studies] will be produced only when attention shifts... [to] the institutional conditions of cultural studies, and especially the changing social composition of tertiary students and teachers" ("Putting Policy" 33). If my own account has helped demonstrate that the pedagogical possibilities that may once have been available in Birmingham are not the same as those subsequently available at other universities with different administrations, different institutional histories, different student bodies, and different disciplinary agendas, it has done so by attending to the very "institutional conditions of cultural studies" of which Bennett speaks.

Raymond Williams came to a similar conclusion about the OU's limited ability to enact a transformative pedagogical practice in his 1986 article "The Future of Culture Studies." Although Williams initially felt that the OU might assist in the broader project of cultural studies by bringing higher education into the homes of adult learners, as he became more familiar with the university he concluded that the technology of the enterprise militated against the project of refashioning higher education. He noted, "[The Open University] lacks to this day that crucial process of interchange and encounter between the people offering the intellectual disciplines and those using them, who have far more than a right to be tested to see if they are following them or if they are being put in a form which is convenient—when in fact they have this more basic right to define the questions" ("Future" 157). As I have detailed here, the version of cultural studies that emerged out of U203 was structurally, and perhaps theoretically, incapable of allowing students to "define the questions" or of providing a forum for "that crucial process of interchange." Indeed, U203 could itself serve as one of Williams's examples "of how in the very effort to define a clearer subject, to establish a discipline, to bring order into the work...the real problem of the project as a whole, which is that people's questions are not answered by the existing distribution of the educational curriculum, can be forgotten" (160).

Bennett has rightly called Williams to task for his idealization of extramural education for adults and, more important, for his failure to recognize that the OU's central achievement was "that it provided open access to degree qualifications," a bureaucratic success that Bennett justifiably declares "wholly new and radically progressive" ("Out in the Open" 143). My own reservations about Williams's assessment of the shortcomings of distance education take a slightly different tack, though: I want to know how he can claim that meaningful "interchanges" between the students and the instructors did not occur. Or, to put a finer point on it, how can I make the same claims about U203 in particular? To substantiate these charges, surely it would be necessary to speak with the students who actually took the course, to interview the course tutors about how they ran their sessions, and to talk with people who "poached" on the course (those who watched but didn't enroll) about the kind of issues U203 brought into their homes. Any account of the course and of the educational experience at the Open University would seem to be incomplete without these other voices. In other words, my familiar methodological reliance on textual traces to build my case about U203 has produced an argument that points to the very limits of taking such an approach. Thus, at this point it would seem that the only way to know what "really" happened in this course is to speak directly with the people who ran the tutorials and the students who took the course. Turning to the ethnographic approach in the next chapter will enable us to see what, if anything, such talk resolves. While ethnography requires that its "informants" speak, does it, in fact, allow for that "crucial process of interchange" Williams demands? Does it allow the "informants" to define the questions that are to structure the investigation? And, if so, what is gained in the process?

Postscript

While the recent spate of budgetary cutbacks at CUNY has substantially altered its open admissions policy,[22] at the Open University the debate about whether the system is or should be serving similarly nontraditional students persists to the present day. In this regard, it can hardly appear as insignificant that the OU only began to collect data on the racial and ethnic backgrounds of its students in 1989, a full eighteen years after the first students entered the system. Preliminary analysis of the data suggests that the OU has not done a good job retaining racial and ethnic minorities either as students or as members of the university's faculty and staff (Woodley, Taylor, and Butcher 157). The authors of this study, Alan Woodley, Lee Taylor, and Bernadette Butcher, are clearly distressed by this finding, as well as by the information they've uncovered indicating that minorities in the university are much less likely to receive credit at the end of the year than other students, even when all other mitigating factors are considered. Woodley's discomfort announces itself most clearly at the end of his report:

> From my own value position, I want to alert the University to the situation and to produce improvements within the system and, as an academic, I expect, and I am expected, to publish useful findings. However, as an employee of the University I have to consider how, in what form, and to whom this information should be released. The University is anxious not to receive bad publicity over what is a very sensitive issue; however, demand for the information is great from outside the university and from within, both by regional staff and by academics developing the "Race and Education" course. Therefore, the process whereby the research data become public knowledge is one of negotiation and even contestation. (167)

At this point, one can only guess what this data will reveal about the racial and ethnic backgrounds of the students who have succeeded in fitting themselves into the OU system: the implication, however, is that the data will show that the university is not and never has been as open "as to people" as Crowther's phrase might have led one to believe. And so, in a turn of events that harkens back to the revolutionary moment at CUNY, the university now finds itself considering whether or not the proportion of minority students admitted to the OU should exceed the proportion in the population at large "in order to compensate for earlier educational disadvantages within these groups" (166).

Thus, although the OU and open admissions at CUNY came into the world at roughly the same time, it is only now, after two decades, that officials at the OU have had to openly confront issues of racial difference and remediation. The research of Woodley, Taylor, and Butcher is helping the university to see that attracting and retaining minority students means not just offering courses in "Black Studies" but also putting together programs in law and accounting, and developing courses "that are designed to improve the study skills of potential students" (168). In part, the OU is able to ignore the fundamental concerns of real students in the world because it delivers its educational lessons at a distance. With a system that ensured that students could not come together and articulate a common set of interests capable of threatening the status quo, the OU allowed the government and its educators to protect themselves from having to come face to face with difference. Thus distance learning, which is popularly thought to guarantee a "color-blind" educational experience, actually serves to conceal the fact that the university itself has not sought to make itself amenable to the needs and desires of those potential students who truly stand outside the system, because, unlike CUNY during the late sixties, it has never been forced to. Consequently, at this "disembodied and airborne" university, where open admissions has, from the beginning, been defined and managed "from above," the result, which can only seem predictable at this point, is a system that rewards the already prepared, diligent, upwardly mobile, generally white, male student, while leaving the rest on their own to fend for themselves as best they can.

5 Teaching Others

Ethnography and the Allure of Expertise

My descriptions of teachers are still from a distance; they ring true, but not true enough. Only after I have really been there with teachers will I be able to show how sensible is the system of unexamined conventional teacher wisdom when viewed from within that system.

(ERICKSON 61, ORIGINAL EMPHASIS)

In this passage, the ethnographer Frederick Erickson points to the gap that exists between his success at describing what teachers actually do in the classroom and his goal of understanding why it is that teachers think and act in such ways. Erickson has faith that there is some animating hermeneutics behind the seemingly irrational, often counterproductive behavior in which teachers engage, a system that makes such behavior seem "sensible" to the teachers themselves. For this reason, Erickson believes that his research will be of value only after he has found a way to see events as his subjects do — only, that is, when he has shown that "teachers, students, administrators, parents, politicians, businessmen, are motivated by good as well as ill, guided by wise as well as foolish elements in their conventional wisdoms, often confused, sometimes acutely aware of what is happening, muddling through" (61). And given that ethnographers are trained to be sensitive to the logics of cultural difference and to attend to the complex interplay between cultural production and societal constraint, it might well seem that ethnographic work on schooling — at least the kind that Erickson strives to produce — would be well suited to the task of solving the problems uncovered in the preceding chapters. That is, from a methodological standpoint, ethnography seems guaranteed to provide an informed, respectful account of students' and teachers' ways of knowing the world that could, in turn, serve as a firm foundation upon which to build a sustainable project of educational reform.

Yet we can be seduced by this rosy account of the ethnographer's privileged access to "the native's" point of view only if we ignore the firestorm of criticism that has, of late, overwhelmed the ethnographic project. Indeed, there is hardly a crime that ethnography has not been accused of committing over the past two decades: ethnography has been described as *the* paradigmatic instance of the "metaparanoia" that is at the root of all humanist practices (P. Smith 97); it has been seen as the work of tourists (Grossberg 388); it has been said to promote "collusion between mass cultural critic and consumer society" (Modleski xii); and, finally, it has been dismissed as a pseudo-science that grants the observer "all of the problems of selfhood," while depriving the subject under observation of such a self (Spivak, "Multiculturalism" 66). This frenzy of criticism is not being produced just by those who don't do ethnography and don't think it should be done; not surprisingly, it's also being generated from within the field itself. There have been calls to recuperate ethnography as "an explicit form of cultural critique sharing radical perspectives with dada and surrealism" (Clifford 12); there have been counterarguments for a fully historicized ethnographic approach that can "penetrate beyond the surface planes of everyday life" (Comaroff and Comaroff xi); there have been efforts to reclaim ethnography's status as a science through the collection of "reflexively cleaned data" that can be interpreted, tested, and challenged by others (Aunger 98). Finally, there has even been a proposal to abandon the term "ethnography" altogether, on the grounds that it denotes neither a "separate category" of research nor "a distinct method" and therefore cannot reasonably be considered a "useful category with which to think about social research methodology" (Hammersley 603).

Amid all this recent controversy, ethnography has, perhaps paradoxically, enjoyed a period of fantastic growth, particularly at "home"; according to Michael Moffatt, anthropologists have "done more research in the United States in the last dozen years than in the entire previous history of the discipline — far more, perhaps twice as much" ("Ethnographic Writing" 205). The reasons for this increased interest in studying the cultures of the United States are not hard to determine: Moffatt gives credit to an overproduction of anthropologists and to "declining transnational access and funding" (205). With more anthropologists and less money to go around, one way for ethnographers to make themselves appealing to government funding agencies, school administrators, and the business community at large is to focus on the educational process: so, during this boom time for anthropology at home, ethnographies of schooling have proliferated in part because, as we will see, they provide the nervous collectivity of parents, school officials, and future employers with ways to come to grips with changes in modern American schools, particularly the consequences of desegregation.

For our purposes, what is significant about the corpus of schooling ethnographies done over the past thirty years is that very little sustained work has been carried out on the culture of undergraduate education, broadly conceived. This may well be because "undergraduates," as a group, appear too well-known to warrant additional study, unlike the more familiar subjects of ethnographies of schooling—marginal high school students, women trying to break into the sciences, or any other structurally disempowered group moving through or outside of the educational system.[1] In other words, the experience of being an undergraduate may seem, on its face, to be universalizable and unchanging over time and, thus, not a fruitful area for ethnographic investigation. Moffatt's *Coming of Age in New Jersey: College and American Culture* stands alone in trying to provide a comprehensive picture of, as he puts it, "the students' mentalities" during their four years at college (xv). Although Moffatt did not pursue his project in the interests of advancing any particular education reform, he warrants extended attention here for three reasons: his work is devoted to gaining a better understanding of the figure who stands at the center of the enterprise of higher education—the undergraduate; his research has since been recommended to professors and administrators as a guide for understanding student experience;[2] and, finally, as a result of the publication of *Coming of Age in New Jersey*, Moffatt was regularly invited by administrators and student organizations from around to country to speak about "college life" and "college fun" in the late eighties. Thus, though Moffatt never intended it, his research led to his becoming a recognized expert of sorts on student culture.

While Moffatt provides us with the opportunity to reflect on one ethnographer's effort to gain "direct access" to "the undergraduate," the work of Shirley Brice Heath, which I discuss in the second half of this chapter, allows us to consider how ethnographic data on students can be used in the service of educational reform. Heath's specific area of concern was to study how language use in three different communities in the Piedmont Valley of the Carolinas differentially influenced the school performance of children from these communities. Once Heath determined that their different "ways with words" led to school failure for children not from the middle class, she set out to train students and teachers to become ethnographers of their home cultures in hopes that the resulting insights would promote the academic success of children from all the communities.

Between them, then, Moffatt and Heath give us two concrete instances of ethnographers at work trying to understand the culture of schooling and the challenges that face those committed to changing that culture. And, because both Moffatt and Heath place "the student" at the center of their investigations, their projects differ considerably from the ones discussed in the previous chapters. They will, for this reason, be treated differently. Specifically, by attending to how Moffatt and Heath read their students and by noting moments in their discussions that reveal contact with, conflict between, or blindness to different ways of knowing the world, I will be working against the grain of their ethnographies, making them tell us what they can about how teachers are trained to see students and the pedagogical consequences of that training. Thus, while I have been concerned in the preceding chapters with reading along the margins of the archive to evince the student's role in the educational process, here the material itself requires a different approach, since the ethnographically oriented classroom places the student center stage. With the student so placed, we might ask, What is there for a teacher to do? What is the content of such a course? That is, what does an ethnographically informed pedagogy look like and to what degree does such a pedagogy truly represent a change in the quotidian practices of the academy?

Before setting out to respond to these questions, I want to make it clear that I take as given that the ethnographer objectifies the Other, usually in order to transform this entity into a unified and stable subject for study and, furthermore, that the end result of this objectifying process is always and inevitably the ethnographer's interpretation of the construction of the Other and not the Other as it is "in itself." While this familiar line of critique is sufficient reason, as we have seen, for many in the academy to reject ethnography on principle, such a response disables the crucial enterprise of assessing the relative merits or failings of any particular ethnographic attempt. And as interest in doing ethnographies of schooling increased dramatically once the effects of federally mandated desegregation policies began to make themselves felt in the sixties, it should be clear that distinguishing between the various uses to which ethnographic findings have been put is not an idle exercise. In any event, making such distinctions certainly was a pressing concern for the many teachers and school systems who turned to ethnography during the sixties and seventies for the conceptual tools and the empirical data they needed to understand, contain, and respond to life in the newly integrated classrooms, where racial difference had suddenly become an inescapable, embodied reality.[3] Indeed, as Dell Hymes, the pioneer of ethnographic work focusing on speaking and communication, saw it at the time, ethnographies of actual language use would help battle the prejudices that surround variant language use among marginalized communities and the prevailing "sense that most people do not deserve better because of linguistic inadequacy" (71). As far as Hymes was concerned, then, ethnography *could* further the ends of democracy by ensuring that people were not discriminated against because they relied on a linguistic code other than Standard English. As we keep Hymes's sense of the promise of ethnography in mind, it seems best that we consider how, in specific instances, ethnographers have addressed the "problem" of racial difference in the academy, if only to better understand the forces that continue to produce this encounter as a "problem."

Coming of Age in New Jersey: Sex and the Student Body

The cover of *Coming of Age in New Jersey* depicts an exasperated student, seated at a desk, head thrown back. Copious tears propel themselves from the student's eyes straight into the air. This abject image comes from a series by Lisa David, who set out to represent what it means to be a student at Rutgers University, the site of Moffatt's research into undergraduate culture and home to his anthropology department.[4] Other images from David's series grace the opening pages of Moffatt's book: there's a student at a desk, head down; a student running to catch a departing bus; a student in bed, saying into the phone, "Mom? Help!"; a student standing before a mountain of books, a clock, and a calendar; a small, featureless, human figure (a student, in other words) propped up in bed, with open books, papers, pencils, glasses, and a coffee cup strewn about. The images, in sum, depict undergraduate life at a large, research university as a solitary, sometime frightening endeavor, where every waking hour is spent either preparing for class, getting to class, falling behind in class, or recovering from class.

In stark contrast to David's — perhaps predictable — images of the loneliness and desperation of undergraduate life, Moffatt offers the reader entry into a thriving world of undergraduate social relations that revolve around the "friendly fun" afforded by "spur-of-the-moment pleasures," such as "hanging out in a dorm lounge or a fraternity or a sorority, gossiping, wrestling and fooling around, going to dinner with friends, having a late-night pizza or a late-night chat, visiting other dorms, going out to a bar, and flirting and more serious erotic activities, usually with members of the opposite sex" (33). The average student, Moffatt discloses, spends about four hours a day engaged in such playful activities and only about two hours a day studying. According to the students' way of counting, though, such statistics are misleading, since they consider the four hours a day they spend in class as time spent studying (33). However one tallies the figures, Moffatt discovered that as far as the students were concerned, "even the fun of college life was a learning experience. And with this claim, the dichotomy between formal education (work, learning) and college life (fun, relaxation) collapsed entirely for the students" (61). Although the students' reasoning here is sure to give traditional educators reason to rage, Moffatt calmly observes that "anthropologically speaking, [the students] were not far from wrong" in claiming that they learned from everything that happened to them in college (61). In fact, what Moffatt sets out to establish in *Coming of Age in New Jersey* is that the most important reason undergraduates pursue higher education in the first place is "college life": this is "their central pleasure while in it, and what they often remembered most fondly about college after they graduated" (29).

Moffatt didn't commence his research with such anthropological insights into student culture in mind, however. Rather, as Moffatt tells the story, he decided to move into the dorms and pass himself off as an older, out-of-state student for a few days in the fall of 1977 "on a whim," partly because he felt, at the age of thirty-three, that he "no longer understood" his students (1). By going under cover in this way, Moffatt hoped to gain a "worm's-eye view" of what it was like to be an undergraduate at Rutgers and to find a way to reconnect with his students now that his own experiences in college "were beginning to feel like very distant times indeed" (1). And, though he little thought this whimsical attempt to reach his students would develop into "serious research," he ended up devoting years to the project:[5] he spent a night a week in the dorms during the academic years 1977–78 and 1984–85; throughout this time, he taught courses that solicited response papers from students on their thoughts about sexuality and the life of the mind; and he put together *The Rutgers Picture Book*, a coffee-table photo album depicting how student life had changed over time at the university. As a consequence of having been so unexpectedly taken with this research, Moffatt came to see that his results had an important role to play in providing an alternative to the mass of "moralizing literature on students and colleges floating around at present." Specifically, he hoped his research would contribute to "a different kind of understanding of what college, college adolescence, and contemporary American culture are all about, from a less-than-elite undergraduate perspective" (xvii).[6]

Before determining exactly what "different kind of understanding" Moffatt wants to communicate, it is worth considering his project in relation to the anthropological ur-text and international best-seller alluded to in his title — Margaret Mead's *Coming of Age in Samoa*. To make sense of this allusion, we need to recall that Mead herself was very interested in educational issues and had gone to Samoa in hopes of contributing to the nature/nurture debate that then (as now) preoccupied the human sciences. Mead returned, of course, having learned that "adolescence need not be the time of stress and strain which Western society made it; that growing up could be freer and easier and less complicated; and also that there were prices to pay for the very lack of complication I found in Samoa — less intensity, less individuality, less involvement with life" (Mead x). Once she has weighed the benefits and the demerits of living in such a "primitive" society, Mead concludes her book with a call to reform educational practice in the West:

> We must turn all of our educational efforts to training our children for the choices which will confront them. Education, in the home even more than at school, instead of being a special pleading for one regime, a desperate attempt to form one particular habit of mind which will withstand all outside influences, must be a preparation for those very influences.... The children must be taught how to think, not what to think. And because old errors die slowly, they must be taught tolerance, just as to-day they are taught intolerance. They must be taught that many ways are open to them, no one sanctioned above its alternative, and that upon them and upon them alone lies the burden of choice. Unhampered by prejudices, unvexed by too early conditioning to any one standard, they must come clear-eyed to the choices which lie before them. (137)

It's a stirring peroration, one that captures Mead's conviction that social forces are entirely responsible for shaping individual actions and beliefs. Given the manifest differences that exist between our complex society and the "simple" society of the Samoans, what we must do, according to Mead, is educate our children at home and at schools in ways that will prepare them for an experience unavailable to such primitive folk — "this possibility of choice, the recognition of many possible ways of life, where other civilizations have recognized only one" (138).

That it's hard to imagine arguing against the notion that students should be taught "how to think, not what to think" is proof that Mead's "radical" proclamations have become commonplaces in our time. Be that as it may, Derek Freeman, one of Mead's harshest critics, has devoted a good deal of his life to assailing the data that led Mead to make such claims about the power of culture and of education. Deploying a methodology that is alternately obsessed with detail and borne aloft by polemical zeal, Freeman sets out to locate Mead's research in its historical moment and to challenge her findings. In so doing, Freeman conjures an image of Mead as a graduate student determined to find evidence that would please her teachers, Franz Boas and Ruth Benedict—evidence that would settle the nature/nurture debate with the eugenicists of her time once and for all. While Freeman devotes much of his book to contesting Mead's observations about life in Samoa point by point, for our purposes his most important work involves historicizing the popular and academic reception of Mead's work, which reveals how it came to be that research done in such apparent haste ended up enjoying lasting, worldwide acclaim. As Freeman would have it, Mead's work has never been subjected to a sufficiently rigorous review because, from the beginning, her depiction of Somoa as a "sexual paradise" engaged the desires of a nation of readers desperate to believe that such sensuous abandon and carefree existence could be found not only halfway around the globe but also somewhere deep inside themselves (Freeman 97). Thus, once *Coming of Age in Samoa* was picked up and cited approvingly by such critics as Bertrand Russell and Havelock Ellis, it wasn't long before Samoa was transformed into an idyllic paradise free of all pain; by the early 1950s, Freeman asserts, Mead's "conclusion about adolescence in Samoa came to be regarded as a proven fact which had demonstrated, beyond all question, the sovereignty of culture" (103).

Whether Freeman succeeds in disproving this "proven fact" is not our concern here.[7] More to the point is how Moffatt responded to the national debate that Freeman's critique sparked. By the winter of 1983, Freeman's critique had been picked up by *Time*, *Newsweek*, the *Wall Street Journal*, and a host of daily publications; Freeman himself had been interviewed on national television and, according to Roy Rappaport, had contributed to creating a situation where "if anthropology was not thrown into public disrepute, it was shadowed by public doubt" (316). Moffatt's own research was carried out during these difficult times and, when he completed his book, he thanked Mead, "her reputation bloodied but still unbowed after the attacks of pygmies, for her original title, which inspired [his own]" (*Coming of Age* xi–xii). By so responding to this important academic debate about Mead's work, Moffatt inadvertently demonstrates his affinity with the subjects of his study, who—he would have us believe—also rely on this discourse of "Undergraduate Cynical," where "moral, ethical, and intellectual positions are rapidly reduced to the earthiest possible motives of those who articulate them" (90). Yet this affinity is not something that Moffatt openly acknowledges. To the contrary, Moffatt is quite concerned throughout his research to establish his own moral, intellectual, and professional superiority to his subjects.

Insisting on this superiority requires a certain amount of deft maneuvering from Moffatt, particularly at the beginning of his project, as he struggles to justify the fact that he *knowingly* misrepresented himself to his subjects by posing as a student. This ruse worked for a few days, allowing Moffatt to live in the dorms, where he could secretly study the intimate lifeways of the undergraduate. It wasn't long, though, before Moffatt's roommates grew suspicious of this older guy who regularly bought the *New York Times*. When confronted, Moffatt immediately confessed that he was actually a professor doing research and presented a letter from the dean verifying his story. To his great relief, his roommates responded as follows:

> None of my five roommates seemed ethically concerned that I had violated their privacy. None of them voiced any formal protest against my methods. They were thrilled when I told them I might write about them, but they seemed a little disappointed when I assured them I would change all their names to protect them. They did feel, a lot less theoretically, that I *had* tricked them, however; and in the next two days they pulled four practical jokes on me. (11, original emphasis)

And, once Moffatt survived this ritual of being "busted" by his roommates, he was welcomed into their community as a "friend" and the viability of his research project was assured (11–12).

It's a happy enough initiation story and as such it fulfills the generic demands of the ethnographic tale, capturing the researcher's transition from unknowing outsider to welcomed participant-observer. But as much as Moffatt would like us to join him as he quickly escorts the ethical concerns raised by his study from the stage, on the grounds that such matters were outside the experience of his "less theoretically" inclined subjects — a group he refers to elsewhere as "my natives" (18) — it's worth pausing to consider why he would expect entering first-year students to feel they could confront him with their "ethical concerns" about his clear violation of their privacy. After all, once Moffatt had established his superior position of authority, shown his credentials, and provided proof that his actions had already been sanctioned by the university's administration, what exactly is it that the students could have said?

But even if the students were publicly silenced by the official approval of Moffatt's actions, they were able to voice a less "formal protest" about Moffatt's intrusion into their world by drawing on what James Scott has elsewhere termed "the arts of resistance" available to all who find themselves in structurally disempowered positions. In this case, Moffatt's roommates stole his clothes, which resulted in the professor appearing naked on a balcony; they filled the professor's shoes with shaving cream; and they put bottles in the professor's pillow so he would deliver a beating to himself when he covered his head to sleep (Moffatt, *Coming of Age* 11). On two other occasions, Moffatt reports, "the wedgie patrol" threatened to pay him a visit (130 n. 16). In other words, the students drew on a repertoire of potentially shaming and certainly annoying antic behavior that they could always say was nothing more than innocent fun. As Scott's work suggests, to see such jokes simply as the kind of "fun" subordinates naturally indulge in is to miss the point that they can also express "a politics of disguise and anonymity that takes place in public view but is designed to have a double meaning or to shield the identity of the actors" (Scott 19). If we turn Moffatt's initiation story on its head, then, we can argue that it captures the students in the act of establishing *their* dominance over their superior, since Moffatt cannot get angry with them about their "native" behavior unless he's willing to expel himself from the very society he hopes to enter.

For whatever reasons, Moffatt doesn't entertain the possibility that the manifest power differential that exists between him, as the professorial, administratively sanctioned observer, and his subjects — the newly arrived undergraduates who find themselves, through no choice of their own, placed under his surveillance — might alter what the students say and how they say it to him. Consequently, Moffatt loses sight of the fact that he hasn't gone out "into the field" so much as he has compelled a certain group of unwitting students to enter his field of expertise. For this reason, he doesn't realize that the students might be studying him, trying to get some purchase on the customs of the peculiar native population he represents. Although the students try repeatedly to reorient Moffatt to the reality of their situation by making it clear to him that, in fact, it is *they* who have arrived to study the ways of the culture *he* represents, the anthropologist turns a deaf ear to his informants and inevitably begins lecturing them on the inadequacy of their perceptions.[8] Ultimately, he's not interested in their ideas, which he already knows too well, or their "artistry," which is, after all, just friendly "busting," but in their social behavior — how they interact as a group, what their rituals and rites of initiation are, and, most important, what they are and aren't up to sexually.

While the notoriety of Moffatt's book is largely the result of what it discloses about these social aspects of student life, the drama of the work is to be found in those moments when the students take control of his project by presenting their version of what being an undergraduate entails. That such moments populate *Coming of Age in New Jersey* is to Moffatt's credit, for he includes much material that attests to the students' dissatisfaction with his representation of their experiences. Indeed, he thanks the students for having improved his analysis, particularly "In continually protesting that the students were generally more variable than I tended to represent them as being during my earlier, participant observation research; in listening to the sexual materials in chapters 5 and 6 with an interest and openness that contrasted strongly with the reactions of many older readers[;]...and in protesting against certain ways in which I denigrated them as intellectual beings [in the final chapter of the book]" (329–30). The students' appreciative listening aside, our concern is with the degree to which their protests were heard and addressed.

It is clear enough why students would have cause to protest Moffatt's portrayal of them as generally shallow beings with little or no interest in the life of the mind when one learns his approach for soliciting the information that led him to this conclusion. Moffatt reveals that his "standard opening question" when interviewing students was to say he "was a man from Mars" and then to ask them: "Why did young Earthlings leave big comfortable homes a few miles away, where all their needs were provided for by their parents, and come to live in these crowded, noisy confines, packed together like sardines?" (92). This is a remarkable way to begin an interview, not only because it draws on a style of questioning best suited to a much younger audience, but also because it reveals the questioner's own assumption that students at a large, public university share a common suburban heritage, including two parents with disposable income, spacious living quarters, and a quiet home life. Moffatt's question shows just how distant he is from the culture he is studying and his sense of how great an imaginative leap one must make to construct students as experts worthy of attention. And, as it turns out, Moffatt's study inadvertently reveals that undergraduates are about as likely to be asked to speculate on the overarching significance of their actions as they are to be interviewed by a Martian.

Despite these manifest problems with Moffatt's method for interviewing his subjects, on one occasion at least, when Moffatt conducted an interview in the public space of a student lounge, his line of questioning led to an engaged argument between two students: Louie, who described coming to school as an opportunity "not only to grow intellectually but to grow independentlywise," and Carrie, who said that college was "a place where suburban brats come, to hang out for four years" (92). Moffatt records the ensuing interchange, intervening only to provide the event with its loose narrative structure: we listen in as the two speakers develop their positions; we are privy to a failed effort by a passerby to derail the discussion; and we are treated to the appearance of "the Stranger," who "had a certain hypnotic charm, reinforced by the reiterative phrases he used, and a man-of-the-world authority reinforced by the density of his easy vulgarisms" (94). But once Moffatt has finished transcribing the Stranger's contribution to the discussion, he abandons the scene, observing only that the Stranger's "tone poem" had "popped the 'cosmic' bubble" produced by Louie and Carrie's concerted efforts to articulate why going to college should matter (94).

Though much that happens during this public argument about the importance of education might be considered banal or overly theatrical to an outside observer, one would expect an anthropologist to mine this scene for what it reveals about alternative conventions for carrying out intellectual work in the dorms, where, unlike the classrooms, participants can openly express passionate beliefs, abandon unpopular positions in the face of skepticism, change the subject, and return to voicing their initial beliefs when the heat has died down. Or the scene might have been examined for what it has to say about internally enforced restrictions among undergraduates that prevent public displays of intellectual engagement, with particular attention paid to the two outside "interruptions" as males sought to engage the attentions of the female discussant, one by speaking of her physical appearance and the other by laying claim to greater knowledge and verbal facility. Or the discussion between Carrie, an African American student, and Louie, whom Moffatt describes as "hustling as usual" (91), could have been analyzed for what it had to say about the public personas students assume when called on to explain their reasons for attending college. Moffatt pursues none of these interpretive routes, however, motivated perhaps by his desire that his chapters be "as open as the state of adolescence itself ideally ought to be" (xvii). Whatever the reason, he leaves it up to the reader to sort this scene out, while he heads off for still greener pastures.

When the reader arrives at Chapter 5, "Sex," and Chapter 6, "Sex in College," it becomes clear that Moffatt includes the business of slogging through life in the dorms to justify his exploration of undergraduate sexual activity. From the moment Moffatt commenced his whimsical project, sex was everywhere: as he says, "in my first couple of days in the dorm, I was finding the generally suppressed sexuality of the coed dorms, which I had never experienced in my own college years, a steamy business, [and?] more than a little stressful for my thirty-three-year-old libido" (9). He introduces the first of his two chapters on undergraduate sex, "Since I had started teaching at Rutgers, I had sometimes wondered what really went on in these new institutions, the coed dorms," and then goes on to observe that an "inevitable middle-aged fantasy about the coed dorms was they were ongoing sex orgies" (181). To his dismay, possibly, while living in the dorms Moffatt found little evidence to nourish this fantasy. Instead, "the undergraduates maintained a set of conventions among themselves, with no detectable adult influence, in which sexual expression and sexual behavior were restrained—if not actually repressed" (182). Unwilling to accept these appearances and armed with statistical information from the university health centers regarding the number of pregnancy tests and abortions performed in a given year, Moffatt set out to devise a way to ask the students about undergraduate sex, their "sexual mentalities," and their sexual behaviors in "safer ways than those provided by the social gossip and by the occasional confidences of dorm ethnography" (186). Incredibly, he finds the safer route to be having students write "anonymous sexual self-reports" for credit in a course he was teaching on the anthropology of sexuality and eroticism.

Here, in part, is the assignment Moffatt presented to his students:

> I'd like you to write a *confidential* paper about your own sexuality. You may write about any aspect of it, in any linguistic style you choose: feelings, behavior, fantasies; best sex you've ever had; worst sex; no sex; frequency of sex; development of your own sexuality through time; pleasures and pains; sex and love; sex and other emotions; anxieties; techniques.
>
> If you're not especially active sexually, don't be intimidated by this assignment; try to write about your eroticism in any way you can. If you *are* sexually active, frank descriptions would be of use to my own research—but I leave such descriptions up to your own choice.
>
> I leave the form of this assignment to you, but I do ask you to be as truthful as possible. For most males, this means avoiding braggadocio; for most females, this means avoiding undue discretion. If you choose to write about fantasies, let me know they're fantasies. (236 n. 17, original emphasis)

This prompt reveals Moffatt's exclusive interest in having students report what they do with their bodies or minds—in having them, in other words, produce the required data (i.e., "frank descriptions") for his research.[9] What the students are not asked to do, tellingly, is to become ethnographers of their own cultures, or to report on what *they* think about what they do or why they think they do it, or even—remember, this assignment does occur in a course on the "Anthropology of Sexuality and Eroticism" — to situate their experiences in relation to the other cultures discussed in the course. In fact, the assignment reserved such comparative work for those squeamish students who found writing the sexual self-report to be "too personal or too excruciating." For this group, Moffatt provides busy work: "compare and contrast the sexual practices of *two* of the *four* cultures on whom we've read ethnography to date" (237 n. 17, original emphasis).

It is reasonable to ask, What was this assignment teaching the students about the culture of schooling? One possible answer is that within this pedagogical approach, the students were being trained to see that their use to the discipline was as "sources of information." For a student to be treated as a data provider and not a knowledge producer is hardly a unique experience in the academy, of course, and thus it should come as no surprise to learn that all but one of the students presented with Moffatt's assignment elected to write about their own experiences rather than write a report on the course lectures — the lone, recalcitrant subject being a "single male, from an east Asian background" (235 n. 15). The rest of the students clearly relished Moffatt's assignment, giving him exactly what he asked for and more. Regardless of whether the responses were frank or not, Moffatt concluded that "most of them sounded true, or they appeared to be fictional in the constructive sense of the term: they employed well-known writing genres to construct and to comprehend experiences that their writers themselves considered to have been real" (189). With this sleight of hand, Moffatt declares his data to be inescapably authentic, showcasing student papers thanking him for the assignment, others testifying to the assignment's having improved the students' own sex lives, and one female student's extended — no doubt reassuring — fantasy about seducing her *French* professor. In each instance, Moffatt bids us to read the student work as "unavoidably honest at the level of values, attitudes, and sexual ideation and as relatively honest at the level of behavior," a move that allows him to argue that the students partake in what he calls "the new sexual orthodoxy," where sex is seen to be *the* central concern of everyone's life (193, 195).

It's a curious argument, given that Moffatt himself provided the prompt that ensured the production of data supporting his conclusion. And, in fact, in his final chapter, "The Life of the Mind," Moffatt cites — but does not respond to — two students who give reason to doubt the overwhelming evidence Moffatt has offered concerning the dominance of this new sexual orthodoxy. The first student, when asked to self-report on her intellectual life, observes that "the opportunity to write about my intellectual life I find even more gratifying than an invitation to anonymously discuss my sexuality....

I've been reading since I was 3 and only started having sex since I turned 20. [So] my 'life of the mind' is also more central to my personality" (271, original ellipsis and brackets). The second student cited comments that "one's study habits [are] just as touchy a subject as one's sexuality and maybe more so" (271, original brackets). Moffatt reveals just how little credence he gives to such statements in a footnote, where he explains that these self-reports were solicited in "large classes in 1986 and 1987" by an assignment that "resembled the one for the sexual self-reports..., though the topic was not as sensitive, and these reports were not anonymous" (311 n. 2). Indeed, Moffatt seems unaware that the student comments he has placed at the opening of his final chapter contradict his assignment's assumption that discussing the "life of the mind" is a less "sensitive" topic for students than "the life of the body."

One could easily argue that these student comments *should* be disregarded, on the grounds that the very publicness of Moffatt's assignment on the life of the mind guaranteed responses that took for granted the importance of thinking: after all, who would openly tell a professor, in a paper for credit, anything else about schooling? Once again, though, rather than entertain the possibility that his students might be responding to the assignment's implicit constraints, Moffatt provides the following account for the students' general satisfaction with the education they had received at Rutgers:

> Like adult ideologues of higher education, most of them believed or hoped, one way or another, that a college education would be a civilizing experience. College should broaden their intellectual horizons, they believed; it should make them into better, more liberal, more generally knowledgeable human beings. At the same time, however, college should have a useful vocational outcome for them.... And this second, vocational meaning of college was—unmistakably—its much more important purpose for most Rutgers students in the late twentieth century. (274–75)

The students, in effect, are understood to be mere functionaries of American ideology about higher education, espousing beliefs that are undercut by their more venal desires for vocational training. And, while Moffatt admits that his presence in the dorms must have restricted the kinds of "spontaneous student-to-student intellectual talks" that undergraduates claimed to value so highly and that they insisted occurred "all the time among themselves, about all sorts of fascinating things," he had reason to believe that "not all the youths who represented themselves as friendly toward the life of the mind in papers like these were real student intellectuals or highly motivated scholars" (298–300). Thus, whereas Moffatt lobbied to establish the unavoidable authenticity of the students' responses about their sexual practices, here he labors in exactly the opposite direction to establish the inauthenticity of the students' experiences with the life of the mind.

But what does Moffatt mean when he insists that there are so few "real student intellectuals"? In a footnote, he guesses that no more than 20 percent of the student population would fit into this admittedly imprecise category, and he goes on to explain that those students he deems "real student intellectuals" were those "youths for whom intellect somehow seemed to be at the core of their identifies,... youths who, if I had a chance to know them as a teacher in a small seminar class, I thought might impress me as outstanding or unusual students" (325 n. 38). To put it another way, because Moffatt couldn't get direct access to the students' experiences of intellectual talk and because he mostly encountered students in large lecture courses, he decided that only a handful of students actually experienced "the life of the mind." While this insight into the declining quality of undergraduate life is meant to be disheartening, Moffatt does his best to conclude his book on an upbeat note by providing portraits of two "student intellectuals, both of them seniors, a male and a female, looking back untraumatically on what they recalled as four happy academic years at Rutgers" (306). There's Joe, an English major and "reformed nerd," and Susan, whom Moffatt describes as "our second and last student pilgrim through the dungeons and dragons of the undergraduate college" (306–7).

It's a striking image to close on, with the student cast in a sacred quest, passing through a fairy-tale landscape filled with the creatures of fantasy. And what this pilgrim has to say about her experience of undergraduate life contradicts much of what Moffatt has presented in the preceding chapters. While she acknowledges the role of college fun and games in her life, she talks also of wandering through the library on her own: "Sometimes I think I learned as much in those hours lounging on the floor between racks as I did in the accumulated classroom time" (309). Such learning never directly registers in the dorms or in the classrooms, of course — or even, apparently, in studies of undergraduate life. Aware of this, the student openly challenges Moffatt's "statement that freshmen and sophomores spend little time discussing anything serious. I've spent every year here involved in late night conversations about a lot more than who was sleeping with who" (308). A page and a half later, Moffatt brings his study to an end, without responding to the student's remarks or commenting on her observation at the conclusion of her undergraduate work that the idea of becoming a professor, specializing in the same subject for thirty years, "bores and terrifies" her (308). In many ways, this student's revulsion at the thought of the life of the professoriate provides a fitting end to Moffatt's study, in which his desire to have students discuss their sex lives has overwhelmed whatever counter-vailing desire the students had to discuss what being an intellectual might mean under their circumstances.

Before leaving Moffatt's book, though, we must attend to the issue that neither Moffatt nor his students were comfortable addressing — race. The place to begin such a discussion is with Chapter 4 of *Coming of Age in New Jersey*, "Race and Individualism," where Moffatt recounts his year visiting an "integrated" coed dorm, Erewhon Third, and the problems he encoun-tered in doing so.[10] The situation on Erewhon Third was as follows: Rutgers had begun admitting significant numbers of minority students between 1968 and 1972. Eventually, leaders from these student populations called for separate dorms to promote a sense of community and to ensure the acade-mic success of minority students. The administration balked at such efforts to "self-segregate" but, in the spirit of compromise, allowed special interest groups to live together. In this case, "the Robeson unit," with a special inter-est in black culture, was allowed to occupy one part of Erewhon Third; the other part of the floor was taken up by white students who "were there ei-ther because the housing computer had placed them there or through a combination of the housing lottery and much more reluctant choices than the Robeson members had made" (145). The floor, in effect, was to serve as a racial crucible for working out relations that have yet to be resolved either in the communities that surround the academy or in the academic depart-ments that surround the dorms.

As one would expect, Moffatt encountered a number of obstacles when he tried to find out what students on the floor thought about race. To begin with, he had difficulty gaining the confidence of the Robeson students:

Even as an older white male, safely encased in my identity as a researcher, *I* sometimes felt intimidated on the Robeson side. Some of the Robeson residents were as amiable and open with me in private interviews as any of the white, low-side residents; others were only grudgingly helpful; and one or two of the older, tougher-looking males on the floor frankly scared me a little with their monosyllabic replies and what struck me as baleful stares. (155, original emphasis)

While Moffatt acknowledges this discomfort with the black students, he sees himself as having no similar difficulties with the white residents on the floor; and, in the absence of such discomfort, he assumed that he could hear and understand what the white residents were saying to him when they spoke of race. Thus, for example, he doesn't hesitate to label the following response to the question "Do you have any problems with blacks on the floor?" as "notable both for its racism and for its sense of illegitimacy of the same":

> I went to a [high] school and I guess I wasn't stuck with college people, and they were very uncivilized, very rowdy and gangy, and...you know, saying they—you say one thing wrong, and forget it! You had fifty of them on your back after school! So I came in with a very bad attitude about them and it's just not getting any better...[The ones at Rutgers] are a lot nicer than just regular ones, cause I guess they're smarter and they know a lot more. (149–50, original ellipses and brackets)

After pointing to the "conflicting attitudes" evident in these remarks and observing that the student described herself as "prejudiced," Moffatt moves on to another example of white students' ambivalence about race (150). What Moffatt overlooks, in the process, is that the student's prejudice arises in response to a particular conjunction of race, class, and educational background: drawing on a long tradition of discrimination, this student distinguishes between "college people" and the masses of "very uncivilized, very rowdy and gangy" folk. While the student initially assumed that this distinction correlated with racial differences, her experiences at the university have brought her original point of view to crisis. In fact, now that she's lived in the dorm, she's been confronted by blacks who are "smarter and...know a lot more" than the ones she encountered in her high school where, it turns out, she was a member of the minority student population.

By labeling this student's response "racist," Moffatt removes it from its complex cultural and historical background. He also avoids drawing attention to the kinship between her discomfort and his own unease with those "older, tougher-looking" black males on the other end of the hall. Given this approach, it seems foreordained that Moffatt would discover evidence that the typical college student has an impoverished notion of culture: indeed, as a result of his investigation, Moffatt concludes that "most of the white students" assumed "people had the right to different opinions...but in many everyday behaviors—those of friend*li*ness, for instance—all normal human beings ought to act similarly, for many daily behaviors were 'natural'" (152, original emphasis). In other words, most of the white students felt that everyone, regardless of race, should be friendly in the same way, have fun in the same way, express themselves in the same way. One could see this as a sign that the students have a "not especially deep or sophisticated" understanding of how culture works, as Moffatt does (153). Or one could argue that the students' shared assumption about "natural," normative social behavior simply reflects the overarching values of the containing institution, which expects all students to demonstrate their intelligence in the same way, regardless of cultural background. To pursue this avenue of thought, though, one would have to be willing to entertain the possibility that it is the institution itself (and the people it most highly rewards) that lacks an "especially deep or sophisticated" working concept of culture.

Rather than go down this perilous road, Moffatt opts instead to hazard yet another "deliberately imprecise" guess about the student population—this time estimating that "between a tenth and a quarter of the white undergraduate student body" were "real racists" at the time he did his study (164). It's hard to know what to make of a methodology that depends on such deliberate imprecision; what is clear, though, is that when it comes to *specific* interactions between students Moffatt knows well, he is reluctant to find evidence of racist intentions. We see this, for example, in Moffatt's reaction to a fight he witnessed on Hasbrouck Fourth in 1984 between Carrie, "a lively black woman with a punk haircut," and Art, a "tall, intense, unpredictable [white male], and every bit as vivid a personality as Carrie" (78). Carrie and Art had once been friendly, but a simmering antagonism had grown between them after Art had complained to the hall preceptor about Carrie's loud music. Carrie responded by threatening Art that she would get some friends "to take care of him" and then allegedly said—within range of Art's hearing—that "you've got to kick [white folks'] asses a few times to make them respect you." A shouting match ensued, spilling over into the lounge and climaxing when Art went "impressively, quiveringly off his head. He screamed at her for what seemed like five minutes. The rest of us went into mild shock" (113).

Moffatt concedes that by the time he wrote up the event, he "had not retained anything of what anyone had actually said, only the emotional tone and the moves the various actors had made" (114). He continues, in a footnote, that "to be fair to Art, I think I *would* have remembered it if he had said anything blatantly racist during his diatribe" (136 n. 38, original emphasis). Although Moffatt does his best to contain the possibility that race figured in the white student's response during this fight, in the end, his efforts fail. In fact, when Art and four other ex-residents of the floor later enrolled in a course where Moffatt presented his preliminary findings about life in Hasbrouck, Art rejected Moffatt's "soft-pedaled" version of the fight and "brought it up again in all its vivid detail" in the class: "He was still angry with Carrie; he apparently still felt that she had introduced racially based threats in an inappropriate way. But after he told the class his version of their fight—referring to Carrie with the phrase 'let's call her *Grace Jones*' and giving her a stereotypic black accent, which she didn't have at all—I felt that I had to make some strong comments from the podium about undergraduate racism at Rutgers" (138 n. 46, original emphasis). Moffatt's response is so automatic that this reaction to his informant's alternative account of the event's significance no doubt felt natural to him. And thus, though Moffatt has tried his best to be "fair to Art," in the end the student has *forced* him to fall back on his professorial authority. The form that authority takes in this instance is, tellingly enough, not a revised analysis of the significance of the event in question but rather another in a long line of lectures from the podium meant to teach students that racism is bad. It's hard to see why this is an appropriate line for an anthropologist to take in this situation, and it's even harder to understand why Moffatt continues to insist, after Art's remarks in his course, that "race was only incidentally important on Hasbrouck Fourth in 1984–85. It was one *possible* subtext of Art and Carrie's fight, though Art was probably just as upset with Carrie as an assertive woman as he was with her as a black" (141, emphasis added).

Moffatt doesn't say how his students reacted to his outburst from the podium. But, it's easy enough to imagine that when Art and his classmates dragged themselves from the lecture hall, some may well have felt duly chastened by their teacher's oration, others may have been puzzled by the animated interchange, and still others might have been angry about what had happened. And, of course, it is not impossible that some students may have left feeling that they had witnessed yet another dramatic performance of the tenuousness of anthropological knowledge, as the teacher attempted to compensate for this necessary uncertainty by laying claim to a higher knowledge and a greater moral authority. We don't know what the students made of this spectacle, but there are very good pedagogical and anthropological reasons for trying to find out. Indeed, as we will see in the second half of this chapter, ethnographic research itself can provide both the method and the materials necessary to engage in more successful interactions with students than we've glimpsed here.

To be fair to Moffatt, though, he is not concerned with pedagogical reform of this kind. In fact, he concludes his study despairing of the possibility of meaningful educational reform. To begin with, he sees Rutgers as typical of American higher education at the end of the century "when it comes to the nature of its current trade-off between research and teaching and when it comes to the often only marginally intellectual mentality of many of its students" (310 n. 1). Thus, after his years "in the field," Moffatt sees only a corrupt industry and inferior human resources. In the face of these apparently overwhelmingly dismal working conditions, he can barely muster the energy to voice approval of the most familiar reform objectives: "more money and social prestige for undergraduate teaching, revised institutional relationships between research and the rest of college in all or most American colleges and universities, and tougher-minded stratifications of research-oriented and teaching-oriented institutions and professors" (310 n. 1). To put it another way, after all his years studying student culture, Moffatt surrenders the possibility of meaningful cultural change, for what else could it mean when an *anthropologist* calls for the spontaneous generation of "more social prestige for undergraduate teaching"? Moffatt doesn't discuss how this increase in prestige would come about, nor does he explain why a "tougher-minded," even more rigidly stratified academic culture is to be desired. Instead, under the smoke screen produced by this empty rhetoric, he retires from the scene of effective political and pedagogical action, but not before he makes the final, obligatory declaration that he would welcome the opportunity to teach differently. The problem, he confesses in his final footnote in the book, lies with the students themselves. While he would love to present them with a more complex picture of what politically critical anthropology looks like, for example, he knows this "doesn't sell nearly as well at the undergraduate level . . . ; the average Intro student seems to like the fairy-tale approach much better. And it is often hard to resist providing what the market demands, especially when one is continually being judged for one's enrollments" (326 n. 43). In the end, then, the students, with their "marginally intellectual mentalities" and their attraction to "the fairy-tale approach" to culture, are the ones ultimately responsible for bringing higher education to its knees.

Ways with Words: Complicity and the Possibility of Reform

Shirley Brice Heath's work with three separate language communities in the Piedmont Valley of the Carolinas from 1969 to 1978 bears a superficial similarity to Moffatt's project studying undergraduate life at Rutgers. Like Moffatt, Heath was interested in learning more about the culture of schooling and about students' experiences of that culture, though her interest is primarily with elementary education rather than college-level instruction. Past this point the similarities end, for Heath both participated in and generated efforts to reform the educational system in the Carolinas. Heath's interest in such work was fostered, in part, by local responses to the federal

mandate regarding desegregation. In the wake of this legislation, communication problems proliferated at the schools and the workplaces: the poor
white residents of "Roadville" and the poor black residents of "Trackton,"
the principal subjects of Heath's study, seemed to have diametrically opposed ideas about the best ways to learn, teach, and use language. To make
matters worse, neither group seemed to fare well when asked to function in
"the townspeople's" world, particularly when it came to school achievement. As a part-time teacher at a local state university in the late sixties,
Heath could see that "Communication was a central concern of black and
white teachers, parents, and mill personnel who felt the need to know more
about how others communicated: why students and teachers often could
not understand each other, why questions were sometimes not answered,
and why habitual ways of talking and listening did not always seem to
work" (*Ways with Words* 2). Heath's task, as she saw it, was to come to an understanding of how these three communities used language, to describe
their differences in detail, and to train teachers in such a way that they
would be prepared to introduce appropriate curricular reforms and teaching methods to address these breakdowns in communication.

Perhaps because Heath's research project set out to determine and, to the
extent possible, remedy the consequences of desegregation, she insists that
Ways with Words not be read as saying that racial difference explains why
the poor white residents of Roadville and the poor black residents of Trackton use language in ways that conflict. A reader who reaches such a conclusion, Heath maintains, would "miss the central point of the [book's] focus
on culture as learned behavior and on language habits as part of that shared
learning" (11). Such a reader would also have failed to understand that the
people of Roadville and Trackton do not use language differently *because*
they are racially different but because they have had "different historical
forces shaping" their language use (10).[11] Having ruled out race as the tran-
scendent determinant of language use, Heath proceeds to do away with
"socioeconomic" explanations as well, on the grounds that over half the
families in the area qualified for in-state social services. And, finally, given
that almost all of her students, regardless of race or class, could shift among
a range of dialects, she joined her students in concluding that "to categorize
children and their families on the basis of either socioeconomic class or
race and then to link these categories to discrete language differences was to
ignore the realities of the communicative patterns of the region" (3).

By neutralizing race and class as explanatory categories from the outset,
Heath was able to shut down those explanations for academic failure most
ready to hand prior to desegregation—that is, "they" speak differently be-

cause of their race or because of their poverty, the other sure sign of "their" innate inferiority. This rhetorical decision also served pedagogical purposes, since it created a classroom agenda that meshed with the needs of the students in Heath's graduate courses—"teachers, who came to advance their degrees and pay levels, and businessmen and mill personnel"—who were fully committed to finding other explanations for the communication problems that confronted them (2). In evaluating Heath's work, then, we must start by noting that her methodological and interpretive decisions were forged in response to a shared need to find a way to talk about race that wouldn't give offense or give rise to violence. Thus, ruling out race and class as determinants reflects an overarching desire on Heath's part and on the part of her students to hold fast to the belief that education has the power to produce a coherent polity, which it achieves by assimilating those outside the system into the system's stable core.[12]

Heath's further determination not to examine as closely the language use of "the townspeople"—the racially mixed middle class living throughout the Piedmont Valley—is clearly related to this need to establish the middle class as the fixed point to which all others, without question, aspire. While Heath studies the language habits of the residents of Trackton and Roadville in great detail, she devotes only one chapter to the ways townspeople use language—a chapter, she assures her readers, that does not repeat the mass of material collected on the middle class by traditional social science but that does verify "the similarities of the lives of [the] townspeople of the Piedmont to those of their counterparts elsewhere" (12). It is against this backdrop of understanding the language use of the middle class as normative and homogenous that *Ways with Words* was written.[13] The first six chapters are devoted to articulating a series of differences between Roadville and Trackton in terms of how the two communities define success, how they teach and learn languages, and how they constitute their oral and literate traditions. The seventh chapter—the one separating the sections titled "Ethnographer Learning" and the "Ethnographer Doing" and the one standing symbolically between the lower-class communities and school success—is the sole chapter on the middle class. The story of *Ways with Words* is, perhaps inevitably, the story of how best to move the masses (in the front of the book) to accept and mimic the values of the middle-class townspeople who live in "Gateway" (in the middle of the book), thereby providing them with a better shot at school success, full employment, and assimilation (at the end of the book).[14]

Heath's work on the differences between how language is used in Roadville and Trackton and how those differences end up producing failure in the schools for children from both communities is a tour de force of ethnographic insight unlikely to be equaled. No other work on schooling is comparable in scope; no other study delivers such a steady stream of pedagogically useful observations about the dynamic interplay between failure in the classroom and success in the home community. This granted, it is worth resting for a moment on the seam in Heath's book where the lower-class communities join with mainstream education, as the juxtaposition of this most familiar object—the middle class—with the foreign worlds of Roadville and Trackton foregrounds education's inescapable role in the business of assimilation. One of the most powerful instances of this juxtaposition occurs when Heath discusses the child-rearing practices of the middle class. Heath casts the differences among the three communities in the following way: in contrast to Gateway, where almost "from conception, the baby [of a townsperson] is treated as a potential conversationalist," babies in Trackton are not understood to be information givers and thus are rarely asked information-seeking questions, while babies in Roadville are addressed almost exclusively in baby talk (245). The difference, then, is that "[Middle-class mothers] assume the baby is attending to their talk, and any response is interpreted in *intentional* and *representational* terms by the mother.... They restate the infant's utterance as they believe the infant intended it, acknowledging that though the infant is not old enough to say what he intends, he is capable of having intentions which can be interpreted by others" (248, original emphasis). In other words, from the moment the newborn enters the middle-class home, the child is constructed as an "intending subject." Unlike residents of Roadville and Trackton, members in these households occupy their time with divining the child's true intentions and representing themselves to others as people who are principally concerned with the business of determining and articulating intentionality. Such an upbringing, as Heath makes clear, is excellent preparation for success in the school system, dovetailing perfectly with an institution whose primary concern is with training students to think about who did what to whom and why.

We can also see a connection between the ethnographer's preoccupation with uncovering intentions, finding patterns, and delineating systems and the child-rearing practices found in the domestic sphere of the townspeople. That is, by teaching teachers and having them, in turn, teach their students to attend to matters of intentionality, Heath effectively is teaching everyone involved in the project how to assimilate the values and lifeways of the middle-class townspeople. Thus, when Heath observes that "in attempting to understand the unconscious rules members of a group follow in their lives, we often look for patterns and themes of behavior which are carried from the home life into other institutions community members themselves control" (201), her formulation dramatizes, in miniature, the set of relationships that underwrite *all* ethnographic projects—there are intending subjects who know and are interested in knowing more (Heath's "we"), and there are others who don't know and who act according to "unconscious rules." With regard to the townspeople, Heath sees little need to elaborate on or to question the links between their ways of using language and the institutions they control. For Heath, her students, and, undoubtedly, the vast majority of her readers, the connection between constructing children as intending subjects and creating classrooms that reward the ability to divine the teacher's intentions is bound to seem obvious, natural, and thus implicitly "known" by all at some unconscious level.

While Heath has little trouble evincing the unconscious rules governing language use in the middle class by having teachers look at the institutions they control, she faces insurmountable difficulties when she pursues a similar strategy with the residents of Trackton. Thus, when Heath turns to the local black church as an example of an institution Trackton controls, she finds herself confounded by the way the church functions and by how hymns get "raised" during the service. Since interviewing both educated and uneducated members of the congregation proves fruitless, Heath's only recourse is to blend the language of her informants with her own critical discourse. So, to explain what happens in the church, Heath writes: "It is a 'sump'n' which allows the raising of hymns that leaders and congregation compose during, in, and for the performance. It is a 'sump'n,' which cannot be articulated by the members that accounts for the process and force by which they sing, tell a tale, compose a story, or pray a prayer" (208–9). Whereas Heath is able to draw on the combined insights of anthropology, linguistics, and education elsewhere in *Ways with Words* to bring to light the rules governing language use in Roadville and Trackton and to tease out the social and cultural forces that redundantly support and reinforce those rules, she hits a wall when it comes to the black church. Her mastery unstrung, Heath can only repeat a term from the Trackton community ("sump'n") in lieu of providing what would look like an "explanation" to someone outside that community.

Thus, despite the best of intentions, Heath's work in the black church would seem to have led her back to the very thing she and her students wanted to avoid—namely, irreducible racial difference, since the church members appear not to have been "taught" how to perform the way they do in church, at least not in any way that either they or Heath would characterize as instruction. In other words, they "just know" and how they know or what they know can't be articulated either by the church members or by the ethnographer of their community—it's just a "sump'n."[15] While Heath tries to cordon off this moment of irreducible difference by restricting it to the relatively secure realm of the sacred, this sense of the unknowability of the Other seeps out into the rest of her work, where the children of Trackton are repeatedly cast in the most favorable light: their learning styles are remarkable for their "flexibility and adaptability," their stories are seen as "highly creative fictionalized accounts," and their relationship to the written word is understood to be one that "opens alternatives" (111, 184, 235). The children of Roadville, by contrast, are described as coming from a community that "allows only stories which are factual" and emphasizes "the teaching of fixed and memorizable statements and labels"; for them, "the written word limits alternatives" (184, 140, 235). One begins to sense in such categorical statements the inevitable reproduction of a set of familiar stereotypes—the crafty, creative, intuitive Tracktonian and the slow, rule-bound, unimaginative Roadvillian.[16]

As troubled as we may be to find these stereotypes confirmed and reinscribed by Heath's research, we should still recognize that by refiguring these stereotypes as the by-products of learned linguistic behaviors, Heath was able to foster the development of desegregated classrooms that afforded the children of Trackton and Roadville a better chance at academic success. In other words, Heath's "complicity" with dominant ideology—her opening move to contain the threat that an emphasis on race and class would have posed to her study, her consignment of irreducible difference to the spiritual realm, and her discovery of literate behaviors that did not openly contradict dominant stereotypical assumptions—allowed her to remain in the educational system and to alter its effects by influencing the thoughts and actions of those who lived and taught in these communities. It is Heath's complicity that makes it possible for her to speak with those in local positions of power; it also enables her to preserve the possibility of meaningfully intervening in the education of the disenfranchised. To accomplish this deft political act, Heath does something unique among the educators we have examined: she openly acknowledges her lack of expertise about the lifeways of the communities her students come from and she then sets out to get her students — who are themselves teachers and managers—to become ethnographers of schooling, researching their own assumptions about appropriate language use in the classroom and in the community at large.[17]

In so doing, Heath not only revises the traditional power relations in the classroom, but she also violates the assumption that the ethnographer should avoid, to the extent possible, changing the actions of those being studied. Consequently, Heath's commitments to her discipline, on the one hand, and to meeting the needs of her students, on the other, come into conflict, which results in a temporary, productive suspension of the distinction between her research and her teaching. We can see this in the final section of *Ways with Words*, where Heath looks at the direct, institutional consequences of her work and tracks the individual initiatives of the various teachers who attempted to design classrooms where they and their students from Roadville and Trackton could "bridge their different ways" (265). In Heath's recounting, once the teachers realized that "they had previously judged their students' habits by the norms of the interactions of the townspeople," they were able to modify their teaching practices and institute curricular reforms that made it possible for the students from Trackton and Roadville to succeed in the classroom (266).

It's a thrilling account, one Heath herself has subsequently deemed "more celebration than description" ("Madness(es)" 265). But, as Kathryn Flannery has noted, the conclusion to Heath's book is more likely than not to be read as "a place where hope for change is dashed," since the creative pedagogical initiatives begun in these heady, tumultuous days—initiatives that allowed previously excluded students to find a voice in the classroom, produced rising test scores, and sustained a vision of eventual school success—all collapsed once Heath left the area (209). Heath attributes the failure of the reform efforts to sustain themselves not to her departure but to larger systemic changes; along with a growing lack of faith in the school systems in the 1980s, there was "a decrease in the autonomy of teachers as competent professionals and an increase in the bureaucratization of teaching and testing" (*Ways with Words* 356). With the crisis transferred to this bureaucratic level, the teachers felt an abatement of "the concrete realities of the new experience of facing black and white students in their classes" that had originally impelled "creative output from teachers and students alike" (357).[18]

Given that Heath's efforts had no lasting outcome, Flannery's insistence that the project *not* be judged a failure is sure to come as a surprise. Flannery argues that while "ethnography as a system of inquiry" was adequate to its particular historical moment, the conclusion to *Ways with Words* shows that "new conditions and new students require some other tactical use of other knowledge attentive to the local, the decentered, the different" (212). In other words, she is suggesting the possibility that the time when ethnographic work was capable of generating insights that would advance efforts to reform the academy may have passed. Though Heath has not embraced this vision of ethnography's limited utility, in reflecting back on the demise of her project she has concluded that it is vital to work against "the holding power of the myth that reform should both improve and persist" ("Madness(es)" 260).

When we keep these recommendations in mind, it seems the only option available to us for assessing Heath's work is to attend quite closely to what she herself defined as success within the moment of her project. In "Ethnographer Doing," Heath tells us that the teachers "used the challenge of integration" to refine the "intuition-based practices" they had used with particularly difficult students in the past and that, once they realized they "had learned unconsciously what to expect of their students so that the classroom could operate in an orderly way," they were then able to provide overt instruction in the codes of politeness that must be respected if the classroom is to function properly (*Ways with Words* 272–79). The story is believable enough: once the teachers began to be able to better articulate what kind of work they wanted their students to do and how they wanted their students to behave, they also began to develop alternative teaching practices for achieving these goals, most notably allowing students to bring their own ways of using language at home into the classroom to be investigated. And, as the story goes, by revising their expectations accordingly, the teachers were able to solicit work that gave nonmainstream students the opportunity to succeed in school without the teachers having to alter or degrade the standards of evaluation. Thus, within this definition of success, the reform effort is seen to have failed once teachers stopped soliciting different kinds of student work and returned to their former ways of teaching.

It's important to recognize what is at stake in this insistence that reigning standards of academic excellence were never put at risk by the teachers' initiatives. Its significance becomes clear when Heath describes how getting the students to become ethnographers of their own cultures helped transform the classroom into a place where the students themselves provided the material to be studied and then participated in producing the interpretations of that material. In one such classroom, we are told, "many [of the students] were 'turned on' to writing in ways which surprised themselves, but this writing was their own, generated by them for purposes which both met their needs and allowed teachers to emphasize school skills of spelling, punctuation, and requirements of style for different purposes" (314). Such claims about student excitement and interest are, of course, generic to arguments in favor of pedagogical innovations. But tellingly, Heath's version of this claim includes the proviso that student enthusiasm did not derail teachers from the serious business of ensuring the continued production of good clean prose. Whether such claims are believable depends on the evidence presented and, in this case, there is less evidence than, as Heath herself has said, "celebration." Thus, in a study that grows out of the conflicts produced by the implementation of desegregation — a study, furthermore, that goes to great lengths to show how stories are differently valued in three competing communities and the consequences of these differing valuations — the classroom is suddenly transformed, in the final instance, into a place where all these conflicts can be erased and all the differing systems of evaluation can peaceably come together. And for this to happen, the teachers needed only to "alter their methods of teaching, but not their standards of judging the mechanics of writing and clarity of writing" (314).

Heath's own research makes it hard to believe that "clarity of writing" could have remained a fixed standard, given the three very different ways that the residents of Roadville, Trackton, and Gateway use language. Yet Heath makes this assertion repeatedly, not only in *Ways with Words* but also in the work that has followed.[19] Thus, when Heath offers a selection from the journal of Zinnea Mae, one of the children from Trackton, she focuses only on the correct spelling and the "seemingly random use of apostrophes and other punctuation marks" in the piece (335–36). What Heath leaves unaddressed is the content of Zinnea Mae's journal: "Childrens back in [the old days] got a lots of education and didn't go to school much. But we go to school nine months and still don't learn too much" (335). Attending only to the surface features, and bidding the readers to do so as well, Heath leaves untouched Zinnea Mae's critique of the school system, with the curious result that her journal entry is showcased as an example of the virtues of pursuing Heath's line of educational reform. Within an educational and investigative system so concerned with *how* things are said — with delineating and transmitting "the unconscious rules" governing the production of proper, error-free language use — *what* gets said is always in danger of being lost or misplaced.[20]

If one similarly scrutinizes how student work is read and understood in the closing section of *Ways with Words*, Heath's claims to have achieved a measure of pedagogical reform seem less grand and the "failure" of the reforms once she departed seems less surprising. For despite Heath's repeated assurances that teachers provided students with a "metalanguage" that allowed them "to talk about acquiring, integrating, and controlling knowledge in school" (342), she provides little evidence to support such a claim, nor does she establish that the teachers themselves had control of such a language. Indeed, if the teachers had gained access to such a metalanguage, why were they unable to find ways to explain the significance of what they were doing in their classrooms to those people who ultimately had the power of determining their working conditions? What the evidence does suggest is that the teachers did not question their own evaluative rules once they had articulated them and that they failed to become conversant in the languages and protocols of their bosses—those bureaucrats who exercised such substantial control over what they were allowed to do in their classrooms. This is, to be sure, an odd fate for a reform program bent on trying to teach the disenfranchised how to read and understand the "ways with words" of other peoples, particularly the ways of those in the dominant classes. Seen in this light, Heath's book presents an important concluding paradox for us to consider: what are we to make of the fact that the teachers in Heath's study asked their students to develop the ability to speak and write across a range of contexts and to think self-reflexively about their own language practices and then didn't hold themselves to the same standards? The answer to this question, as we will see, is to be found not in the weakness of individual teachers but in the cultural norms of the academy, which exert considerable force on our expectations of what may reasonably be asked of a teacher.

Studying Up on Academic Culture: "The Mystique of Interpretive Authority and the Illusion of Scholarly Objectivity"

In the mid-1980s, Elizabeth Sheehan set out to do an ethnographic study of "Irish academics' participation in the public sphere of politics, social reform, and cultural debate" (252). This hardly seems like a project meant to offend the academics involved and yet, from the beginning, Sheehan's research ran into trouble because, as she puts it, "There is some suggestion of bad taste in the notion that one academic should study another, a delicacy of feeling rarely extended by social scientists to the rest of the world" (255). In her case, Sheehan realized that she had upset the refined sensibilities of her subjects in a number of ways: she was a younger, female graduate student studying older, established members of the academic profession; she was a foreigner constructing a reading of indigenous scholars, some of whom were themselves "engaged in developing alternate analyses of their own societies" (253); she was an American anthropologist interested in culture and thus represented both a methodology and an academic tradition that together were stereotyped as "better funded, more influential, but less competent in their research than their Irish or British counterparts"; and finally, her focus on the quotidian concerns of Irish intellectuals was seen to undermine Ireland's claim to "international scholarly prestige, the production of great literature." Thus, as far as Sheehan's informants were concerned, she had put together a project that was a direct threat to "their own status and interpretive authority" (254). As a consequence, Sheehan found she had to contend with a good deal of antagonistic behavior: dismissive responses, repeated requests to show her credentials and prove the depth of her knowledge, the intentional transmission of misinformation meant to mislead her or to damage other informants in the project, and "friendly threats" about the ease with which she could be met at the airport on her return should her write-up prove unfavorable to the concerned parties.

This story takes its shock value from its revelations that trained academics would willfully obstruct efforts to produce knowledge and insight and that they would treat a junior scholar and aspiring colleague with such glaring acts of disrespect. For any student who has been on the receiving end of a teacher's wrath, though, whatever power this story has to shock is quickly replaced by puzzlement that anyone would *ever* think that academics might act otherwise. Indeed, to be truly shocked by Sheehan's experience is to imagine, as teachers and intellectuals are given to doing despite considerable evidence to the contrary, that being educated somehow lifts one up above the reach of material concerns. It is also to imagine that the academy really does provide a collaborative environment populated by colleagues both self-aware and fully humane. The incredible persistence of this vision of academic culture is the subject of the next chapter; here it will suffice to consider Sheehan's conclusion that "the study of intellectuals and their institutions... requires that critical attention be paid to the nature of *our own investment*—as academics and intellectuals, as well as social scientists—in the mystique of interpretive authority and the illusion of scholarly objectivity" (258, emphasis added).

Sheehan ran into such trouble because she was laying claim to a level of expertise that every highly credentialed academic is understood to fully possess by virtue of his or her training—interpretive authority and scholarly objectivity. Consequently, it's not really all that surprising that her subjects responded as they did: after all, what could *she* possibly have to say about them that they couldn't already say about themselves *for* themselves? As an ethnographer, Sheehan had to assume that her subjects might not be fully aware of the forces that controlled their actions, that they might not be the ones best suited to provide an overarching narrative of the codes and conventions of their belief systems, and that they might not be able to achieve the kind of distance from their own situations that enables critical reflection. In other words, she assumed what any ethnographer must assume about her object of study if she is going to do more than simply record and repeat the words of the people being studied. And while the people on the ground in any ethnographic study may well feel the kind of animus and violation that Sheehan's Irish intellectuals felt, usually the research situation itself prevents this discomfort from making itself known, since the researcher is generally "studying down" on subjects who are from a lower class, have less status, or have fewer intellectual accomplishments. By "studying up," Sheehan disrupted what Scott calls "the elite-choreographed public transcript," which consists "of visual and audible displays of rank, precedence, and honor" (Scott 105). For those who believe academics to be free of such "petty," earthbound motives and for those who know otherwise, but say so only in private, the scandal of Sheehan's project lies in its apparent disrespect for the particular "displays of rank, precedence, and honor" that structure academic culture. By asserting her interpretive expertise, despite her status as a young, female, graduate student, Sheehan effectively publicized what Scott calls "the hidden transcript," revealing what is known, but rarely said aloud—namely that academics, too, are consumed by greed, territorial interests, pride, and self-importance.

Scott's analysis of the interaction of dominant and subordinate groups is particularly relevant here, since his research has led him to the surprising conclusion that if anyone can be said to have "false consciousness," it is the members of dominant groups, who dependably show themselves to be the ones "least able to take liberties with those symbols in which they are most heavily invested" (106). Applying this insight to Sheehan's work, we can see that the areas of heaviest investment for academics are those that symbolically represent the academic as the expert, objective interpreter, outside and above the demands of the workaday world. This has certainly been borne out by the preceding discussion of Moffatt's and Heath's research projects, since both studies have been shown to illustrate the degree to which certain founding assumptions about academic expertise must remain unquestioned if the research relationship is to be maintained. In Moffatt's case, we saw how he repeatedly had to reassert his own professorial and moral authority in the classroom and in the dorms when students articulated apparently odious positions that he felt required an immediate response. Heath never acts with such open disregard for her subjects' points of view nor does she adopt a morally judgmental stance when confronted by lifeways that do not accord with her own. And yet, she too could not escape the restrictions of her position as a teacher-trainer—restrictions that required that the normative standards used to evaluate student performance remain unchallenged.

It should be clear that stronger people or better researchers or deeper thinkers could *not* have escaped this structurally produced bind. Heath's example is most instructive in this regard, since it was her very willingness to work with and within the structural constraints of her institutional setting that actually allowed her to open up new teaching and learning possibilities. That Heath's undisguised complicity with (or we might say respect for) the dominant educational system prevented her from making claims about the "radical" aims of her reform project is sure to disturb those who would only be satisfied with a more ambitious program for revising the entire system. With such critics in mind, one could argue that the real threat of ethnographic work like Moffatt's, Heath's, and Sheehan's is in offering incontrovertible proof that the notion of interpretive mastery is always an illusion — an illusion, furthermore, to which academics, regardless of disciplinary affiliation or level of achieved self-reflexivity, can't avoid succumbing. And it is precisely because this illusion is so central to the academic's life that the ethnographic enterprise has attracted so much critical energy over the past two decades. The accusations and recriminations are evidence that academic culture, with its growing commitment to the notion of credentialed expertise, is made frantic by a disciplinary approach that endlessly disproves the long-cherished ideal of the academic's interpretive mastery and objective distance. In this light, much of the animated discussion about the viability of the ethnographic project cited at the opening of this chapter is best read as a sign of a shared desire either to put an end to the production of material evidence that substantiates the limits of academic expertise or to transform that evidence into the kind of highly textualized objets d'art that reinstantiate the need for the academic's learned gaze.

Eschewing these modes of response, but granting the possible validity of Flannery's hypothesis that the ethnographic moment may have passed, I would maintain that the pedagogical value of ethnographic work currently lies in its ability to provide such remarkably vivid accounts of the researcher's limited expertise and of the impossibility of ever fully mastering any social situation. When ethnographies are read with these concerns in mind, as I have done here, they can be shown to detail how the "expert observer's" understanding of the observed event is inescapably circumscribed by disciplinary and personal commitments that, in turn, reveal the research project's equally inescapable complicity with dominant systems of constraint. Such an approach is particularly productive when directed to ethnographies of schooling, giving the lie to the seductive vision of the educator as a free-floating entity and providing in its place a more grounded, perhaps even "fallen," account of how educators and their students work within and against reigning material and discursive conditions. As we have seen in considering the ethnographies written by Moffatt and Heath, the most important and most insistent constraint for research-oriented academic work is that there must come a time during the collection of the data when those being investigated are found to be unable to explain why they are doing what they are doing—a time when their testimony alone cannot make their actions legible to the academic community at large. If no such moment were to arise, no meaningful, interpretive academic labor would be understood to have occurred—one would merely be seen as collecting and preserving materials, archiving resources for future generations to interpret.

When Heath confronts such interpretive moments, she turns to the work of sociolinguistics and anthropology to provide her with the means to transform perceived unconscious behavior into a series of learned rules for social interactions within a given cultural context. And although Moffatt tries to avoid placing himself in this interpretive position, doing his "best to keep [his] tone neutral, to try to describe the students' lives from something like their own attitudinal stances," he acknowledges that his "own moral tone does break through" (*Coming of Age* xvi). This is especially true, he concedes, in the chapters on sex and the life of the mind and whenever fraternities are mentioned. For both ethnographers, it is what might be called the metadiscourse of last resort that plays the greatest role in structuring the imagined program for reform emerging from the study. In Heath's case, the reliance on sociolinguistics translates into providing students with the tools for investigating language use in various contexts so that they can begin to articulate and master the rules deployed within the school system. In Moffatt's case, the struggle between his commitment to descriptive anthropology and his desire to provide a moral response to what he has seen and heard produces occasional pedagogical interventions in class and a general sense that "the problem" is too big to be solved.

What these two examples have shown quite clearly, then, is that using ethnographic techniques does not (and *cannot*) generate the kind of utopian, collaborative interchange evoked at the conclusion to the preceding chapter, where students realize "their more basic right to define the questions," as Raymond Williams put it ("Future" 157). Instead, the subjects of study end up, at one point or another, being transformed into the objects to which questions are posed and upon which reforms are enacted, a process that Gayatri Spivak has described in another context as mingling "epistemic violence with the advancement of learning and civilization" ("Can the Subaltern Speak?" 295). If such "epistemic violence" is an inescapable aspect of institutionalized learning at this time, as I believe it is, then one could argue that this violence occurs within the ethnographic project at the moment the metadiscourse of last resort is brought in to explain and assess the behavior of the subjects constituted by the study. I would even go so far as to locate the specific benefit of ethnographic work—and the force of its threat—in its necessarily making available as texts to be read the voices of those under investigation, *even if those voices must be read in and for their absence.* The multidisciplinary, multidiscursive character of ethnographic work all but guarantees the production of a polyphonic text that can never fully succeed in covering over the epistemic violence that arises in the struggle between the ethnographer's interpreting voice— with its ultimate interest in assimilating the Other—and the voice of the Other that is to be interpreted, whose interests are never and can never be known for certain. The ethnographer may seek to regulate how that material is read in any number of ways (e.g., through selective citation, elision, erasure, translation), but he or she can never fully succeed, because the social context surrounding the collection of the statements can never be fully described or accounted for, nor can the differential in the power relations between the observer and the observed ever be completely stabilized. Consequently, what ethnography endlessly records is that the observer can never, finally, control the unruliness of the observed's text.

Obviously, this situation presents itself whenever any reader confronts any text. But ethnographic work on the culture of schooling is particularly appealing because such work can be made to foreground the pedagogical consequences that follow from the fact that the relationship between teacher/expert and student/text never is "pure" or "unmediated." In other words, the ethnographic approach always embodies the author's attempt to control the rebellion of the material, and the outcome is always a visible, suspicious, often clumsy attempt to master that material and make it behave. This very clumsiness is ethnography's virtue, for in its clumsiness it repeatedly exposes the essentially social mission of the educational enterprise—which is, as the studies discussed here have shown, to acculturate and assimilate the masses, to change the people in the system and not the system itself, and to develop and reinscribe a hierarchy of expertise rather than to recognize the way expertise figures across a broad range of social and cultural practices. If these are, indeed, the reigning ideological constraints that serve to regulate who gets to work in the academy and what work they will do there once admitted, then the question that remains for the final chapter to address is how far these constraining conditions permit the possibility of meaningful educational reform.

6 The Stories That Teach Us

If Julius Getman's progress through the academy were made into a movie, the music would begin to swell just as he was introduced to the Yale Law School alumni. The movie would have already detailed Getman's struggles as the son of working-class immigrants, including his attendance at City College in the early fifties because it was all his parents could afford. It would have followed Getman on to Harvard Law School, shown us his initial difficulties on the job market, and traced his steady rise from his first appointment to the faculty at Indiana University, then to Stanford, and finally to the lofty heights of Yale Law School. At this point, a few choice words about hard work, determination, sacrifice, and success would be heard above the roar of flashbulbs. And then, the credits would roll. With no more mountains for Getman to climb, the story (and his life) would, for all practical purposes, be over: all that remains is to continue writing oft-cited, well-received articles for an ever-increasing audience of admiring peers, on into retirement.

What is surprising about Getman's book *In the Company of Scholars: The Struggle for the Soul of Higher Education* is its refusal to tell this familiar story of the American Dream realized, beginning instead just where "the movie version" of the author's academic career would end—with Getman's decision to join the faculty at Yale. For Getman, the story of his life *begins* rather than ends at this point because his return to the Ivy Leagues as a distinguished professor marked the dawning of his awareness of just how completely he had misunderstood the bureaucratic realities of academic work. Thus, *In the Company of Scholars* represents Getman's efforts to interrogate his own assumptions about the consequences of academic success: as he puts it, "I began this book to articulate my sense of disappointment and alienation from the status I had fought so hard to achieve." Acknowledging that initially he had been swept away by his improbable journey "from a run-of-the-mill teaching position to a unanimous offer to join the faculty at one of the two great law schools in America," Getman confesses that it wasn't long before he "became uneasy with the Yale Law School, critical of its scholarship, and troubled by its smugness" (1–2). Instead of entering into a world of selfless teachers and committed students churning with intellectual energy, as he had expected, he found a community composed of professional academics who were careerist, self-centered, uninterested in teaching, intolerant, ill-informed, opportunistic, absent.

Realizing that *even Yale* could not place him "in the company of scholars" forced Getman to reassess the meaning of his academic success. Indeed, upon reflection, Getman was surprised to discover that *forty years* after his graduation from Harvard Law School, he was still "appalled and angry" at his distinguished alma mater for a host of shortcomings, including "its arrogant assumption of intellectual superiority; its social, intellectual, and professional rating systems; its limited focus; its overemphasis on professional competence; its failure to provide an opportunity to express other aspects of our intellectual ability, such as creativity, empathy, and understanding; and most of all its presumption in setting intellectual limits for people prematurely" (13). With such recollections at the forefront of his mind, Getman commences an examination of what happens to those who have been similarly swept away by stories about the virtues of education's transformative powers only to find themselves, as Richard Hoggart detailed so long ago in *The Uses of Literacy*, the inheritors of a lifelong sense of rootlessness.

It is difficult not to dismiss this familiar criticism of the academy's ways as a kind of infantile complaint—as the yawpings of some wounded inner scholar who dreams of working conditions that promote an otherworldly communion of intellectuals. Certainly, it is odd that Getman, a specialist in labor law and a former general counsel for the American Association of University Professors, could have gotten so far in the profession without discovering that academic labor—with its rigid hierarchies, its elaborate protocols for proper behavior, its restrictive codes of communication, and its relative intolerance and unresponsiveness to difference—can be as alienating as any other form of labor. Nevertheless, to read Getman's dissatisfaction with academic life as evidence of mental weakness or intellectual blindness is to misunderstand how the academy attracts to itself those who imagine it to provide a relatively autonomous work site that is *supposed* to be beyond the reach of everyday concerns and everyday people. One might think that those attracted by this image would recognize its illusory character once they had been exposed to the bureaucratic realities of academic life. The truth, though, is that such exposure to the daily demands of soliciting, assessing, and ordering untold masses of student work only reinforces the general belief that there *must* be other, less constraining situations where *true* scholars and intellectuals are free to do as they please, untrammeled by bureaucratic responsibilities and the burden of grading student papers. In this respect, *In the Company of Scholars* is best read as evidence of just how difficult it is for those who have been highly rewarded by the academic system to come to terms with the essentially bureaucratic nature of the work that awaits them after all their years of laboring to please their superiors. Thus, we find Getman dreaming of himself as engaged in "the struggle for the soul of higher education" instead of seeing himself as what he is—one of a mass of intellectual laborers employed by an essentially soulless social mechanism whose primary function is to create, reinforce, and problematize hierarchical relations among an otherwise undifferentiated citizenry.

In *Domination and the Arts of Resistance*, James Scott makes the provocative suggestion that if such a thing as "false consciousness" may be said to exist, it is to be found not among the disenfranchised, as theories of dominant ideology would have one believe, but among those who have risen through the educational system and have come to believe deeply in its values. When Scott describes this latter group of dominated dominators as having "made sacrifices of self-discipline and control and developed expectations that were usually betrayed," he intimates how wrenching the educational experience can be for those who have come to believe in the academy's promise of mental improvement, social advancement, and cultural and moral superiority (107). For our purposes, Getman perfectly illustrates Scott's hypothesis. By his own account, "like most academics," he believed that the profession would "offer meaning, status, and a pleasant life-style" (2). He persisted in this belief even though his own experiences in graduate school required him to radically reorient his relationship to the social sphere. As Getman puts it, during this time, "I was being transformed in my thinking, speech, and manner from a person whose immigrant, working-class background was obvious into one worthy of mingling with the country's professional, intellectual, political, and social elite" (10). Though at one time Getman had an unwavering faith that it was worth the personal cost of undergoing such a transformation, by the time he is well into his career his faith in the educational process has been replaced, just as Scott would predict, by a profound sense of betrayal. Thus, in return for all his years of diligent study and subservience, Getman finds he is not the inheritor of "meaning, status, and a pleasant life-style," as he had expected; he is just another functionary within a largely indifferent bureaucratic system.

That Scott would have anticipated this course of events doesn't mean that he thinks that such feelings of anger and betrayal are insignificant. In fact, at one moment in his argument, he entertains the possibility that "the system may have most to fear from those subordinates among whom the institutions of hegemony have been most successful. The disillusioned mission boy (Caliban) is always a graver threat to an established religion than the pagans who were never taken in by its promises. The anger born of a sense of betrayal implies an earlier faith" (107). However much one might like to believe this particular story about the nascent revolutionary powers of a constrained, greatly disenchanted intelligentsia, though, Scott himself inadvertently suggests just how easily such threats may be contained by referring to Caliban as the synecdochic representative of the "graver threat" posed to the powers that be. For while it is true enough that Caliban did indeed have designs to overthrow Prospero, his teacher and benefactor, in the end his threat is easily contained. Consequently, he is left to live out a life of isolation with nothing more than his conjuring dreams, while Prospero is restored to his former position of power back in the "civilized" world. In other words, the reference Scott himself supplies suggests that no matter how disillusioned, angry, intelligent, or mystically endowed the disenchanted individual may be, that person is bound to lose out against such a highly organized and highly mutable system for disseminating and extending social power.

Perhaps Scott, like so many scholars before him, has been momentarily swept away by the revolutionary promise of the inherently virtuous extrainstitutional individual; but the overarching argument of his project is useful to us here because it shows how those who have been taken in by this vision of academic purity boil over in rage once they that they have realized too late that there is a profound disjunction between the intellectual life the academy is purported to provide and the bureaucratic life it actually delivers. Evidence of the effects of this realization may be found in any discussion among academics of employment prospects within the profession, where this sense of betrayal and anger is bound to bubble to the surface. There are, for example, the contrasting apocalyptic visions of the transformation of higher education into either vocational training or politically correct brainwashing. There is the lament that we are in the twilight of the profession as we have known it, as may be seen in the steady decline of tenure-track positions and the simultaneous expansion of a large, migratory teaching force, together with the increased demand for accountability and oversight at every stage of the credentialing process. And, finally, there is the pervasive, palpable sentiment among those entering the profession and those already there that being an academic has come increasingly to mean being overworked, underpaid, the object of general scorn, the target of unprecedented levels of scrutiny. In short, everyone seems to agree that the academy is undergoing a radical reformation, but to what end and in response to what forces remains unclear.

While discussion of these issues has tended to stick to the business of lamenting what the academy has become, Michael Bérubé and Cary Nelson have distinguished themselves by moving beyond the comfort of critique to the much riskier work of actually generating proposals for substantially changing the way academics approach the business of education. In the introduction to their jointly edited collection, *Higher Education under Fire*, Bérubé and Nelson demand that academics now "admit that the long-term collapse of the job market is making the logic of graduate apprenticeship morally corrupt" (20). Their reasons for focusing on graduate rather than undergraduate education become clear in the questions they ask us to consider: "What does it mean to face an academic future in which many graduate students will have none? What are the ethics of training students for jobs that few of them will ever have?" (20–21). With these pointed questions, Bérubé and Nelson draw on the ever-serviceable figure of the student to animate their charges concerning the moral and ethical failings of the academy. In so doing, they offer a version of "the student" that has not much concerned us in the preceding chapters: the student that most interests Bérubé and Nelson is the *graduate* student, a persevering entity who is faced with the impossible task of balancing the requirements for joining the profession and staffing the entry-level courses that tenured faculty presumably no longer wish to teach. Within this rhetorical gambit, in other words, the student becomes the embodiment of an accusation—a figure who haunts the academy like a guilty conscience, a constant reminder of the academic's inability to read, let alone control, the market forces that determine whether or not a job stands on the other side of all the courses, examinations, time, and debt that accompany the credentialing process.

In better times, it was easier for everyone involved in the business of higher education to think of "the graduate student" as an apprentice training to enter a vaunted profession—a "secular vocation," as Bruce Robbins calls it. With the collapse of the job market, however, it now requires a great deal more work to conceal or explain away the complicity of academics in the "morally corrupt" business of trading in human capital. Some have insisted that higher education has nothing to do with generating employable end products; others long for the days when students worried more about learning and less about the future; and nearly everyone blames an ignorant public and craven administrators for misconstruing the virtuous work of graduate education as a form of exploitation. Bérubé and Nelson have succeeded in breaking free of this kind of critique in which all is denied and nothing is changed by arguing for a packet of institutional reforms and administrative procedures that would alter the material practices of higher education. They have suggested, for example, reducing the number and size of graduate programs across the country and strengthening the "gatekeeping function" of the master's degree (21). While these reforms would improve the employment picture by reducing the number of applicants competing for work in the academy, Bérubé and Nelson want, reasonably enough, to further improve their students' chances by increasing the number of available jobs. This, they believe, can be accomplished by enjoining universities and colleges to put together attractive early-retirement packages and strenuous posttenure reviews to remove nonperforming faculty members (21). Finally, in the interests of improving the treatment of graduate students prior to their entry into the job market, Bérubé and Nelson call for higher wages and better benefits for teaching assistants, better career counseling, improved training for teaching jobs at nonresearch colleges and universities, and a commitment by faculty to be more faithful in fulfilling their obligations to advance their students careers (22–23).

We will return in a moment to the question of whether or not such reform proposals ever could be enacted. Before doing so, though, I want to point out how heavily these proposals rely on a set of bureaucratic procedures to achieve the essentially social mission of ensuring future employment for current graduate students. Indeed, Bérubé and Nelson show themselves to have a remarkable faith in the power of such procedures to do a good job of discriminating between graduate programs that should be allowed to continue and those that shouldn't, between students who are best qualified to pursue advanced graduate work and those who should be terminated at the master's level, between advanced professors who are fulfilling their pedagogical, scholarly, and professional responsibilities and those who should be enjoined to consider the virtues of early retirement. In fact, Nelson believes so firmly in administered change of this kind that he has since codified his proposals into a "twelve-step program for academia," thereby transforming the massive bureaucratic system of higher education into a dysfunctional entity that needs only to be forced through his prescribed rigorous therapeutic regime to regain its psychic health and moral integrity. To help get the academy back on the wagon, Nelson believes there should be a bill of rights for graduate students and teaching assistants, a union (which could exercise its power, in Nelson's now famous example, by "organizing group shopping trips to other states for all purchases"), and "a year's work for a year's wage" (or, perhaps more helpfully, a year's wage for a year's work). Community colleges should be encouraged to hire Ph.D.'s. Research universities should exchange postdoctoral teachers. The positive accomplishments of the academy should be publicized (22–25). In short, with all the moral authority he possesses by virtue of being an intellectual and not a bureaucrat, Nelson insists that the academy start living up to his standards.

However laudable Bérubé and Nelson's willingness to face up to the fundamentally bureaucratic nature of the educational enterprise may be, it is unfortunate that their insights have not led them to rethink how sustainable reform is achieved in an institutional setting. Because they have not considered this issue, Bérubé and Nelson fall into the "teacher's fallacy" discussed in Chapter 1: that is, they construct the academy itself as an unruly student, bereft of a local history or a set of internal motivations, ready to do the right thing if only told forcefully enough. Trapped in this fallacy, Nelson and Bérubé can't seem to shake the condescending mode of address that certifies their status as "true reformers" outside and above the system; for as Ian Hunter has argued, it is "as the bearer of a prestigious spiritual demeanor and moral authority...that [the figure of the critical intellectual] finds its niche in the school system, alongside the figures of the citizen and the bureaucrat" (xxiii).

Suffused with this moral authority, the scales having fallen from their eyes, Bérubé and Nelson have brought the good news of reform to their colleagues only to be met with a chilly reception. Nelson, for instance, reports being surprised by his colleagues' anger at his efforts to have the administration use some "vacated faculty salaries to increase the size and number of graduate student fellowships" (Cary Nelson 23). And Bérubé, conceding that "we can't do much about the...wholesale conversion of full-time, tenure-track jobs to part-time adjunct positions," can suggest only that we use "our waning sanity and ever-precarious good sense" to decry the inflated requirements for entry-level positions, which have "heightened tensions and worsened working conditions in the profession" (28–29). In the face of such hearty and heartfelt hortatory admonitions, can it really be surprising to learn that the faculty resists, the administration resists, and, following these good examples and relying on the traits that got them into higher education in the first place, the students themselves resist? When the chips are down, no one, it seems, is all that interested in banding together and working for the improvement of all.

Given Bérubé and Nelson's shared commitment to addressing such resistance to collective action head-on, it is worth noting that Nelson has been quite explicit about what part of academic culture is *not* subject to change: "although I have taught composition and enjoyed it, I would now find it *demoralizing and intolerable* to have to grade hundreds of composition papers each semester. There is no way I could do it as carefully and thoroughly as my graduate students do. So what is to be done?" (21, emphasis added). And with this backhanded compliment, praising *his* graduate students for their ability to do work he finds "demoralizing and intolerable," Nelson inaugurates his twelve-step program for reforming the profession. He seems to reason as follows: since he finds reading and responding to the work of beginning students unbearable, the problem he must solve is to propose changes that will improve the employment possibilities of his graduate students without imperiling his own position of privilege. Read in this light, Nelson's calls to shut down marginal graduate programs, to better police the boundaries separating master's and doctoral candidates, and to convince community colleges to hire Ph.D.'s all seem as concerned with preserving the primacy of research institutions as they are with addressing the putative needs of the oft-invoked suffering-but-dedicated graduate student. Presumably, Bérubé and Nelson are banking on the luminous presence of this sympathetic figure to bathe their proposals in the light of righteous indignation, thereby allowing what might seem to be fairly modest changes to assume the aura of radical rehabilitation.

To question Bérubé and Nelson's rhetorical deployment of the long-suffering graduate student is not to deny the exigencies of the current job crisis, nor is it to suggest that graduate programs are doing an adequate job of preparing their students to confront these exigencies. Once we have deflated the rhetorical force of this figure, however, we do have room for a consideration of the paradox that resides at the heart of their proposals: how is it that graduate students can manage to become so skillful at work Nelson and his colleagues find "demoralizing and intolerable"? Is it youthful enthusiasm? naïveté? a natural talent for dirty work? And what does Nelson do to ensure that his students don't end up with his profound distaste for such work, so that when the time comes for them to move into those newly created positions at the local community college, they don't somehow feel they've been betrayed by a system that brought them to the heights of critical theory only to drop them in what they have been so thoroughly trained to see as the academy's deepest valley of practice? Exactly what kind of "career counseling" is going to prepare future members of the profession for the shocking disjunction that exists between the demands of graduate work and the bureaucratic realities of academic employment, whether permanent or temporary?

These—perhaps impertinent—questions are meant to return our attention to the *inescapable* situation that has constrained all of the reform efforts discussed in the preceding chapters, which may be summarized as follows: the academy is not simply a set of administrative, curricular, and pedagogical practices; it is also the people who have been captured and rewarded by those practices. As we have seen, this fact can be dismissed as irrelevant; it can be viewed as a curse hampering reform; it can even be regarded as a manageable problem that can be worked around. We have also seen that while it is certainly true that changing administrative, curricular, and pedagogical practices may alter the experience of higher education for those who enter the system in the future, such changes are unlikely to be seen as desirable by those already resident in the system. And because those already in the system will tolerate only incremental adjustments to their working conditions, the struggle between those who seek to reform the system and those resistant to such change almost naturally gives birth to a rhetorical world where endless calumny gets heaped on those whom the system rewarded in the past—they are lazy, old, ignorant, behind the times, immoral, angry, bitter—and unrestricted praise gets laid at the feet of those about to enter the system—they are honest, hard-working, the best and the brightest, dedicated, patient, thoughtful, sincere. With the battle lines so drawn, those interested in radically altering the bureaucratic delivery of higher education are left with very few options beyond wishful thinking: if only all the people already in the system could be retired or "reeducated," if only an alternative educational regime could be established, if only jobs could be created elsewhere for our students, then it would be possible to achieve economic parity, a measure of social justice, a more humane educational environment, a cultural revolution.

Of course, none of these options is actually available on the local level, but beckoning toward such lofty goals without developing and then acting on a plan for achieving them serves an important institutional function: it reinstantiates the critical intellectual as the academy's moral conscience—the lone voice of the dreamer who is fundamentally opposed to the senseless but indomitable forces motivating the bureaucrats who populate the administration. To escape the thunderous rhetoric that inevitably results when such archetypes come into contact, however, one need only observe that these figures—the abused student, the earnest reformer, the entrenched faculty, the indifferent administration, the incompetent profession—are all stock types, dutifully fulfilling the parts assigned to them in the melodrama of educational reform. To be sure, recognizing that persistent calls to reform academic practice have a generic form does not deprive those calls of their urgency, for whether the call is made by Paulo Freire, Allan Bloom, or Cary Nelson, the unfolding drama about the vulnerable individual who must contend with seemingly immutable and certainly unreasonable rules and regulations inevitably captures the essence of the working conditions everyone faces in our highly bureaucratized world. The greatest horror in this drama is for the individual to be swallowed up by this world and become part of its undifferentiated mass of paper pushers. We see this horror arise in Nelson at the very thought that he might be required to descend back into the business of composition instruction, which, with its incessant circulation and assessment of student work, is from his perspective the academic equivalent of being returned to the secretarial pool. To be demoted to such a station is to lose one's hard-earned prestige: it is, quite literally, "*de*-moralizing," since the demotion is seen to deprive the intellectual of the critical distance necessary to assume an institutionally sanctioned position of moral superiority over others.

By focusing on educators who have sought to reform academic practices, I have departed from this more common understanding of "critical work" as the province of those who generate critique. Indeed, one might say that I have tried to "re-moralize" the intellectual mired in bureaucratic necessities, daily teaching requirements, mandatory acts of assessment. In closing, I would like to consider why this critical reversal in itself fails to provide the analytic tools necessary for constructing reform projects that are both feasible and humane. After all, we have seen that the general assumption of an agonistic relationship between academics and administrators serves important therapeutic and structural functions. It doesn't follow, however, that problematizing the assumed distinctions between intellectual and bureaucratic labor will assist those committed to developing curricular, pedagogical, and evaluative reforms that will actually alter how the academy goes about its business and who it employs to do that business. Indeed, there are good reasons to believe that problematizing this relationship might impede progress toward such reforms, since blurring these boundaries deprives intellectuals and reformers of the very moral authority they draw on to generate and defend their proposals. To put this another way, all intellectuals who commit themselves to reforming the academy immediately get caught up in an inescapable structural contradiction: the moment the reform effort moves from the planning stage to implementation, the intellectual is in danger of becoming entrapped by the bureaucratic machinery necessary for designing, delivering, and then assessing the new educational product or experience the proposed reform seeks to make available to those en route to the academy.

Confronted with such seeming dirty work, teachers at all levels regularly convene to lament that "education is now being treated as if it were a business," determinedly ignorant of the fact that, as the preceding analyses have clearly shown, education has been a business *for well over a century* and is sure to remain one for the foreseeable future. Because bureaucratic detail and business interests are seen to be inimical to our fond notions about the pursuit of knowledge — ideally a selfless act, a spiritual adventure, a pure quest for truth — discussion about how to discriminate between different ways of carrying out the business of higher education has floundered. Consequently, those who have been willing or have been compelled to do the work of setting admissions standards, designing curricula, establishing appropriate modes of assessment, and generating adequate grievance procedures — those people, in other words, who have had to choose between one set of bureaucratic practices and another — have been left to labor in a kind of critical darkness.

It has been one of my concerns here to show that, historically, laboring in this critical darkness has not prevented those committed to reforming the academy from devising a range of strategies for coming to terms with the administrative demands that simultaneously constrain and enable the educational enterprise. Standing outside the system, one can declare oneself an "alien," as Matthew Arnold did, and critique the government's management of social affairs from afar; standing against the research system, one can construct a curriculum that is expressly antivocational, as Hutchins and Adler did at the University of Chicago and Buchanan and Barr did at St. John's; standing against the system that promotes a belief in disinterested knowledge, one can assist students in seeing the presence of business interests in the seemingly neutral area of popular culture, as U203's course team did at the Open University; and finally, standing against systems of racial and economic discrimination, one can train teachers to rethink their assumptions about language use in the classroom, as Shirley Brice Heath has done. But whether one withdraws from the administrative realities of a system that ceaselessly solicits and assesses student work, as Arnold attempted to do, or one immerses oneself in that business in hopes of altering what it is that students are asked to do and how their efforts are to be evaluated, as all the other reformers discussed here sought to do, the only certain outcome is that the reformer's dream of escaping institutional constraint will *never* be realized. Things will never work out exactly as planned; the results will never be just what was expected; contingencies will always arise; unanticipated resistances are certain to proliferate. Consequently, to enjoy some small measure of success, any effort at reform must be conceived of not as an isolated act but as an ongoing process that forever needs to be tended to, monitored, and nurtured. The educational system, in other words, will always reveal itself not to be fixed once and for all by some pronouncement from on high or by some set of well-thought-out reforms that have been implemented, but rather to be perpetually in need of fixing.

For most who work in the academy, the inescapability of this dynamic, which retards progress in *any* given direction, is the source of considerable frustration. It is yet one more argument about the virtues of retiring to the security of one's own classroom or office, where one's designs can, presumably, be realized more immediately, if on a much smaller scale. And, to be sure, given the complexities involved in effecting institutional change, the maze of macro- and microbureaucratic detail to be negotiated, the certitude that, at best, whatever gains can be made will only be achieved incrementally over broad stretches of time, and the inevitable disappointments along the way, there are good reasons for seeing the effort to reform academic practice as fool's work. Indeed, once one factors into the reform equation the necessity of addressing the concerns of those already employed in the business of higher education, the enterprise may seem utterly hopeless. To glimpse just how profound are the mental and psychological barriers that impede the actual work of reforming work practices in the academy we need only recall that Nelson finds demoralizing and intolerable not the business of concocting a "twelve-step" program for the profession that will *never* be adopted, but the very thought that he might be required to participate in the instruction of entry-level students. And by insisting that he *could not* do such work as well as his graduate students, Nelson exemplifies a strain of the profession that strategically represents itself as beyond the reach of instruction, remediation, retraining, reform — as, in effect, an unteachable, depleted human resource.

We need not despair as we recognize the prevalence of such sensibilities in the academic community, however. Rather, understanding this mind-set can be the first step in constructing a reform project that addresses not only the administrative mechanisms that govern academic life but also the cultural realities produced by those same mechanisms and deeply felt by those employed in the business of education. In other words, conceding that institutional reform is inevitably constrained by the presence of those already in the system means accepting that the thoughts, desires, and motivations of those whom the system has rewarded must be respectfully engaged if such reform is to have any chance of success. The collapse of Hutchins's efforts at the University of Chicago, discussed at length in Chapter 3, most vividly illustrates the dangers of dismissing the concerns of the resident workforce, since Hutchins could sustain his sweeping reforms only as long as he wielded enough power to silence and terrorize his foes. During this period, Hutchins's detractors did what any group with limited access to cultural power does when under attack: they hunkered down and waited out the storm, participating in all the time-honored forms of resistance at the disposal of those who labor in immense bureaucratic systems. Some luminaries resigned in spectacular fashion, some tenured faculty carried on public skirmishes with the president and his followers, but most members of the community participated in the reforms as required, dragged their feet when it was expedient and prudent to do so, and sighed in relief when the system returned to something like its former orientation. Similarly, when Barr and Buchanan sought to uproot the faculty, staff, and student body in Annapolis and take the Great Books program on the road, no one followed them, because to have done so would have been, in all respects, an act of pure folly, one that would have demanded that the followers renounce all ties to the local community, abandon the campus, and willingly give up the hard-won comfort of knowing what lay ahead in exchange for an evanescent vision of what Barr and Buchanan insisted would have been a better life.

As these examples show, treating real members of the academy—be they students, teachers, or administrators—as disembodied ideas to be discarded or moved about at will inevitably undermines any effort to institute sustainable reform, since these players in the drama of higher education exist not as ideas but as historical beings, with reasons for their actions and thoughts that are not necessarily amenable to revision through argumentation or even through the imposition of administrative force. In this regard, intellectuals, administrators, and students are no different from anyone else who works in a large bureaucratic system: they need to be *persuaded* that change is necessary, they would prefer to exercise some control over how change is implemented and assessed, and they want to be certain that the proposed changes will not make their own work obsolete or more difficult. If these conditions aren't met—and they almost never are—then the affected parties offer public conformity and private resistance, engaging in what Scott calls an "undeclared ideological guerrilla war" that is fought with "rumor, gossip, disguises, linguistic tricks, metaphors, euphemisms, folktales, ritual gestures, anonymity" (137). However understandable it may be that even the most well-intentioned efforts to reform academic practice provoke such divided responses, by way of conclusion I would like to consider the degree to which this resistance to change and perceived sense of powerlessness can be put to work improving academic working conditions.

To complete the trajectory of this book's argument, which has moved from the past to the present, from the "alien" to the local, I draw my closing example from a graduate seminar I have taught for the past two years in the English department at Rutgers University. In this case, as with those that have preceded it, it is worth considering the multiple forces motivating and constraining all the players in the field. This seminar, "The Teaching of Writing," is required for all graduate students assigned to teach the introductory composition course, EN101, for the first time. Like all required courses, both the graduate seminar and EN101 tend to be perceived by those in attendance as elementary, inessential, perhaps even the product of a punitive administrative gesture. Furthermore, in the wake of the efflorescence of Foucauldianism, this particular graduate seminar is likely to be seen as a disciplinary mechanism that openly relies on panopticism to exercise its power: the graduate students *must* all teach out of the same textbook; they *must* meet the Writing Program's requirements for the minimum number of assigned drafts and revisions; they *must* conform to the Writing Program's standards for responding to and assessing student work; they *must* pass the seminar in order to continue teaching in the program; twice a semester, they *must* submit their student papers, along with their comments, grades, and assignments, for outside evaluation; and, finally, they *must* continue to abide by these requirements and submit to this review for as long as they continue to be employed by the program. In short, in exchange for tuition remission, a modest annual stipend, and health benefits, the graduate students *must* agree to submit to the demands of the Writing Program. They are not free to teach what they like. They are not free to teach as they might like. They are not free to teach whomever they would like.

On its face, this would not appear to be the ideal teaching situation. And, in fact, the seminar can't help but begin in an atmosphere fraught with tension, because the student-teachers' presence in the seminar is institutionally compelled, because the Writing Program further constrains what it is the student-teachers are allowed to do in their classrooms, and, finally, because the student-teachers are pursuing advanced graduate work that has no obvious relation to their instructional tasks. As Scott might have predicted, many of the graduate students in the seminar find sufficiently ambiguous ways to communicate their genuine sense of having been betrayed by a system that requires them to receive such instruction: after all, they feel quite keenly the genuine disjunction between the content of their education, which has entailed struggling to understand postmodern theory, to master the evolving canon of postcolonial fiction, to plumb the depths of literary history, and to cover the areas in their comprehensive exams, and the content of their employment, which requires them to find ways to communicate with students for whom stringing together two coherent paragraphs is an achievement. Aren't their intellectual powers being wasted in such menial labor? Hasn't something gone terribly wrong with the system that has produced this sharp disjunction between the education they're receiving and the work that is being required of them? Couple these well-warranted misgivings with the other emotions that accompany the work of teaching—the persistent fears of inadequacy, the frustrations of not capitalizing on unexpected moments in class discussion, the unfamiliarity with a new system of instruction—and all the necessary ingredients for a pitched pedagogical battle seem to be in place.

These are the emotional realities that define the seminar at its outset and they are among the constraints that I must respect and work with as part of my responsibilities toward this particular student population. Of course, given the power relations that further constrain all the players in this drama, it would certainly be possible to proceed as if these concerns did not exist, a strategy that would allow the seminar's discussions to focus exclusively on the narrowest, most instrumental understanding of what writing instruction entails—namely, the business of producing expository prose that is well-organized and relatively free of surface errors. In some ways, providing a course of this kind would be easier on everyone: it would reduce a rich area of intellectual inquiry to the mechanical work of prose tidying—a kind of scholarly chore best carried out quickly so as to make even more room for the work the graduate students must complete in order to continue their progress toward their degrees. Obviously, offering such a course would hardly be unprecedented in the history of composition studies, which is littered with just such instrumentalist approaches to the business of training entry-level students to write. Whatever appeal there might be to teaching such a course, though, doing so would clearly violate the standards that my department and the director of the Writing Program have set for teacher training at Rutgers. Thus, even if my disciplinary training didn't prevent me from representing the work of composition studies as "demoralizing and intolerable"—which it does—the local culture at my home institution would militate against my reducing this central departmental responsibility to the equivalent of a dreary stint in purgatory.

Such departmental requirements also reflect local decisions about what graduate students must know in order to function professionally. And, as anyone who follows recent trends in academic hiring can attest, the truth is that regardless of how graduate students in English may *feel* about the work of teaching composition, most of the available jobs require the instructor to spend considerable time working with entry-level students. As we have seen, there are plenty of examples of academics who decry this fact, seeing in it evidence of everything from a collapse in academic standards (why admit students who can't write?) to the bureaucratizing of the university. But even those who voice such longings for the academic life of some bygone era must concede that the relatively brief period when being an English professor meant teaching exclusively in the area of one's expertise to a self-selecting student populace is all but over. This is not to say that there are *no* jobs available that free one to teach what one wants, when one wants, in the way one wants, to the students one wants or that it is *completely* impossible for someone entering the field to land such a job. It is rather to recognize that regardless of talent and expertise, most graduate students aiming to enter the profession at this time can anticipate spending a significant part of their teaching career working with entry-level students, participating in an educational exchange that bears almost no resemblance to the kind of exuberant pedagogical fantasies portrayed in *The Dead Poets Society*.

At the risk of breaking with the professional consensus that this shift in the job market and the ongoing redefinition of what constitutes work in the profession is wholly to be lamented, I would like to suggest that this shift in the job market is better understood as an opportunity for anyone truly interested in becoming a public intellectual, anyone committed to improving the educational chances of the disenfranchised, and anyone who has more than an academic interest in the work of theorizing and disentangling encounters with difference. The twilight of the profession, in other words, can also be seen as the slow dawning of a new profession, one that may well be more committed to meeting the needs of students on the margins of the academy, more responsive to the concerns of the local community, and more prepared to set in motion a range of pedagogical and bureaucratic practices that can provide instruction in the arts of working within and against systems of constraint. That I find these possibilities exciting and even desirable does not mean I have forgotten that this vision of what the profession might evolve into is not the vision that lures most people to graduate school, nor does their attractiveness enable me to ignore the great deal of agony, disappointment, and anger that this shift in the job market has occasioned. To the contrary, thinking about the profession as it is and as it might become has compelled me to convene a graduate seminar on "The Teaching of Writing" in which those preparing to enter the profession are encouraged to consider together what a career of teaching and scholarship entails, whether they want to pursue such work, and what standards they might draw on to assess whether or not any given career should be deemed a success.

In the seminar itself, these issues take concrete form once the graduate students begin to confront the challenges of learning how to read the student writing that is being produced in their own courses. As they attempt to gain an understanding of the Writing Program's standards of assessment—struggling, for instance, to see what distinguishes an "A" from a "B" paper—the frustration with the course and with the Writing Program mounts. Accustomed as they are to the free play of semiosis in their own work, they are disturbed to discover that at this evaluative moment, there are no absolutely clear-cut guidelines to follow, that the methods of assessment are context-specific, that the work expected of the beginning students appears so demanding, and that the standards appear too high and the course of instruction too difficult. As it turns out, much of the course pivots on determining the source of their general frustration with the business of commenting on and grading student work, for concealed within this emotional (and therefore knowing) response resides a range of controlling assumptions about what it means to teach and learn in the academy. While this frustration surfaces in different ways for different students, it is inevitably tied up with a dissatisfaction at discovering how limiting the business of teaching can be.

Obviously, few teaching situations have as many devices for constraining and observing instructors as the one I've described here, a circumstance that often leads beginning teachers to posit the existence of a different kind of teaching where one can teach what one wants in the way one wants, assigning the grades one deems fair according to one's own standards. But while it is certainly true that there are less overtly constraining teaching situations, the important point to recognize is that *all* teaching positions in accredited programs require a terminal assessment of student work. This unavoidable process of soliciting, assessing, and responding to student work constitutes the core of the business of education, whether one is teaching entry-level students how to navigate academic prose, assisting advanced undergraduates construct independent research projects, guiding graduate students toward the successful completion of a dissertation, or commenting on submissions to an academic journal. It is doubtless the case that varying amounts of prestige accrue to those engaged in the different manifestations of this evaluative work, but the central activity of reading and assessing the labor of others remains the same, whether the labor is that of a first-year student, an advanced graduate student, a metaphysical poet, or a postmodern theorist. Thus, the absolutely predictable anxiety that emerges around the business of grading papers and the consequent desire to escape to a realm of employment where this work is less carefully scrutinized can't be understood as a discomfort with power, though it is frequently explained in these terms. Rather, this anxiety *must* be read as an expression of distress at discovering the essentially bureaucratic nature of teaching in the academy: one's work, regardless of how dutifully carried out, thoughtfully planned, or brilliantly presented, inevitably leads to a moment when students generate some response that can then be assessed. No matter what happens in the classroom, the seemingly homogenous mass must be hierarchized into varying levels of success. And even for those teachers who enjoy this evaluative work quite a bit, the business of separating the wheat from the chaff inevitably appears as a distraction from the more important work of delivering a good lecture, producing a solid piece of research, serving on an important panel at a national conference.

For those who believe that being a teacher is supposed to lead to absolutely autonomous working conditions, that the intellectual and the bureaucrat are antithetical entities, and that academic standards are not negotiable and subject to change over time, the experience of actually working in the academy is bound to be experienced as a betrayal of some sacred trust. There is no question that this felt sense of betrayal is both profoundly painful and all but completely disempowering. Indeed, the academic presses dependably churn out their annual load of bookshelf-bending diatribes about the collapse of the university, the struggle for the soul of higher education, and the imperiled academy precisely because the discovery of the bureaucratic nature of academic work is *always* news to a workforce that has been lured by the promise of academic freedom and the unbounded pleasures of the life of the mind. Perhaps the time is ripe, though, to leave off critiquing the academy for having failed to make good on its promise to deliver a meaningful, morally sacrosanct life and to begin, instead, to work within the fiscal and bureaucratic constraints that both enable the academic enterprise and limit its scope. With regard to teaching, this means recognizing that one is inescapably implicated in a bureaucratic system and therefore the best one can do is to commit oneself to the seemingly impossible project of becoming a "good bureaucrat." As noxious as such an idea is sure to sound to most, given the negative connotations of the word, this proposal is bound to appear positively repulsive to those for whom the virtues of bureaucracy are inconceivable.

It is true enough that when weighed against the pleasures that moral outrage affords, the promise held out to those who would reconsider the relationship between intellectual and bureaucratic work is modest indeed: by letting go the ideology of the intellectual's exclusively critical function, one gains the opportunity to experience a real sense of agency in the world of local academic affairs. By "a real sense of agency," I do not mean that in faithfully carrying out one's teaching duties, assigning grades fairly, promoting the academic success of all students regardless of race, class, sexual orientation, gender, or political leanings, and serving on departmental and university-wide committees one will somehow change the nature of academic work. This certainly won't happen. But to think of agency only as the ability to alter massive cultural structures, to shift the thinking of large numbers of people, or to perform any number of similarly grand feats of conversion is to effectively remove agency from the realm of human action, since no individual, working alone, has ever achieved any of these goals. If, however, agency is understood as learning how to work within extant constraints, as an activity that simultaneously preserves and creates the sense of self-worth that comes from participating in the social world, it becomes feasible to think of the higher education as ideally providing all under its power both training in and opportunities to experience the arts of such agency.

In order to make progress toward this goal, students, teachers, and administrators must develop a sufficiently nuanced understanding of how power is disseminated in a bureaucracy to see that *constraining* conditions are not *paralyzing* conditions. Such an understanding is always well within reach; as soon as one enters the school system and begins to learn about its ritualized practices, its shortcomings, its prejudices, and its strengths, one inevitably discovers that "relatively autonomous" working spaces are there to be found. Under these conditions, it isn't long before all students realize that not all teachers have the same standards, require the same amount or kind of work, respond in the same way, demand the same level of respect and punctuality, act according to the same protocols of behavior, and ascribe to the same ethical or political belief systems. Unfortunately, this common experience is generally called on to support a surprisingly unsophisticated analysis of the dynamics of power in a bureaucracy. That is, even as they perceive a spectrum of constraint, students, teachers, and administrators alike tend to analyze this spectrum in exclusively dyadic terms. There are those places where one is free—for the student, this means those rare classes where the teacher values one's work; for the teacher, this sense of freedom is likely to arise in response to being allowed to decide the content of instruction; for the beleaguered administrator, freedom may come only when one is on vacation, away from the reach of the office. And, then, there are all the other places where one is paralyzed, where one's work is nothing more than empty response to mandatory requirements—for teachers, students, and administrators, this could well describe the vast majority of experiences within the school system. When this is how life in a bureaucracy is understood and experienced, it is not surprising that fantasies of escape and thundering jeremiads about the system's gross inequities result.

It is important to recognize that such outraged responses are functional at a certain level, since they successfully reinscribe each player in his or her role in the academy's melodrama. This does not mean, however, that the speaker succeeds in attaining some less tainted space. For, as we have seen, even those most interested in reforming the system have found it impossible to escape the bureaucratic machinery of assessing and evaluating the work of others. And, as we have also seen, all the fulminating moral posturing in the world does nothing to change this essential aspect of modern life. So what remains, for those who want to change what can be changed, is tinkering on the margins of the academy—altering admissions standards; contributing to the slow, sustained, all-but-anonymous work of designing curricula that are more responsive to a range of learning practices and cultural backgrounds; training teachers to think differently about the assumptions underlying the idea of native intelligence; participating actively in hiring decisions; and providing instruction at all levels in the arts of discovering the possibilities that emerge when one sets out first to enumerate and then work on and within extant constraints. Such modest adjustments won't overthrow the university, of course. Nor will capitalism be brought to its knees. Nor, finally, will the manifest social injustices of an institution that trades in the business of naturalizing and then hierarchizing the citizenry's culturally produced differences be permanently eradicated. The most one can hope for is that fostering the development of this hybrid persona—the intellectual-bureaucrat—will produce an academic environment that rewards versatility as well as specialization, teaching as well as research, public service as well as investment in the self. But by providing students with the opportunity to rethink the assumed opposition between the academy and the business world, the intellectual and the bureaucrat, it may just be possible also to promote the development of sensibility that can bear thinking creatively about administrative matters—a state of mind that will seek to ensure that institutional working and learning conditions approach the humane ideal that resides at the core of all efforts to democratize access to higher education.

The academy is actually already well positioned to make the modest shift necessary to begin working in this direction. Recent work in cultural studies and postmodern theory, as well as ongoing efforts to understand sub-ject-formation in relation to race, class, and gender, has provided much of the critical knowledge that being a "good bureaucrat" requires. That is, one who would take on the hybrid persona of the intellectual-bureaucrat would apparently have to possess remarkable tolerance for ambiguity, an appreci-ation for structured contradictions, a perspicacity that draws into its purview the multiple forces determining individual events and actions, an understanding of the essentially performative character of public life, and a recognition of the inherently political character of all matters emerging from the power/knowledge nexus. All of these attributes are highly valued on the contemporary critical scene; all of them might be put into service in the act of brokering administered change. While the critical knowledge available could assist in redirecting attention to the bureaucratic realities and exigencies of higher education, this project also has at its disposal a workforce that brings with it a storehouse of lived experience that necessar-ily includes successful strategies for navigating a bureaucratic system and ideas about ways to make the system function more efficiently, if not more humanely.

While this wealth of critical and experiential knowledge would seem to provide a promising foundation upon which to construct an academic cul-ture that valued the anonymous labor of the intellectual-bureaucrat more highly, it would be foolish to imagine that the predictable revulsion at the notion of bureaucratic work can be overcome either by reasoned argument or by gestures toward the body of evidence documenting the collapse of a market for purely intellectual labor. One need only try to find a positive representation of a bureaucrat to understand how deep the enmity for this kind of labor runs. After all, from a commonsense perspective, what possi-ble attraction could there be to the work of pettifogging, paper-pushing, rule-bound, ring-kissing, social automatons? Indeed, the search for a posi-tive representation of the bureaucrat reveals how bureaucracies figure across the entire narrative spectrum as the social space that true individuals avoid at all costs. For regardless of whether the particular bureaucrats rep-resented are personnel from the military, government services, law enforce-ment, education, or the political sphere, generic conventions require that all dignity, honor, and glory go to those who distinguish themselves from this faceless mass of "men in suits" and their duplicitous behavior.

A rare and particularly instructive exception to this rule is *Citizen X*, Chris Gerolmo's 1995 film about the real-life effort to capture the Soviet se-rial killer Andrei Chikatilo. The story's opening is conventional enough: it pits Viktor Burakov, a newly assigned police forensics expert, against a large, utterly unconcerned, and immobile bureaucratic system. Thus, when Burakov announces to his superiors that a serial killer is responsible for the death of thirteen young children whose bodies have been discovered spread about the local countryside, the knowing viewer can't be surprised when the massive Soviet bureaucracy dismisses his allegations on the grounds that serial killing is "a decadent Western phenomenon." When Burakov takes his complaint to his immediate superior, Col. Mikhail Fetisov, he is told that the panel leader who refused his request for assistance "may be a stupid man, but he is in charge."

While *Citizen X* commences with this familiar opposition between the intellectual and the bureaucrat, the film is remarkable in that it resists the equally familiar resolution to this conflict, where the intellectual either triumphs over or is roundly defeated by the mindless bureaucratic machine. Perhaps because the film strives to be responsible to the historical record, it opts for a murkier course, recasting Burakov's eight-year search for Chikatilo as the story of a diligent investigator's attempt to reconcile himself to the inescapable realities of a bureaucratic world where, more often than not, a stupid man is, indeed, in charge. Burakov—the intellectual, the expert, the detective—is by no means a willing or happy student during this process of "reeducation," of course. It is not difficult to understand his frustration and rage: he has discovered a pattern that points to the existence of a serial killer; he has followed procedure and brought his discovery to the attention of his superiors; and he has had to watch helplessly as his superiors demonstrate that they have no higher interest than preserving their own power and prestige. The intellectual has detected a problem, but he can't find a way to make the bureaucrats care about the problem, and so he boils over in anger.

Fetisov sees and understands Burakov's frustration and tries to explain to him that there is *no way* around the bureaucratic system: "The only way that I have been able to get anything done," he says to the detective, "is behind closed doors, by hoarding favors, by bribing, by wheedling." Such an "explanation" simply further fuels Burakov's rage, which in turn compels him to blurt out to his superior the observation that, while time is being wasted in such indirection, children will continue to die at the hands of the unknown serial killer. What Burakov can't understand, because he has given himself over to his moral outrage, is that Fetisov is well aware of consequences of the bureaucracy's relative inaction: "It will take all our strength to suffer these outrages, but suffer them we must because we are the people who have to catch this monster. You and I. As you may have noticed, no one else is even willing to try."

Again, with the lives of innocent children weighing in the balance, it is not surprising that Burakov finds little solace in Fetisov's words. In fact, as far as Burakov is concerned, he's merely been treated to some faceless bureaucrat's automatic and insincere expression of regret. Consequently, as Fetisov turns to leave, Burakov concludes the exchange by issuing the accusation that is always ready to hand when the moral figure of the intellectual and the unprincipled figure of the bureaucrat square off. "You care about nothing but making your superiors happy," he says to Fetisov, to which his superior replies, "You're right. I should spend more time trying to alienate them. Perhaps you could teach me." As the search drags on and the killings continue (Chikatilo was ultimately convicted of murdering fifty-two children), Burakov continues to treat Fetisov with the contempt one reserves for one's moral inferiors. Thus, when Fetisov informs Burakov that some amusing gossip about a high Soviet official has surfaced during the interrogation of a prisoner, Burakov sneers, "You think a man is what he says, don't you, Colonel?" Once more, Fetisov responds with words that Burakov cannot understand: "He is if he talks for a living." Burakov, the idealist, presses the point, insisting that "a man is what he fights for." Fetisov replies, without any apparent regrets, "Well, I don't fight for anything."

At this point in the action, Burakov and Fetisov appear to embody the antithetical interests of the intellectual and the bureaucrat—the former determined to capture a real threat to society, the other enjoying a salacious glimpse into someone else's private life. As it turns out, though, Burakov's contemptuous moral superiority has prevented him from recognizing the importance of the gossip Fetisov has overheard. He hasn't attended to what Fetisov has told him about how change is effected at the upper echelons of a bureaucracy, where people are employed, by and large, to talk for a living. It is only later, when Burakov realizes that Fetisov has successfully deployed the gossip he's overheard to neutralize Burakov's most powerful critic, that Burakov comes to appreciate Fetisov's ability to manipulate the bureaucratic system dominating both of their lives.

From that point on, Burakov and Fetisov begin to learn from each other. Burakov figures out how to manipulate his superiors to achieve his own ends and he concedes that often it is necessary, as he puts it, to "sprinkle a little sugar" in order to have the investigation function smoothly. For his part, Fetisov finds his tolerance for the stupidity of his superiors has receded and, in its place, an overwhelming passion for finding the killer surfaces, filling him with such rage that he is unable to act effectively at a crucial moment in the investigation. Thus, at the film's climax, with Chikatilo in custody but refusing to confess to Fetisov's superior from Moscow—a man hungry for the glory of having closed the case—it is Burakov who is able to convince Fetisov's superior to step aside so that the psychologist, Bukhanovsky, might have a chance with the prisoner. When it matters most, Burakov shows that he has come to understand why it is so important to learn how to work within bureaucracy's constraints and that doing so need not compromise the ends one desires. Thus, when Bukhanovsky emerges from the cell, having elicited Chikatilo's confession, his final judgment concerns not the serial killer, whose guilt was known all along, but rather the relationship between Burakov and Fetisov, where the moral ground seems much less firm. Parting company with the intellectual and the bureaucrat, Bukhanovsky says simply, "May I say that together you make a wonderful person."

This is a fitting sentiment to close on, as it captures what is, at this historical moment, the essential and necessarily symbiotic relationship that exists between the intellectual and bureaucrat, each of whom depends on the other to make the work that they do possible and meaningful. It is certainly the case that the academy can continue to operate, as it has from the outset, by seeing work in these spheres as fundamentally opposed. And there are undoubtedly compelling reasons for steadfastly refusing to entertain the possibility that these two spheres might be made to function in concert. However, for those of us weary of feeling utterly powerless—those of us interested in translating into a workable plan of action the dissatisfaction with institutional life that makes itself known everywhere in all of our lives—overcoming the deep revulsion we all feel for the bureaucratic conditions that simultaneously constrain and enable our labor in the academy may well be the best chance we have for shaping how the business of intellectual inquiry gets carried out in the future. That is, if shifts in the job market and in hiring trends do indeed signal that the academy is undergoing a radical reformation at the hands of economic powers over which no single individual or corporate entity exercises control, the best strategy available to anyone seeking to enter or remain in the profession may well involve fabricating for oneself and for the academic community at large some inhabitable version of the intellectual-bureaucrat.

Notes

Chapter 1. Thinking with Students: Deliberations on the History of Educational Reform

1. For more on the failure of the academic left to rebut Bloom's critique of higher education, see J. Miller. While Miller is concerned with highlighting the resilience of Bloom's argument after a decade of assault, I prefer to draw attention to the unquestioned assumption that refuting Bloom might be of any material consequence at the level of educational practice.

2. Stanley Fish and Dinesh D'Souza, for example, went on tour from September 1991 to March 1992 debating all matters curricular before capacity crowds at college campuses across the nation. See Fish 51–101 for his contributions to these debates.

3. In this way, Graff's proposal in *Professing Literature* illustrates the dynamic relationship that exists between a given historiographic approach to education and what subsequently becomes imaginable as a reform project: studying "the conflicts" leads to an argument for "teaching the conflicts." My own work demonstrates this dynamic as well, since my interest in various institutional constructions of "the student" has led me to argue for the importance of seeing the business of educational reform as intellectual work that is carried out in specific, bureaucratic contexts.

4. For my extended analysis of the relationship between Graff's historical approach and his subsequent reform proposals, see R. Miller, "Composing English Studies." See also Graff's response, "Conflict Pedagogy," and my rejoinder, "Ships."

5. Rose illustrates what is to be gained by moving beyond the official documents and debates of the educational sphere and into actual classrooms.

6. For a critique of methodologies that depend on generating a felt sense of surprise, see Guillory; for a critique of the current reliance on narrative in the academy, see Simpson, *Academic Postmodern*. These critiques do not apply to my use of surprise and of narrative, however. Far from seeking to deploy my own sense of surprise as evidence of what Guillory calls a "quasi-exteriority to the institution" (244), my methodology involves situating moments of surprise precisely within an educational history that permeates the purportedly "private space between the master and the disciple"—a space that is, in fact, overwritten by the curriculum, dominant teaching practices, and the structure of the institution itself. Furthermore, while Simpson sees the academic turn to narrative as a longing for a return to "preprofessional culture" (62), my concern here is to demonstrate that "telling a story" about learning is a historically and discursively constrained act: what can be said about the scene of instruction is restricted by, among other things, the insistence that this experience be described as a voyage from ignorance to understanding. By acknowledging these constraints and working within them here, I aim not to forge some purer communion with the reader but rather to establish my place inside the profession and my awareness of its cultural commonplaces.

7. Richard Nice, the translator of *Distinction*, offers a definition of misrecognition that draws on a common pedagogical event: " 'Misrecognition' (*méconnais-*

sance) combines subjective non-recognition (blindness) with objective recognition (legitimation); for example, a teacher who observes his pupils' 'gifts,' or lack of them, and who imagines he is indifferent to social class, objectively helps to legitimate the causes and effects of cultural inequality" (in Bourdieu, *Distinction* 566 n. 46).

8. See Aronowitz and Giroux, for example, who object to "the mechanistic notions of power and domination and the overly determined view of human agency that characterizes much of [Bourdieu's] work" (83). The "dialogic method of knowledge acquisition" that Aronowitz and Giroux support is no less mechanistic, however: to achieve this "dialogic method," for instance, they recommend that teachers "be required to themselves become intellectuals in the technical sense, that is, attain a degree of mastery over the legacy of high culture as well as assimilate and validate the elements of students' experience, which is intimately bound with popular culture" (158). This additional training would, in turn, lead to the eventual collapse of the market for cultural capital: "The point [of revising teacher training in this way] is not to reproduce high culture; the point is to make these works a part of our popular culture and eventually, on the basis of selection, eliminate their canonical status entirely" (159).

9. While the history of composition studies is undoubtedly populated with instrumentalist approaches to language acquisition and instruction, anyone who characterizes the entire field as favoring a technobureaucratic mission misunderstands how cultural capital circulates in this realm of the profession and is wholly unaware of the field's ongoing debate about the role of "the personal" in writing instruction. For his purposes, though, Guillory is content to allow composition to figure as the beachhead on which "the technobureaucrats" have secured a foothold for launching their attacks on the essentially antibureaucratic work of literary studies.

10. At the end of *Cultural Capital*, Guillory acknowledges that there is no chance that the aesthetic experience will be universalized, since "socializing the means of production and consumption is only a thought experiment" (340). These final words are apparently meant to bear a certain self-ironic pathos, with their reference to Marx's "thought experiment" in *The German Ideology* about life in a communist society where, as Guillory puts it, "no one is a painter because everyone is (or can be)" (338).

11. On this point, my overarching concern with how commitments to theoretical, methodological, ideological, and evidentiary purity prevent the intellectual from acting on or analyzing the "impure" world of lived experience overlaps with Guillory's effort to explain why interest in the aesthetic has declined. Guillory attributes this decline to "the discourse of purity" that has suppressed the obvious fact that "the experience of *any* cultural work is an experience of an always composite pleasure" (336, original emphasis). As I will show, pedagogical materials and the artifacts of educational reform, more generally, rarely imagine the student as capable of "an always composite" response to the experience of schooling.

12. We are, of course, always awash in such statistical information, which means both that there is always evidence to support radically opposed programs of reform and that there is always an argument for collecting more information before acting. This doesn't mean that all this information is essentially useless, however.

For example, according to the *New York Times*, a recent study has confirmed—once again—that economic class plays the most significant role in determining school success, thereby providing evidence in support of the argument for expanding the availability of financial aid to low-income families (Honan). Furthermore, this report's finding that a child's aspirations with regards to higher education have been solidified by the eighth grade makes it clear that university-level reforms only affect a population already dramatically reduced by teaching and testing practices at the lower levels. Thus, to become engaged in the process of designing and implementing workable plans that will address the problem of producing and nurturing a desire for advanced education—indeed, even to recognize this as a problem—is to accept one's enmeshment in a bureaucratic system that necessarily views the population as a site of problematization in need of better management.

Chapter 2. Ministering to a Mind Diseased: Matthew Arnold, Her Majesty's Inspector

1. See, for example, Lipman: "Why, a century and a quarter after its initial appearance, should we read *Culture and Anarchy*? My answer is simple. Because we need culture, and we have anarchy" (213).

2. The relationship between educational practices in India and Great Britain is, in fact, much more complicated than Said's brief account allows. Before the British began forcing the people of India to speak and study English, they were importing Indian pedagogical practices into the British educational system. Dr. Andrew Bell, who recorded seeing in India "a youth of eleven years of age, with his little assistants under him, teaching upwards of fifty boys," is credited with bringing the "monitorial method" of instruction to Great Britain, where it was adopted by the two philanthropic organizations responsible for educating the poor (qtd. in Hyndman 17).

3. While Super admits he is "probably alone in thinking that Arnold meant this obviously exaggerated statement (as it must have seemed to him) from one of his father's private letters (where, for all we know, it was meant humorously) as fun" (qtd. in Walcott 130 n. 70), Keating makes a much more compelling case for seeing this passage as evidence of the depth of Arnold's commitment to bringing about a cultural change. As Keating puts it, for Arnold to "have spoken so strongly for culture without wishing to make it prevail would have been to become the aesthetic trifler his critics tried to see him as" (234).

4. To be sure, Arnold's writing shows up in important documents of educational reform. But citation does not necessarily establish influence: it can be read just as well as a strategy for gaining approval for decisions made elsewhere. Arnold is cited, for example, at the beginning of the Newbolt Report, as the committee sets about launching its argument that teaching English can serve to create a national culture: "Matthew Arnold, using the word in its true sense, claimed that 'Culture unites classes.' He might have added that a system of education which disunites classes cannot be held worthy of the name of a national culture. In this respect we have

even fallen away from an earlier and better tradition" (*Teaching of English* 6). As Baldick points out, though, Arnold did not in fact write "Culture unites classes," but rather that culture "seeks to do away with classes" (qtd. in Baldick 95). And, of course, in using Arnold to harken back to an "earlier and better tradition," the authors of the Newbolt Report forget that Arnold saw his own time as having itself "fallen away from" a former ideal. In other words, to determine the degree to which Arnold's thinking actually shaped this document, which misquotes him and repackages his moment as an occasion for nostalgia, one would need to pursue the kind of historical approach to educational reform that I outlined in Chapter 1.

5. All citations from Arnold's *Reports on Elementary Schools* are taken from the Marvin edition.

6. That Arnold thinks Shakespeare's plays are best read as poetry is clear from the fact that two of the ten "touchstones" of high poetic quality he refers to in "The Study of Poetry" come from Shakespeare's plays, none from his sonnets (169–70).

7. While not specifically concerned with this example, Willinsky argues that this division of intellectual labor between what students and critics are meant to do with poetry is the Arnoldian legacy that has been passed on to those who work in English Studies. We will see, however, that as an inspector of schools, Arnold was hardly free to pose questions of his own choosing to the students: although the examination question appears to be Arnold's, it is actually the state's way of transforming the act of reading into a measurable event.

8. It wasn't until I. A. Richards's system of reading protocols was institutionalized that the estimation of poetic quality was rescued from this silent interiority and made into a visible object subject to public evaluation. For more on how Richards's exam moved English Studies away from mere " 'fact-grubbing' on the one hand and vague impressionism on the other," see Baldick 155–56; Bové 39–78.

9. Contrary to those who imagine Arnold as having possessed some unique insight into the educational process, Ball insists that "there is little in the views [his School Reports] express to distinguish them from those of other Inspectors; indeed, much of what Arnold had to say before the time of the Revised Code, as to fees, pupil-teachers, class-teaching, infant schools and schools too poor to benefit from the Minutes of 1846, had already been said many times by the Inspectors" covered in her study (233–34).

10. For a consideration of the theory and practice of the monitorial method, see Silver and Silver.

11. Although Arnold's career and his thinking were profoundly influenced by his work for this commission, Pattison makes no mention of this time of government service in his memoirs.

12. In this regard, Foucault is uncharacteristically nostalgic when he laments the replacement of the instruction of apprentices in guilds by exam-driven instruction in schools (187–91). Foucault overlooks the many for whom the guild system would never have validated "an acquired aptitude," whereas the examination system, because it functions as a "constant exchanger of knowledge" (187), has come over time to afford many of these formerly excluded people the opportunity to enter into the system of exchange. Here, as elsewhere, Foucault's preference for subjugated invisi-

bility as opposed to disciplinary subjugation exposes the borders of his utopian vision.

13. The table of examination standards that accompanied the Revised Code, a copy of which may be found in Appendix 1 of Fearon, provides a shining example of one such a *tableau vivant*. Fearon distinguishes "examination" and "inspection" in the following way: "many a teacher, who, if his school had been only examined, would have set his failures down to bad luck, has been convinced by a thorough but kindly inspection, that he has only himself to blame for them, and that it is his own fault if such failures ever recur" (2).

14. Though Lowe is regularly reviled by educational historians for the role he played in determining the shape and the content of elementary instruction in Britain, Sylvester argues convincingly that Lowe "did not invent the principle of payment by results. The idea was already common coin when Lowe decided to implement it as a policy for financing public elementary schools" (57). Corroborating this point, Winter notes that well before Lowe's ascendancy to power, Kay-Shuttleworth had "directed inspectors to hold examinations in reading, writing, and arithmetic, and to withhold funds from schools where the results were unsatisfactory" (177).

15. Arnold reiterates this point in his General Report for 1867, where he informs his superiors, "The truth is, what really needed to be dealt with, in 1862 as at present, was the irregular attendance and premature withdrawal of scholars, not the imperfect performance of their duties by the teachers; but it was far easier to change the course of school instruction and inspection, and to levy forfeitures for imperfect school results upon managers and teachers, than to make scholars come to school regularly and stay there a sufficient time" (*Reports* 112).

16. For evidence that these predictions were warranted, see Kay-Shuttleworth's argument that "Any grant, the amount of which is determined by individual examination after a certain attendance at School, tends to cause the neglect of the irregular, dull, and migratory scholars whom *it does not pay to teach*; while, on the other hand, grants proportionate to the average attendance of scholars are a direct inducement to fill the School, but not to teach the children, if such grants are not accompanied by conditions as to the number of the teaching staff" (15, original emphasis).

17. One of Arnold's General Reports is actually cited in the Newcastle Report as evidence of why the examination process itself needed to be reformed. Having highlighted Arnold's description of examining 150 students in just an hour and a half, the report observes, "such an *examination* is only one in name. It is really *an inspection* rather than an *examination*, and cannot apply the test and stimulus, particularly to the lower classes, which a real inquiry into their knowledge secures" ("Report on Popular Education" 230, original emphasis).

18. In 1864 Lowe himself was censured for "mutilating" the reports that spoke unfavorably of his reforms and, shortly thereafter, resigned his position in the Education Department. For a remarkable account of these proceedings, see Winter 188–93.

19. This aversion to practical details was evident in Arnold's working life as well. Fitch records of his colleague, "the details of administration, the framing of syl-

labuses and schedules, and the laying down of the legal conditions under which the public grant should be assessed and distributed, were tasks not to his mind. But when questions of principle were involved, he was frequently consulted, and we who were his colleagues received from him at times very weighty and practical suggestions" (177).

20. For all the claims about Arnold's prophetic powers, the truth is that the move toward free, universal, compulsory education in Britain came as a direct result of the extension of the franchise, which Arnold had steadfastly opposed (see Simon 354–56). Lowe had also inveighed against allowing a greater percentage of the male population to vote, but once it was clear that the franchise was going to be expanded, he, in that unprincipled fashion which defines the life of a bureaucrat, came to support broader educational reforms, so that those in power could "conquer back by means of a wider and more enlightened cultivation some of the influence which they have lost by political change" (qtd. in Simon 356).

Chapter 3. "Education for Everybody": Great Books and the Democratic Ideal

1. This chapter draws on archival material from two different locations: the Houghton Library at Harvard University, Cambridge, Massachusetts (identified HL in the text), which houses the Buchanan papers, and the Maryland Archives in Annapolis, Maryland, which house the papers for St. John's College. Materials drawn from the Maryland Archives are identified in the text as coming from the Buchanan Correspondence (SBC), the Barr Correspondence (BC), or the Klein Correspondence (KC).

2. Macdonald did take a certain delight in entertaining the possibility that his review was responsible for the poor sales of the "densely printed, poorly edited, overpriced and over-syntopiconized collection" in the early fifties (258).

3. Although the University of Chicago has retained the rhetoric of having a "common core" for undergraduates, this core is now composed of a set of rubrics within which there are a range of electives. Nowhere does the catalogue evidence a commitment to Hutchins's vision of what should constitute an undergraduate's education. Rather, it explains that revisions in the university's curriculum were made to ensure "that the tension inherent in contemporary academic life—between the demand for specialization and the need to provide common learning for members of a democratic society—would be resolved in a way consonant with the College's established mission" (*Courses and Programs of Study* 3).

4. See, for instance, Gilbert and Gubar; Said; Spivak, "Multiculturalism"; Gates, "The Master's Pieces" and *Notes*; hooks; McDowell.

5. Denby is the exception here: his best-selling account of returning to the classroom to relive Columbia's yearlong course in Western classics records and reflects on student discussions of the Great Books precisely because the author feels such serious textual work is passing away from the world.

6. Erskine made these recommendations to the Great Books Foundation, a nonprofit organization established in 1947 to take over the University of Chicago's adult

education program. A subsequent study of adult learners participating in the foundation's program made clear that such recommendations were unnecessary since, in practice, the approach self-selected a homogenous group of participants: "in spite of any differences in sex, job, religion, age, generation, etc., most of the people [in the Great Books program] will be talking with others who have pretty much the same aims, and very seldom will they be talking across the table to someone who has a radically different conception of the purposes of the program" (Davis 40).

7. For a more general history of curricular reform at Columbia, see Bell.

8. For a detailed account of the tensions produced by the University of Chicago's obligation to provide undergraduate education and its desire to establish itself as a research rival to the Eastern universities, see McNeill 1–17.

9. According to McNeill, Mason was not a casualty of the battles between those university factions committed to research and those determined to revise the undergraduate curriculum, as his sudden resignation might suggest; rather, the hasty departure was occasioned by a "private, domestic scandal" (McNeill 171 n. 1).

10. While this bureaucratic reorganization ended up profoundly influencing the shape of undergraduate education at the university, Hutchins would later say that it had been accomplished "primarily in the interest of administrative simplification" (Hutchins, "State of the University" 2–3).

11. This appointment, one of Hutchins's first acts as president, had a catastrophic effect on the university's philosophy department: Adler's contemptuous attitude, combined with the faculty's growing suspicions about Hutchins's motives for bringing him to the university, caused the chair of the department, J. H. Tufts, to resign from his administrative position and three other prominent members of the faculty — George H. Mead, E. A. Burtt, and Arthur E. Murphy — to resign from the university (Ashmore 86–87).

12. Acknowledging the shortcomings of one's past educational experience is a central component in the narratives of those committed to advancing the cause of the Great Books Program. For examples, see C. Van Doren 6; Stringfellow Barr, qtd. in Wofford 87; Mellon 178; Wofford iii.

13. Near the end of his tenure as head of the university, Hutchins had this to say about his administrative style: "As I look back over the last twenty years, I am inclined to think that I have tended to put too much faith in mechanical changes" (*State of the University* 15). He observed as well, "Not much can be expected from hortatory resolutions" (16). As we will see, the history of the Great Books approach at Chicago bears out Hutchins's grim self-assessment of his lasting influence.

14. Hutchins was, in fact, called to testify before the senate of Illinois in 1935 to explain why students at the University of Chicago were required to read the *Communist Manifesto*. His defense of academic freedom in general, and of his faculty in particular, was so compelling that the department store magnate Charles Walgreen, who had originally brought the complaint to the state senate, was convinced to present the university with a substantial gift to establish the Charles R. Walgreen Foundation for the Study of American Institutions. See Ashmore 128–32; Kogan 250–52.

15. See Adler, *Reforming Education* 66–88, for an example of these incendiary charges.

16. Olson confirms Adler's assessment of McKeon's way of teaching the Great Books (304).

17. For an elaboration of this notion that the Great Books and their readers forever carry on a conversation with one another, see Hutchins, *Great Conversation*.

18. For the extraordinary story of how the University of Chicago acquired the *Encyclopaedia Britannica*, see Kogan 247–62; Hyman 249–59.

19. According to Barr, Buchanan refused to accept the presidency on the grounds that he never answered his mail, agreeing to become dean only when Barr made it clear that he wouldn't become president of the college without his friend's help (qtd. in Wofford 88).

20. In a "Memorandum on the College," dated 5/24/37, Buchanan recommends presenting the resident faculty with two options: the college could either be shut down in 1938 or it could be reorganized. If the first option were to be pursued, it would mean that everyone would lose his or her job. If the second option were followed, everyone would have a chance to keep his or her job. If the faculty decided to adopt the second option, however, they needed to understand that the president would "be the sole judge of whom he will retain or invite to his faculty" (SBC, "Memorandum" 11). And in a letter from Barr to Hutchins (BC, 9/28/38), Barr describes the old faculty as doing a fairly good job of gearing up for the New Program, but notes that the AAUP had been "brought down on [his] head" for terminating teachers still under contract.

21. The college continues to promote this vision of itself by distributing a recruitment catalogue that announces, "The following teachers will be returning to St. John's this year . . ." before listing the names of the authors of the Great Books. This idea has been reiterated in the college's recent "Statement of Educational Policy," written by Eva Brann, longtime tutor and current dean of the Annapolis campus. In this statement, Brann catalogues the sixteen tenets that constitute the school's "radical pedagogy," including the belief that "WE ARE NOT PROFESSORS, and perhaps not even teachers. We are tutors, guardians of learning, at most" ("Statement" 15, original emphasis).

22. To this day, the college does not rely on SAT scores in evaluating applicants to the program. Admission is based on how the applicant responds to five essay questions that solicit, among other things, a discussion of the student's most important reading experience. As Eva Brann explains in her essay "The Program of St. John's College," "We find that except for occasional sad cases, self-selection is the best guarantee of aptitude; the desire to learn outweighs questions of talent" (10).

23. Mellon was originally drawn to the program by a favorable article in *Life* magazine. Although he had already graduated from Yale and studied at Cambridge, Mellon decided to become an undergraduate once again in the fall of 1940. After about six months of struggling with the mathematical and scientific components of the curriculum and "very conscious of being nearer in age to the instructors than to the students," Mellon "gave it up for the life of a soldier" (Mellon 181). Despite the brevity of his stay, Mellon had an abiding fondness for the college and made a series of contributions over the following years that kept the college going, beginning

with a grant of $78,000 in 1941 to address problems with the physical plant (Weigle 10, 53).

24. In a letter of "recommendation," Jacob Klein asserted that many people felt that Buchanan "probably overestimated the average ability of students, the depth of their desire to learn, their devotion to the quest for truth" (KC, 11/22/57).

25. See Huber, who surveys upper-division literature classes and concludes that "the major works and authors remain preeminent in the courses surveyed, though nontraditional texts were cited among the works respondents had recently added to their required readings" (52).

Chapter 4. Cultural Studies for the Masses: Distance Education and the Open University's Ideal Student

1. Accounts of these events vary widely. In his Presidential Report for 1970–72, Marshak asserts that the "militant leadership of the Black and Puerto Rican student body" was responsible for the occupation of the South Campus (12). Traub credits the college's "black club, the Onyx society" with providing the initial impetus for changing the admissions policies at CUNY (48). According to Traub, an offshoot of the Onyx society, the Committee of Ten, worked in concert with members of the Puerto Rican student group, PRISA, to formulate the list of demands that were presented to President Buell Gallagher. When those demands were not met, "a handful of black and Puerto Rican students padlocked the gate leading to South Campus, refusing to allow white students to enter under any circumstances" (49). In yet another version, Lavin, Alba, and Silberstein cite a press release from the BPRSC announcing their "willingness to join white student groups to fight the budget cuts" as evidence that economic pressures played a major role in precipitating the student uprising at City College (11). By their account, the BPRSC called for a boycott of classes on April 21, 1969, for three reasons: the failure of the student protests to convince then-Governor Rockefeller to significantly alter the funding of the CUNY system, the fear that these the budget cuts would further diminish the presence of minority students in the City University system, and the dissatisfaction with the administration's response to the students' earlier demands. The next day, "some two hundred members of the BPRSC entered the south campus . . . sealing off half the College's territory and eight of its twenty-two buildings," and "the following day a white group took over another building in a show of support for the BPRSC" (11–12).

2. Traub notes that pictures of the burning auditorium "made the top of each network newscast" and that one of the candidates then seeking to become mayor of New York, Mario Procaccino, "exploited the footage in [his] campaign commercials as if it were Kristallnacht" (53).

3. The other members of U203's course team were Tony Aldgate, Geoffrey Bourne, David Cardiff, Alan Clarke, Noel Coley, David Elliott, Ruth Finnegan, Francis Frascina, John Golby, Graham Martin, Colin Mercer, Richard Middleton, John Muncie, Gill Perry, Bill Purdue, Carrie Roberts, Paddy Scannell, Grahame Thompson, Ken Thompson, and Bernard Waites.

4. See Harris 45–70 for a fuller discussion of how production requirements constrain the writing schedules of the course teams and restrict the possibilities of revision. See Rumble for a more detailed economic analysis of these same issues.

5. Because of this unexpectedly high completion rate, the OU ended up flooding the market with newly degreed students just as the recession was beginning to hit hardest. Indeed, according to Robert McFadden, "by the 1980's [the OU] was awarding more degrees than Oxford and Cambridge combined" (B15). With this in mind, Simpson has argued that the OU's increased production of newly degreed students indirectly served to turn up the heat at Cambridge during Colin MacCabe's famous tenure battle there, because Cambridge "responded to the challenge [of the changing market] not by reorganizing its ever more limited resources but by digging in and refusing to discuss change" ("New Brooms" 261).

6. While this kind of numbers juggling may have assuaged Perry's fears about OU's realization of its mission, McIntosh, Woodley, and Morrison argue after further analysis and study: "Now that the Open University has established its credentials it must concentrate its efforts on becoming more 'open.' While its early years saw some increase in the proportions of students with low educational qualifications and in the manual trades, little progress has been made since then" (193). And, a decade later, Woodley, Taylor, and Butcher report that the university has generally failed to retain ethnic minorities as either students or as members of the university's faculty and staff. For more on this issue, see this chapter's postscript.

7. For examples of such discussions, see the following articles in *Screen Education Notes*: Berry, "Film" and "Materials"; Pye; Bark; and all of nos. 4/5 (1972) and 8 (1973).

8. During this time, Len Masterman offered a third position on the importance of this new area of study, when he argued that film's immediate accessibility makes it the perfect medium for instructing students not destined for the university, a group he describes as "largely composed of those who have never experienced literature's 'civilizing' influence" ("Film" 21). Masterman subsequently revised this position in light of his experiences teaching "low stream kids" in the sixties and seventies, having developed "quite low tolerance thresholds for the elitism of much film culture and criticism" (*Teaching* xiv). As a result, he found himself "increasingly guided in [his] teaching by the dominant media experiences of pupils and students," coming to the conclusion that "if a critical education is to be of any value at all, then it will need to be firmly grounded in the life-experiences of each learner" (xiv). As we will see, this third position — that film was easier to understand than other modes of representation — is one that neither of the warring parties at *Screen* or *Screen Education* was willing to entertain.

9. This last term was suggested by the Editorial Board in *Screen Education*, no. 21 (1976–77), to designate the process of students' making films.

10. One could also argue that the movement toward high academic status reflected a need to move away from students whose life experiences might directly challenge the emergent discipline's assumption that the disempowered were in need of a "serious political education." For an example of such a challenge, see Goodwin, who discusses a course he designed to illustrate the biases of the media to a largely unknowing student body. However, he found himself teaching students

who were the wives and children of coal miners then engaged in a bitter national strike—students, in other words, who knew quite well the power of the media to shape events to meet the interests of the dominant classes. Goodwin's essay illustrates how the student that is constructed in theory and the student with a history in the world are not identical, the latter serving to disturb the assumptions that produced the former if the actual student is allowed to speak and be heard.

11. The reply is signed by the following: Ben Brewster, Elizabeth Cowte, Jon Halliday, Kari Hanet, Stephen Heath, Colin MacCabe, Paul Willemen, and Peter Wollen. The four resigning members were replaced by six new members: Richard Dyer, John Ellis, Christine Geraghty, Annette Kuhn, Steve Neale, and Geoffrey Nowell-Smith.

12. When I interviewed Colin MacCabe about this time on the journal, he said: "Questions of education weren't exactly ignored or repressed. We were not interested in the dominant educational orthodoxy at all." This is borne out in MacCabe's response to my follow-up question regarding whom he would name as representing this dominant position: "After the 1976 split, there were no representatives of progressive [i.e., student-centered] educational opinion on the board. There were some of the board committed to educational questions but hostile to progressive views and there were others who were not interested in education at all" (interview with author, April 10, 1991).

13. Nor is it the case that "hard" (i.e., structuralist) theory took the high road to *Screen*, while "soft" (i.e., culturalist) theory found a happy community in *Screen Education*. Hall, for instance, provides a critique of *Screen*'s use of psychoanalytic theory remarkably similar to the one proffered by Buscombe et al., diverging only in his commitment to developing "an adequate concept of 'struggle' in ideology" ("Emergence" 161).

14. During the past decade, *Screen* (the journal is never referred to by its longer, official name) has turned out two issues devoted solely to pedagogy: 24.2 (1983) and 27.5 (1986). In 1989, when the British Film Institute did away with SEFT entirely, *Screen*'s ownership and its editorial offices were transferred to the John Logie Baird Centre in Scotland where, the new editors assured its readers, it would be "difficult for *Screen* to maintain a pretence any longer that it is not an academic journal" (Editorial Board 3).

15. The overlap with U203 is not just discursive: some figures surface in both contexts. Colin MacCabe appeared as one of many scholars who made presentations to the U203 course team, while Ed Buscombe (one of the resignation signatories) and Geoffrey Nowell-Smith (one of the replacements for the resignation signatories) also "helped in various ways" (T. Bennett, "Out in the Open" 152 n. 1). And, as we will see, Bennett himself contributed to *Screen Education*.

16. Consider, for instance, Womphrey's assessment of the student responses to the block on "Form and Meaning": "U203 students found Block 4 very hard going. Hardly any OU units have been rated more difficult than U203 15 and 16 ["Reading and realism" and " 'Reading' popular music," respectively]; Unit 16 is in the bottom 1% of OU units for 'interest,' and Units 15 and 16 are in the bottom 10% as regards high workload" ("Feedback Block 4" 3).

17. Bennett was prompted to provide his 1996 account of U203, "Out in the Open: Reflections on the History and Practice of Cultural Studies," by my essay " 'A Moment of Profound Danger': British Cultural Studies away from the Center," which puts forth a substantially abbreviated version of the argument I'm making here.

18. It is worth recalling Keddie's concern with relevance in this regard: in the highly visible arena of education at the OU, downplaying student "experience" might well have been perceived as a necessary step for realizing a higher disciplinary status.

19. The summer session, which included a stay at Blackpool Beach, may have afforded just such an opportunity. For reasons that are not entirely clear, the IET did not solicit evaluations for this part of the course, which in itself suggests that that office did not see the session as integral to the course. Cubitt, in contrast, uses the summer session as the cornerstone of his appeal to save U203 from cancellation (92–93). Ian Purser, a student in the course, recalls the journey to Blackpool: "I certainly didn't feel that we were intended to condemn Blackpool and its culture. What came over to me was the fascination of the intellectual middle-class for an earthier, less inhibited culture, that of working-class Northern England, a combination of admiration for its vigor and vulgarity, and amusement and/or horror at some of its forms (e.g. the wax museum showing exhibits of gruesome murders and car-crashes)" (letter to author, October 11, 1994).

20. Obviously, I have not provided an exhaustive study of the forces that shaped the pedagogical encounter in U203. Ian Purser notes, for instance, that the political events occurring at this time also had an obvious influence on the reception of this course. Specifically, the Conservatives' return to power in Britain in 1979 "brought with it a return to 'red-menace' rhetoric, talk of the 'enemy within' and an increasingly hardline stance in the Cold War. To be left-wing was to be unpatriotic, and flag-waving was brought to a new pitch by the Falklands War in early 1982" (letter to author, October 11, 1994).

21. In describing what it was like to teach at CCCS during the sixties and early seventies, Hall recalls that "it was impossible for us to maintain for very long the illusion that we were teaching our graduate students from some established body of knowledge, since it was perfectly clear to them that we were making it up as we went along" ("Emergence" 17).

22. In the summer of 1995, CUNY announced that it would "no longer accept students judged unable to complete all remedial work within the freshman year" (Jones A1). It further declared that beginning in the fall of 1996, it would "limit the number of remedial courses students at the four-year colleges can take" (Bernstein). Amid the general declarations of the failure of open admissions, a new study by David Lavin and David Hyllegard, *Changing the Odds: Open Admissions and the Life Chances of the Disadvantaged*, which surveyed "students who entered the City University under the open-admissions policy, [has] found that more than half received bachelor's degrees, sometimes more than a decade later, and [that] they went on to better-paying jobs as a result" (Arenson A1). Apparently, earlier studies failed to consider how long it would take students to complete their degrees, with the result that many who were still inching toward completion were counted as dropouts.

Chapter 5. Teaching Others:
Ethnography and the Allure of Expertise

1. There are many excellent ethnographies of high school students, including Ogbu, *Next Generation*; Willis; MacLeod; Foley; Heath and McLaughlin. Aside from Moffatt, *Coming of Age*, the only other sustained ethnographic study of undergraduates is Holland and Eisenhart, which focuses on women in college. One need only consider the huge success of the documentary film *Hoop Dreams*, which concludes when the two aspiring basketball stars enter college, to get a glimpse of schooling's master narrative, which places the drama of the process in the transitional space of secondary education: once the aspirants have moved through this space, they no longer evoke the same degree of interest or sympathy and so the story must be over.

2. Baker, for instance, states that Moffatt "has written a book every professor should read, especially those who teach in large state universities." And, Baker continues, *Coming of Age in New Jersey* is "one of the most thoughtfully crafted case studies of undergraduate culture that has ever been written in the field of higher education" (54). Wilkinson describes Moffatt as "a multi-talented, multi-disciplinary scholar of higher education who writes without a trace of gobbledygook. He deserves a wide following" (160). Thelin characterizes the work as "beautifully written, carefully researched...a classic" (105). And Ebner praises Rutgers for fostering "an admirably high standard" for academic freedom by allowing Moffatt to pursue his "extraordinary ethnographic work" (354–55).

3. For example, John Ogbu was hired by the Stockton Unified School District in 1968 to study their bilingual educational project in order that they might understand the disappointing performance of minorities in the school system (Ogbu, *Next Generation*). At the same time, on the other side of the country, Heath's graduate courses in anthropology and linguistics had started to fill with teachers who desperately wanted help finding ways to understand the new student populations that confronted them (Heath, *Ways with Words*).

4. It is, as chance would have it, where I am employed as well.

5. In his review article ("Ethnographic Writing" 210), Moffatt places himself in an elite group of anthropologists who spent from six to ten years in the field.

6. Moffatt's choice of words here reveals his own investment in class distinctions among institutions: the undergraduate perspectives are "less-than-elite" because the students involved in his study go to Rutgers, not Harvard. And, as we will see, this fact about the student population is meant to suggest that their perspectives on higher education are both more representative and less worthy of being taken seriously that those of their counterparts in the Ivy Leagues.

7. In his balanced review of Freeman's critical reevaluation of Mead's work, Rappaport concludes that Freeman has missed the crucial point that Mead produced both better science and better myth than the eugenicists she was arguing against. As Rappaport puts it, "the choice, if choice there is, for any individual or society is not between myth and no myth but among accounts contending for mythic status. We will be well served if those we choose [in the future] are as humane and liberating as the text Mead gave us" (347).

8. As a representative of the values and conventions of academic culture, Moffatt is strikingly consistent in presenting himself as someone who knows better than the students themselves do the intentions behind their actions. Thus, when one of his roommates seeks to engage him in what the student might well have felt was a scholarly discussion, asking the anthropologist if "blacks have a better survival instinct than whites," Moffatt's response is immediate: " 'Well, for a start,' I replied, 'the question is a racist one' " (*Coming of Age* 17). When the same student described college students from the sixties as "rebels without a cause," in contrast to his own "more mature" generation, Moffatt reacts with a list of alternative adjectives for the undergraduate population: "How about more quiescent, more apathetic, and more apolitical?" Following this outburst, Moffatt observes only that the student "looked embarrassed and asked me to tell him what those words meant" (17). From our vantage point, it is worth asking what the student is meant to learn about academic culture from such an interchange—besides that his teacher perceives him to have racist thoughts, an impoverished sense of history, and a rudimentary vocabulary.

9. This is a standard aspect of Moffatt's research methodology. When he wanted to know how students feel about race, he handed out an anonymous questionnaire, where students were instructed to give "their real opinions on the questions, however embarrassing they might be, rather than the polite ones that they usually felt they had to offer up in public" (*Coming of Age* 177 n. 26). And, when Moffatt came across a review of *Ferris Bueller's Day Off* with which he disagreed, he handed out a questionnaire to his students that asked, among other things, if they would want Ferris as a friend and what they thought Ferris would be doing at age forty-five ("Do We Really Need 'Postmodernism'?" 372 n. 1, 373 n. 5).

10. Moffatt renamed all the dorms in his study, noting that "readers who don't recognize the source of the 'Erewhon' in Erewhon Hall have only themselves and their shoddy educations to blame" (*Coming of Age* 21 n. 3). Readers who do recognize the source, however, might wonder at the appropriateness of this particular allusion, which transforms these college living quarters into Samuel Butler's fictionalized world that is the inversion of our own.

11. Heath herself has subsequently used *Ways with Words* to make statements about the reading and writing of African Americans in general. See, for instance, Heath, *Ways with Words* 368, and "Sense" 15.

12. Ogbu's ethnographic work has managed to keep its focus squarely on minorities in the educational system without disposing of the categories of class and race. As a result, he has reached conclusions about the existence of "caste-like minorities" in the United States that would, no doubt, have disturbed the students in Heath's class. See Ogbu, *Next Generation* and *Minority Education*.

13. Heath and Shelby Anne Wolf have subsequently coauthored a book that explores how it is that the children of "townspeople" come to learn the arts of imagination that promote success in school.

14. Heath has since said that given the chance to do the book over again, she would omit the "Ethnographer Doing" section entirely. Although she insists she "would have written a better book had [she] stuck to writing about the communities and their settings of work and leisure" ("Madness(es)" 266), what makes her

book remarkable is that it moves from research to reform. To excise the "Ethnographer Doing" section would be to return the work to the normative realm of conventional, descriptive ethnography. As Heath's more recent work on inner-city youth groups reveals, she fortunately has not confined her subsequent work to this safer realm, insisting instead on using ethnographic research as the basis for developing policy from the ground up (see Heath and McLaughlin).

15. That the literate practices of the black community should end up ultimately escaping final analysis will not surprise some. Henry Louis Gates Jr. has asserted, for instance, that African Americans learn "how to 'signify' " as part of their adolescent education, which involves "ever punning, ever troping, ever embodying the ambiguity of language" ("The 'Blackness of Black' " 286). And Mae Henderson has argued that "black women must speak in a plurality of voices as well as in a multiplicity of discourses," a practice she calls "speaking in tongues" (277). Others, though, might be troubled that in Heath's study this unspeakable knowledge is seen to show itself only when blacks are singing in church and not when they are at home teaching their children to speak and read or when they are moving about in the secular world.

16. Heath has subsequently acknowledged that her "comfort level was highest in Trackton where themes, tastes, and smells of [her own] life as a child among Trackton-like children played again and again for [her]" ("Madness(es)" 264).

17. This approach has led Heath to advocate consistently on behalf of African Americans and other minorities, arguing that their potential contributions to the evolving workplace have yet to be recognized. Indeed, she has gone so far as to say that "traditional oral and literate habits of Black Americans match the demands and needs of employers in the late 20th century far better than those of most classrooms" ("Oral and Literate Traditions" 372).

18. Ironically, the micromanagement of classroom practice that followed in the wake of this bureaucratization of the schools ended up making it possible for two of the children of Roadville to grow up and become teachers. As Heath reports, these two "like the individualized instruction mandates of their districts, feeling secure in 'knowing what it is [they] have to do each day' " ("Madness(es)" 257). Heath even attributes the entrenchment of "step-by-step learning and standardized testing" to the fact that more and more Roadville women have come to see teaching as a viable career option (260–61).

19. See, for example, Heath and Thomas, where Heath asserts that letter writing and research on early language use helped her subject, "T," show "increased confidence in expressing herself, some improvement in her command of the mechanics of writing, and development of an ability to write a well-formed friendly letter and to summarize facts in a narrative style" (67). See, as well, Heath and Mangiola, where the benefits of cross-age tutoring are extolled: "By the end of the term the students' transcriptions of their own data had become so expert, and their methods of analysis so keen, they could determine subtle sentence structure differences between native speakers and non-native speakers and differentiate 'real' conversations from invented ones or literary dialogue" (32).

20. Heath's interest in Zinnea Mae is ongoing: see Heath, "Oral and Literate Traditions"; "Children of Trackton's Children"; and "Fourth Vision." This long duration of their relationship has allowed Heath to study Zinnea Mae's children, who have been raised in a tenement in Atlanta. Because these children show none of the signs of verbal facility and playfulness displayed by the Trackton children discussed in *Ways with Words*, Heath has been compelled to revise her view that the ways of using language within a given community change very slowly ("Children of Trackton's Children" 500).

Bibliography

Adler, Mortimer. *Philosopher at Large: An Intellectual Biography.* New York: Macmillan, 1977.

———. *Reforming Education: The Opening of the American Mind.* Ed. Geraldine Van Doren. New York: Macmillan, 1988.

Alvarado, Manuel, Cary Bazalgette, and Jim Hillier. "Editorial." *Screen Education,* no. 15 (1975): 1–3.

Alvarado, Manuel, and Richard Collins. "Editorial." *Screen Education,* no. 14 (1975): 1–3.

Arenson, Karen. "Study Details CUNY Successes from Open-Admissions Policy." *New York Times* May 7, 1996: A1.

Arnold, Matthew. "The Code Out of Danger." 1862. *Complete Prose Works* 2:247–51.

———. *The Complete Prose Works of Matthew Arnold.* Ed. Robert H. Super. 11 vols. Ann Arbor: University of Michigan Press, 1960–77.

———. *Culture and Anarchy.* 1869. *Complete Prose Works* 5:85–256.

———. "The Function of Criticism at the Present Time." 1864. *Complete Prose Works* 3:258–87.

———. *Letters of Matthew Arnold, 1848–1888.* Ed. George W. E. Russell. 2 vols. New York: Macmillan, 1896.

———. *The Letters of Matthew Arnold to Arthur Hugh Clough.* Ed. Howard Foster Lowry. London: Oxford University Press, 1932.

———. "Literature and Science." 1882. *Complete Prose Works* 10:53–73.

———. *The Popular Education of France.* 1861. *Complete Prose Works* 2:3–211.

———. *Reports on Elementary Schools, 1852–1882.* Ed. F. S. Marvin. London: Wyman and Sons, 1910.

———. *Reports on Elementary Schools, 1852–1882.* Ed. Sir Francis Sandford. New York: Macmillan, 1889.

———. *Schools and Universities on the Continent.* 1867. *Complete Prose Works* 4:15–328.

———. "The Study of Poetry." 1880. *Complete Prose Works* 9:161–88.

———. "Three Public Speeches of Arnold's, 1873–1877." *Complete Prose Works* 8:373–75.

———. "The Twice-Revised Code." 1862. *Complete Prose Works of Matthew Arnold* 2:212–43.

Aronowitz, Stanley, and Henry Giroux. *Education under Siege: The Conservative, Liberal, and Radical Debate over Schooling.* South Hadley, Mass.: Bergin and Garvey, 1985.

Ashmore, Harry S. *Unseasonable Truths: The Life of Robert Maynard Hutchins.* Boston: Little, Brown, 1989.

Aunger, Robert. "On Ethnography: Storytelling or Science?" *Current Anthropology* 36 (1995): 97–130.

Baker, Paul J. Review of Michael Moffatt, *Coming of Age in New Jersey. Academe*
September–October 1990: 54–55.

Baldick, Chris. *The Social Mission of English Criticism, 1848–1932.* Oxford:
Clarendon, 1987.

Ball, Nancy. *Her Majesty's Inspectorate, 1839–1849.* Edinburgh: Oliver and Boyd,
1963.

Bark, Charles. "Film and Examination." *Screen Education Notes,* no. 4 (1972): 17–19.

Barr, Stringfellow. Barr Correspondence. MSA T 1404. Maryland State Archives,
Annapolis, Maryland.

Bell, Daniel. *The Reforming of General Education.* New York: Columbia University
Press, 1966.

Bennett, Tony. Introduction. *Politics, Ideology and Popular Culture 1.* Block 5: Unit
18 of *Popular Culture: A Second Level Course.* Milton Keynes: Open University
Press, 1981. 3–4.

———. "Out in the Open: Reflections on the History and Practice of Cultural
Studies." *Cultural Studies* 10 (1996): 133–53.

———. "Popular Culture: A 'Teaching Object.' " *Screen Education,* no. 34 (1980):
17–29.

———. "Popular Culture: History and Theory." *Popular Culture: Themes and
Issues 2.* Block 1: Unit 3 of *Popular Culture: A Second Level Course.* Milton
Keynes: Open University Press, 1981.

———. "Popular Culture and Hegemony in Post-War Britain." *Politics, Ideology,
and Popular Culture 1.* Block 5: Unit 18 of *Popular Culture: A Second Level
Course.* Milton Keynes: Open University Press, 1981. 5–30.

———. "Putting Policy into Cultural Studies." *Cultural Studies.* Ed. Lawrence
Grossberg, Cary Nelson, and Paula Treichler. New York: Routledge, 1992. 23–37.

———. "Stand Back and Study the Daily Round." *Sesame.* May/June 1981.

Bennett, William J., ed. *The Book of Virtues: A Treasury of Great Moral Stories.* New
York: Simon and Schuster, 1993.

Bernstein, Emily M. "CUNY Gives High Marks to Freshmen." *New York Times*
December 10, 1995: A49.

Berry, David. "Film and Television Studies at Stockwell College." *Screen Education
Notes,* no. 4 (1972): 9–15.

———. "Materials for Teaching about Television." *Screen Education Notes,* no. 3
(1972): 21–26.

Bérubé, Michael. "Standard Deviation: Skyrocketing Job Requirements Inflame
Political Tensions." *Academe* November–December 1995: 26–29.

Bérubé, Michael, and Cary Nelson, eds. "Introduction: A Report from the Front."
*Higher Education under Fire: Politics, Economics, and the Crisis of the
Humanities.* New York: Routledge, 1995. 1–34.

Bethell, Andrew. "Eyeopeners." *Screen Education,* no. 41 (1982): 67–81.

Bloom, Allan. *The Closing of the American Mind.* New York: Simon and Schuster,
1987.

Boucher, Chauncey Samuel. *The Chicago College Plan.* Chicago: University of
Chicago Press, 1935.

Bourdieu, Pierre. "The Corporatism of the Universal: The Role of Intellectuals in the Modern World." Trans. Carolyn Betensky. *Telos*, no. 81 (1989): 99–110.

———. *Distinction: A Social Critique of the Judgement of Taste.* Trans. Richard Nice. Cambridge, Mass.: Harvard University Press, 1984.

Bourdieu, Pierre, and Loïc J. D. Wacquant. *An Invitation to Reflexive Sociology.* Chicago: University of Chicago Press, 1992.

Bové, Paul. *Intellectuals in Power: A Genealogy of Critical Humanism.* New York: Columbia University Press, 1986.

Brann, Eva T. H. *The Program of St. John's College in Annapolis, Maryland, and Santa Fe, New Mexico.* Annapolis, Md.: St. John's College Press, n.d.

———. "Statement of Educational Policy." *Reporter* December 1991: 14–15.

Brewster, Ben, Elizabeth Cowte, Jon Halliday, Kari Hanet, Stephen Heath, Colin MacCabe, Paul Willemen, and Peter Wollen. "Reply." *Screen* 17.2 (1976): 110–16.

Buchanan, Scott. "Awakening the Seven Sleepers." *Scott Buchanan: A Centennial Appreciation of His Life and Work.* Ed. Charles A. Nelson. Annapolis, Md.: St. John's College Press, 1995. 1–14.

———. Buchanan Correspondence. MSA T 1406 and MSA T 1099. Maryland State Archives, Annapolis, Maryland.

———. The Papers of Scott Buchanan. bMS Am 1992. Houghton Library, Harvard University, Cambridge, Massachusetts.

Buchler, Justus. "Reconstruction in the Liberal Arts." *Columbia College on Morningside.* Ed. Dwight C. Miner. New York: Columbia University Press, 1954. 48–135.

Buscombe, Edward, Christopher Gledhill, Alan Lovell, and Christopher Williams. "Statement: Psychoanalysis and Film." *Screen* 16.4 (1975–76): 119–30.

———. "Why We Have Resigned from the Board of Screen." *Screen* 17.2 (1976): 106–9.

Chambers, Iain. "Rethinking 'Popular Culture.'" *Screen Education*, no. 36 (1980): 113–18.

Citizen X. Dir. Chris Gerolmo. Home Box Office, 1995.

Clifford, James. *The Predicament of Culture: Twentieth-Century Ethnography, Literature, and Art.* Cambridge, Mass.: Harvard University Press, 1988.

Comaroff, John, and Jean Comaroff. *Ethnography and the Historical Imagination.* Boulder, Colo.: Westview Press, 1992.

Connell, W. F. *The Educational Thought and Influence of Matthew Arnold.* London: Routledge and Kegan Paul, 1950.

Courses and Programs of Study: The College. The University of Chicago, 1996–1997. Chicago: University of Chicago Press, 1996.

Cubitt, Sean. "Cancelling Popular Culture." *Screen Incorporating Screen Education* 27.6 (1986): 90–93.

Davis, James. *A Study of Participants in the Great Books Program, 1957.* [White Plains, N.Y.]: National Opinion Research Center, [1960].

Denby, David. *Great Books: My Adventures with Homer, Rousseau, Woolf, and Other Indestructible Writers of the Western World.* New York: Simon and Schuster, 1996.

Dewey, John. "President Hutchins' Proposals to Remake Higher Education." *Social Frontier* 3.22 (1937): 103–4.

D'Souza, Dinesh. *Illiberal Education: The Politics of Race and Sex on Campus.* New York: Free Press, 1991.

Dzuback, Mary Ann. *Robert M. Hutchins: Portrait of an Educator.* Chicago: University of Chicago Press, 1991.

Ebner, Michael H. "Anthropology in a University Village." *Virginia Quarterly Review* 66 (1990): 348–55.

Editorial Board. "Editorial." *Screen* 31.1 (1990): 1–5.

Educating Rita. Dir. Lewis Gilbert. Acorn Pictures, 1983.

Elbow, Peter. *Writing without Teachers.* New York: Oxford University Press, 1973.

Erickson, Frederick. "What Makes School Ethnography 'Ethnographic'?" *Anthropology and Education Quarterly* 15 (1984): 51–66.

Erskine, John. *The Memory of Certain Persons.* Philadelphia: J. B. Lippincott, 1947.

———. *My Life as a Teacher.* Philadelphia: J. B. Lippincott, 1948.

"Extract from the Minutes of the Committee of Council on Education." *British Sessional Papers, House of Commons.* Ed. Edgar L. Erickson. Readex Microprint. January 4, 1840.

Fearon, D. R. *School Inspection.* London: Macmillan, 1876.

Ferguson, Bob. "Practical Work and Pedagogy." *Screen Education,* no. 38 (1981): 41–55.

Ferguson, John. *The Open University from Within.* London: University of London Press, 1975.

Fish, Stanley. *There's No Such Thing As Free Speech: And It's a Good Thing Too.* Oxford: Oxford University Press, 1994.

Fitch, Sir Joshua. *Thomas and Matthew Arnold and Their Influence on English Education.* New York: Charles Scribner's Sons, 1897.

Flannery, Kathryn Thoms. "In Praise of the Local and Transitory." *The Right To Literacy.* Ed. Andrea Lunsford, Helene Moglen, and James Slevin. New York: MLA, 1990. 208–13.

Foley, Douglas E. *Learning Deep in the Capitalist Heart of Tejas Culture.* Philadelphia: University of Pennsylvania Press, 1990.

Foucault, Michel. *Discipline and Punish: The Birth of the Prison.* Trans. Alan Sheridan. New York: Random House, 1979.

Freeman, Derek. *Margaret Mead and Samoa: The Making and Unmaking of an Anthropological Myth.* Cambridge, Mass.: Harvard University Press, 1983.

Freire, Paulo. *Pedagogy of the Oppressed.* Trans. Myra Bergman Ramos. 1970. New York: Continuum, 1989.

Gates, Henry Louis, Jr. "The 'Blackness of Blackness': A Critique of the Sign and the Signifying Monkey." *Black Literature and Literary Theory.* New York: Methuen, 1984. 285–321.

———. "The Master's Pieces: On Canon Formation and the African-American Tradition." *South Atlantic Quarterly* 89 (1990): 89–112.

———. *Notes on the Culture Wars.* New York: Oxford University Press, 1992.

Getman, Julius. *In the Company of Scholars: The Struggle for the Soul of Higher Education*. Austin: University of Texas Press, 1992.

Gideonse, Harry D. *The Higher Learning in a Democracy: A Reply to President Hutchins' Critique of the American University*. New York: Farrar and Rinehart, 1937.

Gilbert, Sandra M., and Susan Gubar. *The Madwoman in the Attic: The Woman Writer and the Nineteenth-Century Literary Imagination*. New Haven: Yale University Press, 1979.

Godsen, P. H. *How They Were Taught: An Anthology of Contemporary Accounts of Learning and Teaching in England, 1800–1950*. Oxford: Basil Blackwell, 1969.

Goodwin, Andrew. "Striking Contrasts: Media Studies at Northern College." *Screen Incorporating Screen Education* 26.5 (1985): 92–102.

Graff, Gerald. *Beyond the Culture Wars: How Teaching the Conflicts Can Revitalize American Education*. New York: W. W. Norton, 1992.

———. "Conflict Pedagogy and Student Experience." *College Composition and Communication* 46 (1995): 276–79.

———. *Professing Literature: An Institutional History*. Chicago: University of Chicago Press, 1987.

Grossberg, Lawrence. "Wandering Audiences, Nomadic Critics." *Cultural Studies* 2 (1988): 377–99.

Guillory, John. *Cultural Capital: The Problem of Literary Canon Formation*. Chicago: University of Chicago Press, 1993.

Hall, Stuart. "Cultural Studies and Its Theoretical Legacies." *Cultural Studies*. Ed. Lawrence Grossberg, Cary Nelson, and Paula Treichler. New York: Routledge, 1992. 277–94.

———. "The Emergence of Cultural Studies and the Crisis of the Humanities." *October* 53 (1990): 11–23.

———. "Notes on Deconstructing the Popular." *People's History and Socialist Theory*. Ed. Raphael Samuel. London: Routledge and Kegan Paul, 1981. 227–40.

———. "Recent Developments in Theories of Language and Ideology: A Critical Note." *Culture, Media, Language*. London: Hutchinson, 1980. 157–62.

Hammersley, Martyn. "What's Wrong with Ethnography? The Myth of Theoretical Description." *Sociology* 24 (1990): 597–615.

Harris, David. *Openness and Closure in Distance Education*. Philadelphia: Falmer Press, 1987.

Heath, Shirley Brice. "The Children of Trackton's Children: Spoken and Written Language in Social Change." *Cultural Psychology: Essays on Comparative Human Development*. Ed. James Stigler, Richard Schweder, and Gilbert Herdt. Cambridge: Cambridge University Press, 1990. 496–519.

———. "The Fourth Vision: Literate Language at Work." *The Right To Literacy*. Ed. Andrea Lunsford, Helene Moglen, and James Slevin. New York: MLA, 1990. 289–306.

———. "The Madness(es) of Reading and Writing Ethnography." *Anthropology and Education Quarterly* 24 (1993): 256–68.

———. "Oral and Literate Traditions among Black Americans Living in Poverty." *American Psychologist* 44 (1989): 367–73.

———. "The Sense of Being Literate: Historical and Cross-Cultural Features." *Handbook of Reading Research, Volume II.* White Plains, N.Y.: Longman, 1991. 3–25.

———. *Ways with Words: Language, Life, and Work in Communities and Classrooms.* Cambridge: Cambridge University Press, 1983.

Heath, Shirley Brice, and Leslie Mangiola. *Children of Promise: Literate Activity in Linguistically and Culturally Diverse Classrooms.* Washington, D.C.: National Educational Association, 1991.

Heath, Shirley Brice, and Milbrey W. McLaughlin, eds. *Identity and Inner-City Youth: Beyond Ethnicity and Gender.* New York: Teachers College Press, 1993.

Heath, Shirley Brice, and Charlene Thomas. "The Achievement of Preschool Literacy for Mother and Child." *Awakening to Literacy.* Ed. H. Goelman, A. Obert, and F. Smith. Exeter, N.H.: Heinemann Educational Books, 1984. 51–72.

Heller, Joseph. *Catch-22.* New York: Simon and Schuster, 1961.

Henderson, Mae Gwendolyn. "Speaking in Tongues: Dialogics, Dialectics, and the Black Woman Writer's Literary Tradition." *Changing Our Own Words.* Ed. Cheryl Wall. New Brunswick, N.J.: Rutgers University Press, 1989. 16–37.

Hirsch, E. D. *Cultural Literacy: What Every American Needs to Know.* Boston: Houghton Mifflin, 1987.

Hoggart, Richard. *The Uses of Literacy.* Boston: Beacon Press, 1961.

Holland, Dorothy C., and Margaret A. Eisenhart. *Educated in Romance: Women, Achievement, and College Culture.* Chicago: University of Chicago Press, 1990.

Honan, William H. "Income Found to Predict Education Level Better Than Race." *New York Times* June 17, 1996: A18.

hooks, bell. *Teaching to Transgress: Education as the Practice of Freedom.* New York: Routledge, 1994.

Huber, Bettina. "Today's Literature Classroom: Findings from the MLA's 1990 Survey of Upper-Division Literature Courses." *ADE Bulletin* Spring 1992: 36–60.

Humphreys, Joseph Anthony. *Changes in Certain Aspects of the College of the University of Chicago Following the Inauguration of the New Plan (1931).* Chicago: University of Chicago Libraries, 1936.

Hunter, Ian. *Rethinking the School: Subjectivity, Bureaucracy, Criticism.* New York: St. Martin's Press, 1994.

Hutchins, Robert Maynard. *The Great Conversation: The Substance of a Liberal Education.* Vol. 1 of *Great Books of the Western World.* Chicago: Encyclopaedia Britannica, 1952.

———. *The Higher Learning in America.* New Haven: Yale University Press, 1936.

———. *The State of the University, 1929–1949.* Chicago: University of Chicago Press, 1949.

Huxley, Leonard, ed. *Thoughts on Education: Chosen from the Writings of Matthew Arnold.* New York: Macmillan, 1912.

Huxley, Thomas H. "Science and Culture." *Science and Education: Essays by Thomas H. Huxley.* 1898. New York: Greenwood, 1968. 134–59.

Hyman, Sidney. *The Lives of William Benton*. Chicago: University of Chicago Press, 1969.

Hymes, Dell. *Language in Education: Ethnolinguistic Essays*. Washington, D.C.: Center for Applied Linguistics, 1980.

Hyndman, Michael. *Schools and Schooling in England and Wales: A Documentary History*. London: Harper and Row, 1978.

"Instructions to Inspectors of Schools: Extracts from Minutes of the Committee of Council on Education." *British Sessional Papers, House of Commons*. Ed. Edgar L. Erickson. Readex Microprint. January 4, 1840.

Jones, Charisse. "CUNY Adopts Stricter Policy on Admissions." *New York Times* June 27, 1995: A1.

Kay-Shuttleworth, Sir James. *Memorandum on Popular Education*. 1868. New York: Augustus M. Kelley, 1969.

Keating, Peter. "Arnold's Social and Political Thought." *Matthew Arnold*. Ed. Kenneth Allott. Athens: Ohio University Press, 1976. 207–35.

Keddie, Nell. "What Are the Criteria for Relevance?" *Screen Education*, no. 15 (1975): 4–11.

Klein, Jacob. Klein Correspondence. MSA T 1405. Maryland State Archives, Annapolis, Maryland.

Kogan, Herman. *The Great EB: The Story of the Encyclopaedia Britannica*. Chicago: University of Chicago Press, 1958.

Lavin, David E., Richard D. Alba, and Richard A. Silberstein. *Right versus Privilege: The Open-Admissions Experiment at the City University of New York*. New York: Free Press, 1981.

Lipman, Samuel. "Why Should We Read Culture and Anarchy?" *Culture and Anarchy*. Ed. Samuel Lipman. New Haven: Yale University Press, 1994. 213–27.

MacArthur, Brian. "An Interim History of the Open University." *The Open University Opens*. Ed. Jeremy Tunstall. London: Routledge and Kegan Paul, 1974. 3–20.

MacCabe, Colin. "Class of '68: Elements of an Intellectual Autobiography, 1967–81." *Theoretical Essays: Film, Linguistics, Literature*. Manchester: Manchester University Press, 1985.

———. Interview with author. University of Pittsburgh, Pittsburgh, Pa., April 10, 1991.

Macdonald, Dwight. "The Book-of-the-Millennium Club." 1952. *Against the American Grain: Essays on the Effects of Mass Culture*. New York: Da Capo Press, 1983. 243–61.

MacLeod, Jay. *Ain't No Makin' It: Leveled Aspirations in a Low-Income Neighborhood*. Boulder, Colo.: Westview Press, 1987.

Maclure, J. Stuart, ed. *Educational Documents: England and Wales, 1816 to the Present Day*. 5th ed. New York: Methuen, 1986.

Marshak, Robert. *Problems and Prospects of an Urban Public University: A Report*. New York: City College, 1973.

Masterman, Len. "Film and the Raising of the School Leaving Age." *Screen Education Notes*, no. 6 (1973): 21–24.

————. *Teaching the Media*. New York: Routledge, 1990.

McDowell, Deborah E. *"The Changing Same": Black Women's Literature, Criticism, and Theory*. Bloomington: Indiana University Press, 1995.

McFadden, Robert. "Harold Wilson, Twice British Prime Minister and Old Lion of Labor Party, Dies at 79." *New York Times* May 25, 1995: B15.

McIntosh, Naomi. "The OU Student." *The Open University Opens*. Ed. Jeremy Tunstall. London: Routledge and Kegan Paul, 1974. 54–65.

McIntosh, Naomi, with Judith A. Calder and Betty Swift. *A Degree of Difference: The Open University of the United Kingdom*. New York: Praeger, 1977.

McIntosh, Naomi E., Alan Woodley, and Val Morrison. "Student Demand and Progress at the Open University-The First Eight Years." *Distance Education: International Perspectives*. Ed. David Sewart, Desmond Keegan, and Borje Holmberg. New York: St. Martin's, 1983. 170–94.

McNeill, William H. *Hutchins' University: A Memoir of the University of Chicago, 1929–1950*. Chicago: University of Chicago Press, 1991.

McRobbie, Angela. "Editorial." *Screen Education*, no. 38 (1981): 1–3.

Mead, Margaret. *Coming of Age in Samoa: A Psychological Study of Primitive Youth for Western Civilization*. 1928. New York: William and Morrow, 1973.

Mellon, Paul. *Reflections in a Silver Spoon: A Memoir*. New York: William Morrow, 1992.

Miller, James. "The Academy Writes Back: Why We Can't Close the Book on Allan Bloom." *Lingua Franca* 7.3 (1997): 59–66.

Miller, Richard E. "Composing English Studies: Towards a Social History of the Discipline." *College Composition and Communication* 45 (1994): 164–79.

————. " 'A Moment of Profound Danger': British Cultural Studies away from the Centre." *Cultural Studies* 8 (1994): 417–37.

————. "Ships in the Night Revisited: A Response to Gerald Graff." *College Composition and Communication* 46 (1995): 279–82.

"Minutes of the Committee of Council on Education, August 25th, 1846." *British Sessional Papers, House of Commons*. Ed. Edgar L. Erickson. Readex Microprint.1847.

Modleski, Tonia. Introduction. *Studies in Entertainment: Critical Approaches to Mass Culture*. Ed. Tania Modleski. Bloomington: Indiana University Press, 1986. ix–xix.

Moffatt, Michael. *Coming of Age in New Jersey: College and American Culture*. New Brunswick, N.J.: Rutgers University Press, 1989.

————. "Do We Really Need 'Postmodernism' to Understand *Ferris Bueller's Day Off*? A Comment on Traube." *Cultural Anthropology* 5 (1990): 367–73.

————. "Ethnographic Writing about American Culture." *Annual Review of Anthropology* 21 (1992): 205–29.

————. *The Rutgers Picture Book: An Illustrated History of Student Life in the Changing College and University*. New Brunswick, N.J.: Rutgers University Press, 1985.

Nash, Mark. "Editorial." *Screen* 22.4 (1981): 1–7.

Nelson, Cary. "Lessons from the Job Wars: What Is to Be Done?" *Academe* November–December 1995: 22–25.

Nelson, Charles A. Preface. *Scott Buchanan: A Centennial Appreciation of His Life and Work, 1895–1968.* Ed. Charles A. Nelson. Annapolis, Md.: St. John's College Press, 1995. i–ii.

Nice, Richard, trans. *Distinction: A Social Critique of the Judgement of Taste.* By Pierre Bourdieu. Cambridge, Mass.: Harvard University Press, 1984.

O'Brien, Gerry, and Pat O'Brien. "Culture Shock: A Student Viewpoint." *Sesame* August 1982.

Ogbu, John U. *Minority Education and Caste: The American System in Cross-Cultural Perspective.* New York: Academic Press, 1978.

———. *The Next Generation: An Ethnography of Education in an Urban Neighborhood.* New York: Academic Press, 1974.

Olson, Elder. "Richard McKeon." *Remembering the University of Chicago.* Ed. Edward Shils. Chicago: University of Chicago Press, 1991. 300–306.

O'Shea, Alan, and Bill Schwartz. "Reconsidering Popular Culture." *Screen Incorporating Screen Education* 28.3 (1987): 104–9.

Pattison, Mark. *Memoirs of an Oxford Don.* 1885. Ed. Vivian H. H. Green. London: Cassell, 1988.

Perry, Walter. *The Open University: History and Evaluation of a Dynamic Innovation in Higher Education.* San Francisco: Jossey-Bass, 1977.

Pye, Douglas. "Film and English Studies at Berkshire College of Education." *Screen Education Notes,* no. 4 (1972): 3–8.

Rappaport, Roy A. "Desecrating the Holy Woman: Derek Freeman's Attack on Margaret Mead." *American Scholar* 55 (1986): 313–47.

"Report on Popular Education in England [The Newcastle Report]." 1861. *British Sessional Papers, House of Commons.* Ed. Edgar L. Erickson. Readex Microprint. 1861.

Robbins, Bruce. *Secular Vocations: Intellectuals, Professionalism, Culture.* New York: Verso, 1993.

Rose, Mike. *Possible Lives: The Promise of Public Education in America.* Boston: Houghton Mifflin, 1995.

Rumble, Greville. *The Planning and Management of Distance Education.* New York: St. Martin's Press, 1986.

Ryall, Tom. "Editorial." *Screen Education Notes,* no. 6 (1973): 1–3.

Said, Edward W. *The World, the Text, and the Critic.* Cambridge, Mass.: Harvard University Press, 1983.

St. John's College in Annapolis: Catalogue for 1939–1940. Annapolis, Md.: St. John's College Press, 1940.

Scott, James. *Domination and the Arts of Resistance: Hidden Transcripts.* New Haven: Yale University Press, 1990.

"Second Level Course Examination 1987. U203 Popular Culture." Open University. October 23, 1987.

Shakespeare, William. *Macbeth.* Ed. George Lyman Kittredge. New York: John Wiley, 1967.

Sheehan, Elizabeth. "The Academic as Informant: Methodological and Theoretical Issues in the Ethnography of Intellectuals." *Human Organization* 52 (1993): 252–59.

Shils, Edward. "Robert Maynard Hutchins." *Remembering the University of Chicago.* Ed. Edward Shils. Chicago: University of Chicago Press, 1991. 185–96.

Silver, Harold. *Education as History: Interpreting Nineteenth- and Twentieth-Century Education.* London: Methuen, 1983.

Silver, Harold, and Pamela Silver. *The Education of the Poor: The History of a National School, 1824–1974.* London: Methuen, 1974.

Simon, Brian. *Studies in the History of Education, 1780–1870.* London: Lawrence and Wishart, 1960.

Simpson, David. *The Academic Postmodern and the Rule of Literature: A Report on Half-Knowledge.* Chicago: University of Chicago Press, 1995.

———. "New Brooms at Fawlty Towers: Colin MacCabe and Cambridge English." *Intellectuals: Aesthetics, Politics, Academics.* Ed. Bruce Robbins. Minneapolis: University of Minnesota Press, 1990. 245–72.

Smith, J. Winfree. *A Search for the Liberal College: The Beginning of the St. John's Program.* Annapolis, Md.: St. John's College Press, 1983.

Smith, Paul. *Discerning the Subject.* Minneapolis: University of Minnesota Press, 1988.

Spivak, Gayatri Chakravorty. "Can the Subaltern Speak?" *Marxism and the Interpretation of Culture.* Ed. Cary Nelson and Lawrence Grossberg. Urbana: University of Illinois Press, 1988. 271–316.

———. "Questions of Multiculturalism." *The Post-Colonial Critic: Interviews, Strategies, Dialogues.* Ed. Sarah Harasym. New York: Routledge, 1990. 59–68.

Super, Robert H. "Notes to Arnold's Speech at the Royal Academy." Arnold, *Complete Prose Works* 9:478.

Sylvester, D. W. *Robert Lowe and Education.* Cambridge: Cambridge University Press, 1974.

The Teaching of English in England. London: His Majesty's Stationery Office, 1921.

Thelin, John R. Review of Michael Moffatt, *Coming of Age in New Jersey. Educational Studies* 21 (1990): 103–5.

Thompson, John O. "Popular Culture: The Pleasure and the Pain." *Screen Education,* no. 41 (1982): 43–52.

Traub, James. *City on a Hill: Testing the American Dream at City College.* Reading, Mass.: Addison-Wesley, 1994.

Tyack, David, and Larry Cuban. *Tinkering toward Utopia: A Century of Public School Reform.* Cambridge, Mass.: Harvard University Press, 1995.

Van Doren, Charles. *The Joy of Reading.* New York: Harmony Books, 1985.

Van Doren, John. "Scott Buchanan." *Reporter* Winter 1995: 10.

Verduin, John R., Jr., and Thomas A. Clark. *Distance Education: The Foundations of Effective Practice.* San Francisco: Jossey-Bass, 1991.

Walcott, Fred G. *The Origins of Culture and Anarchy: Matthew Arnold and Popular Education in England.* Toronto: University of Toronto Press, 1970.

Watkins, Evan. *Work Time: English Departments and the Circulation of Cultural Value.* Stanford: Stanford University Press, 1989.

Weigle, Richard D. *Recollections of a St. John's President, 1949–1980.* Annapolis, Md.: St. John's College Press, 1988.

Wilkinson, Rupert. Review of Michael Moffatt, *Coming of Age in New Jersey*. *Journal of American Studies* 25 (1991): 159–60.

Williams, Raymond. *Culture and Society*. 1958. New York: Columbia University Press, 1983.

———. "The Future of Cultural Studies." 1986. *The Politics of Modernism*. Ed. Tony Pinkney. New York: Verso, 1989. 151–62.

———. "Open Teaching." 1971. *Raymond Williams on Television*. Ed. Alan O'Connor. New York: Routledge, 1989. 139–42.

Willinsky, John. "Matthew Arnold's Legacy: The Powers of Literature." *Research in the Teaching of English* 24 (1990): 343–61.

Willis, Paul. *Learning to Labour: How Working Class Kids Get Working Class Jobs*. Farnborough: Saxon House, 1977.

Wilson, Harold. Forward. *The Open University*. By Walter Perry. San Francisco: Jossey-Bass, 1977.

Winter, James. *Robert Lowe*. Toronto: University of Toronto Press, 1976.

Wofford, Harris, Jr. *Embers of the World: Conversations with Scott Buchanan*. Santa Barbara, Calif.: Center for the Study of Democratic Institutions, 1970.

Wolf, Shelby Anne, and Shirley Brice Heath. *The Braid of Literature: Children's Worlds of Reading*. Cambridge, Mass.: Harvard University Press, 1992.

Womphrey, Bob. "U203 (1982) Popular Culture Student Feedback Block 1 (Units 1–3)." Survey Research Department, Open University. June 1982.

———. "U203 (1982) Popular Culture Student Feedback Block 2 (Units 4–8)." Survey Research Department, Open University. July 1982.

———. "U203 (1982) Popular Culture Student Feedback Block 3 (Units 9–12)." Survey Research Department, Open University. August 1982.

———. "U203 (1982) Popular Culture Student Feedback Block 4 (Units 13–17)." Survey Research Department, Open University. September 1982.

———. "U203 (1982) Popular Culture Student Feedback Block 5 (Units 18–23)." Survey Research Department, Open University. October 1982.

Womphrey, Bob, and Robin Mason. "U203 (1982) Popular Culture Student Feedback: Overview of Whole Course." Survey Research Department, Open University. February 1983.

Woodley, Alan, Lee Taylor, and Bernadette Butcher. "Critical Reflections on Developing an Equal Opportunities Action Plan for Black and Ethnic Minorities." *Reforming Open and Distance Education: Critical Reflections from Practice*. Ed. Terry Evans and Daryl Nation. New York: St. Martin's, 1993. 150–68.

Young, Hugo. *The Iron Lady*. New York: Farrar, Straus, Giroux. 1989.

Index

Index

Humphreys, Joseph, 93
Hunter, Ian, 13, 31, 34, 37–41, 44
Hutchins, Robert Maynard, 86–88,
    92–102, 113, 116–19, 203–5, 222–24
Huxley, Leonard, 52
Huxley, T. H., 54
Hyllegard, David, 228
Hyman, Seymour, 121
Hyman, Sidney, 224
Hymes, Dell, 161

In the Company of Scholars, 193–96
Institute of Educational Technology,
    128–29, 142, 228

Kay-Shuttleworth, Sir James, 60, 221
Keating, Peter, 77, 219
Keddie, Nell, 135–36, 228
Keiffer, John, 85, 107
Klein, Jacob, 225
Kimpton, Lawrence, 87, 102
Kogan, Herman, 223–24

Lacan, Jacques, 137, 141
Lansdowne, Lord Henry, 59–60
Lavin, David, 228
Liberal Arts, Inc., 113–15
Lingen, R., 69
Lipman, Samuel, 219
"Literature and Science," 54, 57
Loose Canons, 12
Lovell, Alan, 136–37
Lowe, Robert, 69–73, 221–22
Lowell, Amy, 90
Lubbock, Sir John, 47

MacArthur, Brian, 125
Macaulay's Minute of 1835, 51
Macbeth, 55–57, 77–78
MacCabe, Colin, 138–39, 227
Macdonald, Dwight, 86, 222
MacLeod, Jay, 229
Mangiola, Leslie, 231
Marshak, Robert, 225
Marvin, F. S., 52, 220

Mason, Charles, 92, 223
Mason, Robin, 142–43
Masterman, Len, 226
Marx, Karl, 98, 218
McDowell, Deborah, 222
McFadden, Robert, 226
McIntosh, Naomi, 130–131, 226
McKeon, Richard, 99–100, 113, 115, 224
McLaughlin, Milbrey, 229, 231
McLeod, Ian, 126
McNeill, William, 94, 100, 223
McRobbie, Angela, 139
Mead, George, 223
Mead, Margaret, 163–64, 229
Mellon, Paul, 112, 116, 223–25
Memory of Certain Persons, The, 89
Mill, John Stuart, 13
Miller, James, 217
Modleski, Tonia, 158
Moffatt, Michael, 44, 158–77, 188–91,
    229–30
Morley, David, 123
Murphy, Arthur, 223

Nash, Mark, 140
National Society, 59
Nelson, Cary, 12 , 197–200, 202, 204
Nelson, Charles, 85
Newcastle Commission, 62–69
Newcastle Report, 72, 221
Nice, Richard, 217–18
"Notes on Deconstructing 'The
    Popular,' " 144

O'Brien, Gerry and Pat, 143
O'Conor, Herbert, 111
Ogbu, John, 229–30
Old Dominion Foundation, 112, 115–16
Olson, Elder, 224
Open University, 119, 122–55, 203
Origins of Culture and Anarchy, The, 53
O'Shea, Alan, 145

Pattison, Mark, 64, 220
Pedagogy of the Oppressed, 18